M000036047

Real Estate Market Valuation and Analysis

Real Estate Market Valuation and Analysis

JOSHUA KAHR
and
MICHAEL C. THOMSETT

WILEY

John Wiley & Sons, Inc.

Published by John Wiley & Sons, Inc., Hoboken, New Jersey.
Published simultaneously in Canada.

For general information on our other products and services, or technical support, please contact our Customer Care Department within the United States at 800-762-2974, outside the United States at 317-572-3993 or fax 317-572-4002.

Wiley also publishes its books in a variety of electronic formats. Some content that appears in print may not be available in electronic books.

For more information about Wiley products, visit our web site at www.wiley.com.

Library of Congress Cataloging-in-Publication Data:

Kahr, Joshua, 1974-
    Real estate market valuation and analysis / Joshua Kahr and Michael C.
  Thomsett.
        p.   cm—(Wiley finance series)
    Includes bibliographical references.
    ISBN-13: 978-0-471-65526-8 (cloth/cd-rom)
    ISBN-10: 0-471-65526-0 (cloth/cd-rom)
    1. Real property—Valuation.   2. Real estate investment.   I. Thomsett,
  Michael C.   II. Title.   III. Series.
  HD1387.K3135 2005
  333.33'2—dc22

                                                          2005012597

Printed in the United States of America.

10   9   8   7   6   5   4   3   2   1

Contents

Preface—A *Practical* Approach

"**H**ow much is it worth?"
    Every investor begins with this question. The question of *value* is at the core of the decision. It is the essence of the decision to buy one property and to reject another.

Value is a complex topic because it is partly subjective and partly determined by outside forces. A particular piece of property—whether residential, commercial, or industrial—will be valued based on its location, improvements, zoning, competition, local employment, and the availability (or lack of availability) of other, similar properties. For the serious analyst, the question should be, How is real estate value properly determined? There are numerous methods and theories available, some scientific and others utilizing inaccurate statistical bases or national (rather than regional or local) trends. We propose the use of scientific methods and, at the same time, an overlay of practical considerations regarding local markets, risk tolerance, cash flow, experience, tax benefits, and real estate-focused fundamental analysis. Just as stock investors recognize the importance of the fundamental analytical tools in the selection of stock, the same approach can and should be used in the analysis of real estate.

It is neither possible nor advisable to try to determine value based merely on a visual inspection or other nonfundamental indicators. Such decisions are better made based on comparative shopping and analysis and a thorough comparative approach to the *entire* real estate market. Ironically, some investors make a decision to purchase without careful and thorough analysis and, in some cases, without even defining the means for assigning value. For some consumers, a property is worth whatever its listed price may be, or whatever a real estate broker says. Considering that the same consumers are likely to purchase automobiles with greater care, this is a puzzling way to buy real estate. A car buyer will likely visit two or more dealers and, at the very least, take cars out for a test drive. Why comparison shop for $20,000 cars but impulse-buy a $250,000 investment property or residence?

The example of the impulse-buying real estate buyer is the extreme. Most people are not that impulsive. However, real estate investors *are* faced with the problem of how to analyze real estate values and, if they are to succeed, they also need to develop the means for reliably analyzing the real estate they are considering buying. What factors determine value? What are the appropriate means for comparison between like-kind properties? Why does a subtle difference in location make a vast difference in price?

These and similar questions are enormous challenges for the real estate investor. We cannot shop for property based on a single criterion, and we cannot limit our examination to the same criteria in all cases. For example, it is not prudent to shop for commercial rental property using the same valuation methods as we use when buying residential property. We cannot even make the same underlying assumptions about two similar properties in different locations. The collective economic, demographic, and local factors affecting real estate values have to be studied and analyzed collectively if we are to make an informed decision. Real estate analysis can be performed by anyone; however, it is not enough to place trust in a broker or seller, and we cannot pick real estate from classified advertising. Those media are starting points in the search; informed decisions rely on more detailed analysis and study.

It is a mistake to rely on others to identify value without further study. Even so, a vast number of investors do not ask the right questions or even know what questions to ask. Those who do inquire usually limit their dialogue to one with a real estate broker, who may not even be conversant in the art of real estate analysis. Most state tests for real estate licensing are surprisingly easy and require little in the way of actual analytical knowledge. Emphasis is usually placed on more mundane matters such as knowing how to fill in the standard forms for real estate contracts; agent and broker liability and how to prevent it; and knowing about buyer and seller rights and duties. Few real estate agents can provide advice on estimating cash flow, analyzing relative value and investment potential, or the current state of local supply and demand.

Even so, the buying public (including many mom-and-pop investors) presumes that the real estate broker has the answers. The broker's job is to move property onto the market, and the more properties they close, the more commission they earn. Emphasis is placed on bringing together a willing seller and a willing buyer. But as many prospective buyers often overlook, the broker usually works for the seller. Consequently, so the process of real estate analysis—which is of greater interest to buyers than to sellers—is not within the bundle of motivations that the broker has in mind. Therefore, if you do not know how to critically analyze real estate values and you depend on the assurances of a broker, you are on your own.

This book addresses the problems of analyzing real estate with several possible readers in mind. A number of investors allocate a portion of their capital to real estate through direct ownership, partnerships, or pooled investments (mortgage pools, for example, operate much like mutual funds, with portfolios consisting of mortgage debt rather than stocks or bonds). Business and real estate students and professors will also find this reference to be valuable in developing—at the very least—an approach to issues of valuation and investment in real estate.

The book has been organized to present material in a *practical* manner. What does this mean? Many years ago, a workshop was held at a conference for stockbrokers. One of the audience members asked a panel, "How can we do a better job helping our clients to make investment decisions?" One of the panel members advised, "Pretend it's real money."

We are going to offer the same advice in this book. When we use *theory* by itself, we can have all of the answers. However, to make theory practical, we also need to provoke thought within ourselves. We ask basic questions and try to provide answers that may surprise many readers. Good rule-of-thumb advice, whether conceptual or practical, is valuable as a starting point; but we want to go beyond, to help our readers to think of money invested in the real estate market as *real* money, and not just as an exercise in the theoretical process of investing.

We begin with three chapters that discuss real estate analysis overall. These topics are essential for all investors, consumers, and students of real estate topics. Chapters 4 through 6 discuss specific popular types of property and isolate their unique features. The analysis of each type of real estate rests largely with the features each type of property contains. Thus, valuation of single-family residences (Chapter 4) will not be identical to the process of analysis for multi-unit properties (Chapter 5) or retail properties (Chapter 6). Chapters 7 through 9 examine valuation and means for analysis of nonresidential investment properties: office and industrial (Chapter 7), lodging and tourism (Chapter 8), and mixed-use real estate (Chapter 9).

Throughout the book, our goal has been to provide useful tools in the form of statistical information, examples, charts and graphs, and case studies. The organization and format of the book is intended to ensure that the information can be absorbed and converted to practical applications.

CHAPTER 1

The Essence of Analysis

Analysis is an elusive process; whether investor, appraiser, or student, understanding the essential points to consider is itself a difficult process. In this chapter, we introduce the fundamental methodology as a starting point for deciding whether an investment makes sense. We examine the question, Who uses market analysis and why? Finally, we demonstrate how raising capital for investment purposes must be premised on a foundation of solid analysis.

Knowing the right questions to ask is a wise starting point in any inquisitive task. Otherwise, we cannot identify the underlying assumptions necessary to arrive at an *informed* conclusion. A market analysis may have several different meanings, just as a *real estate market* is not necessarily going to mean the same thing to different people. We recognize a definition of real estate market as

> *the interaction of individuals who exchange real property rights for other assets, such as money. Specific real estate markets are defined on the basis of property type, location, income-producing potential, typical investor characteristics, typical tenant characteristics, or other attributes recognized by those participating in the exchange of real property.*[1]

We also need to recognize that *analysis* may fall into several distinct and separate functions within the broad function of market analysis.

BASIC MARKET ANALYSIS CONCEPT—AN OVERVIEW

We view *market analysis* as a broad overview of supply and demand attributes for property, including site-specific and local factors and current as well as emerging competition. To begin, we provide some basic definitions. Additional definitions may also be found in the book's Glossary. *Studies that focus on the market include*:

> *Analysis of local economies*: Studies the fundamental determinants of the demand for all real estate in the market.
>
> *Market analysis*: Studies the demand for and supply of a particular property type in the market.
>
> *Marketability analysis*: Examines a specific development or property to assess its competitive position in the market.

Studies that focus on individual decisions include:

> *Feasibility analysis*: Evaluates a specific project as to whether it is likely to be carried out successfully if pursued under a proposed program. May relate to developability. Most often related to financial feasibility.
>
> *Investment Analysis*: Evaluates a specific property as a potential investment. Usually incorporates specific financing in the analysis, and may evaluate alternative financing options to select most appropriate financing or consideration of income taxes. Emphasis is on risk and reward, sensitivity analysis, and internal rate of return.

With these definitions in mind, the value of the market analysis becomes apparent. It is a study that tries to identify the market for a particular real estate product. Why would we want to understand the market? Real estate markets are *not* efficient markets like the stock market, and pricing does not occur every day.

Whenever someone undertakes a real estate transaction, a market analysis must be performed. This could range from an informal process to a two-inch-thick book.

Three key questions should be answered by the study:

1. Will there be users to rent or buy the proposed product?
2. How quickly and at what rent or price will the proposed project be absorbed in the market?
3. How might the project be planned or marketed to make it more competitive in its market?

In market analysis, three phases are involved: collection of data, analysis, and recommendations. It all starts with data, which may be found in many places.

Primary, or *raw* data is unanalyzed, often collected in person by the analyst. It may include reading classified ads, new development announcements and legal notices, or Census data. *Secondary* data has gone through the analytical process by someone else, who tells the analyst what to conclude. Secondary data has bias.

The analyst needs to consider bias for all types of data. For example, even primary data may include unintentional bias. Even Census data may include undercounts of immigrants, as one example. Secondary data helps the analyst develop a sense of the market, but primary data is much more valuable and accurate.

Think of the data as coming from two sides—demand and supply—and in that order. Why? On the demand side, the analyst includes:

- Population, number of households, and demographic characteristics.
- Income, affordability, and purchasing power.
- Employment, by industry or occupation.
- Migration and commuting patterns.
- Other factors.

On the supply side, the following are included:

- Inventory of existing space or units.
- Vacancy rates and character of existing property inventory.
- Recent absorption of space, including types of tenants or buyers.
- Projects currently under construction and proposed.
- Market rents/sale prices and how they differ by location and quality.
- Features, functions, and advantages of existing and proposed projects.
- Terms and concessions.

Information sources are not limited, either. Analysts may include, among other sources newspapers, Census and private databases, tax rolls, advertisements, and maps—in other words, any source that reveals something of interest.

The value of direct interviews should not be forgotten in this information-gathering process. The analyst may interview brokers, owners, urban planners, local officials, and so on. Interviews provide guidance and open the analyst's eyes. The goal in the interview is to ask as many people as many questions needed to understand the marketplace in order to synthesize a complete picture.

The data gathering process should be thought of as *competitive intelligence*. Market analysis should be tied in with an understanding of the psychology of the different players. In order to understand whether a proposed project is real, we need to understand the game of business. It is not enough to just say what is going on; we need to understand the players involved. Going even further, it is not just enough to know the players. The analyst also needs to know the local government. In the real estate business, government is your largest partner. If you want to do a project, you need to understand how the political framework either supports or hinders you based on the desires of elected officials.

Market analysis is generated by virtually everyone in real estate:

Private Sources of Analysis

Appraisers.

Brokers (leasing and sales).

Developers.

Investors.

Asset managers.

Lenders.

Public Sources of Analysis

Urban planners.

Economic development consultants.

Public agencies.

It is interesting to determine—and to study—whether private and public analyses mesh or even agree in their conclusions. There are certain ways that the two sides may be specifically biased. In the private sector, market analysis is used to maximize profits (and to reduce losses by reducing market risks). However, the goals of the public sector are often quite different, including a context of impacts beyond profitability or feasibility, such as density, traffic, or design.

Is there such a thing as an unbiased analysis? The answer: Yes. Whichever one *you* are doing.

The serious analyst—absence of bias aside—should be keenly aware that the process itself invites bias. The analyst cannot fall in love with a project and remain objective.

One effective method for identifying market analysis is by taking note of which group or groups use the analysis. These may include developers/builders, investors and lenders, designers, marketing managers, local governments, appraisers, assessors, tenants and occupants, sellers, purchasers, landowners, and property managers. Within the context of identifying the end-user, it also is important to note that the market analysis data feeds into the process of feasibility analysis. The two phases—market and feasibility—are directly affected by the analyst's conclusions about market area.

Defining the market area can be broken down into attributes of the question, What location and physical space make up the market area? This includes natural features, constructed barriers, population density, political boundaries, neighborhood boundaries, type and scope of development, and location of the competition. This level of analysis next leads to a study of primary and secondary trade areas. Some important considerations define how accurate the analyst's work will be. For example, do you use geographic rings to define the trade area? Putting it another way, is the trade area a circle? In practice, trade areas are actually formed by travel time and other market factors, and true trade areas are rarely suitable to explain with the use of perfect circles. For example, residential zoning and commercial clusters may more accurately define the trade area.

Following the gathering of data, the next step is to analyze. A site's advantages and disadvantages can be studied and compared in terms of zoning and comparisons to the competition: location/linkage to other services and properties, rent or purchase price, unit sizes, occupancy costs, parking ratios, building/project amenities, technology, security, and maintenance (current expense level *and* any deferred maintenance).

In performing the range of analytical tasks, one aspect of real estate valuation within the broader scope is the more concentrated *analysis of local economics*. This study of supply and demand is viewed as specific to a narrowly focused region or city. Furthermore, whereas market analysis tends to be associated with the economic conditions affecting valuation of a particular property or property type, analysis of local economics applies to all real estate within a region.

We also want to make a clear distinction between market analysis and *marketability analysis*. The latter is a study of the relative competitive position of a project within the existing market and anticipated market trends in the near future.

While studies such as these (market analysis, local economics, and marketability) tend to be broad-view market studies, two additional types of analyses are more specific to a particular project. First is the process of *feasibility analysis*, which is intended as a study of whether the numbers work, given the current perception about how a project should proceed, what it will cost, and who will buy or rent the property. The range of analysis includes a feasibility study, which we examine later in this chapter. However, the analysis is a larger process focused on financial questions but intended as a critical review. If the financial aspects of the project are impractical, it needs to be modified so that questions relating to financial feasibility produce more favorable answers.

A related process is called *investment analysis*, and it looks at the same financial questions but from the investor's point of view. Feasibility—usually associated with developers and project management—is a part of the developer's market analysis, whereas investment analysis takes the same issues and examines them with a different set of choices. A developer may tend to compare various projects, sites, and real estate markets; an investor is likely to compare potential real estate investments to nonreal estate alternatives as well. The investor will, of course, review financing considerations as part of the analysis; however, financing is not isolated to investors alone. Lenders and potential lenders will perform a variation of investment analysis to analyze risk and to identify the most appropriate type of project financing. Overall, investment analysis, whether performed on behalf of equity investors or potential lenders, will want to include an analysis of cash flow, tax benefits and costs, and comparative return analysis.

To what extent should analysis go? Is it expensive, formal, and time-consuming in all situations, or should the extent of the process be determined by the project? For an experienced speculator, for example, who is familiar with local conditions and trends, an analysis may include a quick and informal study of a specific property. For an outsider, analysis may involve a more detailed study. For someone requiring local approval or extensive financing, that analysis may be a thorough research on many levels.

An expanded definition explains how analysis continues to work after initial decisions have been made concerning where, when, and how to build a project. Market analysis and research are not isolated functions occurring only at the very front processes of the project but are best utilized throughout:

> *Market analysis is a crucial part of the initial feasibility study for a real estate project, but it does not end there. Market research continues to play an important role in shaping the project throughout its development and management phases. Market analysts are commonly consulted for repositioning strategies after a project is up and running and the developer realizes that absorption does not meet projections. As many types of market analysis exist as variations in development projects, stages of development, and interests being served.*[2]

In its final form, analysis may be published as a market study or a feasibility study. In some cases, these are one and the same. However, we make a clear distinction. Market analysis, as a collective process, includes an identification of the timing for demand; the direct relationship between demand and supply (the analysis of which should consider the role of competition), and calculations of investment rates of return.

MARKET STUDY AND FEASIBILITY STUDY: THE DISTINCTIONS

A *market study* should always begin by answering specific questions that may be raised by lenders or equity partners, or by investors themselves. The document has added value as well. For example, regarding subdivision developments, a survey among developers and bankers concluded "that a well-documented market survey was a key component of the appraiser's report."[3] Such a survey often is mandatory in defining the market area itself. That definition phase should be the first step, according to a real estate research company's president, who also advises that "all market analysis should focus on three basic areas of evaluation: the site, the demand for the product, and the supply of comparable products.[4]

The issues of site plus supply and demand analysis lead us to a series of critical questions:

1. Is there adequate demand for the improvements existing or proposed, so that assumed vacancies will be low? This should include analysis of population demographics, income, employment, and growth forecasts. Additional market components beyond the analysis of supply and demand may go to price segmentation and coordination with marketability (development concept in the context of the market, current available sites versus what end-users want, and market absorption analysis, for example).
2. Is there a market demand for such improvements and how readily will the development be sold on the market? How will the proposed development impact on current supply in the immediate area (local market) and the broader market (regional)?
3. How will the development be paid for, and what is the source of funds?

These three questions will be expressed in the next chapter in a somewhat different form, that of *supply and demand*. We recognize three forms of supply and demand, involving tenants, real estate acquisition/sale, and financing. For now, we want to review these important questions and even expand upon them in defining the scope of a market study. To continue, a market study will also include the following questions, concerned with marketability rather than with the conditions of the market:

4. What competitive developments exist and how should *this* project be designed, planned, and marketed to effectively compete? In other words, what is the specific development concept in terms of site plan, architecture, design, and the proposed market itself (tenant, shopper, user)?

5. What relevant factors affect our determination of the market? (Consider the effects of local employment trends, population mix, and even the existence or lack of similar properties.) What is needed in the market today, and how does this development address that demand? Can the design and concept of this development be improved, and if so, how?

These five questions—involving questions of supply and demand—are at the heart of the market study. In comparison, a *feasibility study* focuses on financial aspects of a proposed development or acquisition. While the financial aspects of market analysis and valuation may be viewed as coldly factual, a lot of room for interpretation is likely to be found. The numbers reflect varying forms of reality, but the whole question comes back to supply and demand and the marketability of a project concept. Expressing this in market terms, "three possible courses of action . . . exist in real estate feasibility: (1) a site in search of a use, (2) a use in search of a site, and (3) an investor looking for a means of participation."[5]

What is the purpose of the feasibility study? If we view it simply as a means for crunching numbers, then the value of the report will be limited. In fact, number crunching can and should provide a developer, builder, or potential investor with a far more important outcome: the determination of whether the risks of proceeding are justified. A skeptical approach—assuming a project will *not* work—is often a smart approach. One business consultant explained this aspect of feasibility:

> The first goal of a feasibility study or business plan should be to determine whether or not the potential entrepreneur should actually take the plunge . . . the default conclusion should be that the [project] will not succeed. Thus, the plan must convince potential investors [and] lenders . . . that the [project] will succeed.[6]

Another expert has observed that the process of feasibility analysis should relate more to what will work and less to what the costs will be, a concept that often is forgotten in numbers-oriented feasibility work. That expert observed that

> *. . . the steps necessary to evaluate the economic feasibility of a project are frequently confused with a variety of other tasks. Often this confusion leads to the recital of various statistics dealing with population size, growth rates, average income, median home selling price, employment growth, unemployment listings, and the like. Too often the result is that pure statistical information is substituted for the analytical process necessary to determine the economic feasibility of a project. . . . Some believe the [analyst's] role should be limited to answering the question "what is it worth?" and leaving the question "will it work?" to others."*[7]

We can accurately define *feasibility*—at least in part—as the matching between various elements of supply and demand, expressed in terms of cost and benefit. The kinds of questions you will find in a feasibility study are broader in scope because these various elements are complex; however, the primary areas involved will include:

- What is the target market for the proposed development? (In retail projects, the target has two components: potential tenant stores, and shoppers, so the target needs to be evaluated with both of these groups in mind. In residential projects, the target may be either a home-buying family or a renter, depending on the project and scope envisioned in the development process. Mixed-use projects are especially complex regarding target markets. For example, in urban areas such as Manhattan, some projects involve retail shopping areas and hotel, residential, and recreational features in a single complex.
- What comparable properties are on the market, and how will competition affect pricing in our case? (If a lot of similar properties exist, does it make sense to build another? If so, why?)
- What is the performance level and market demand of the competition? (This may include vacancy rates in multi-family complexes or sales in a mall, for example.)
- What level of *financial* performance is projected? Specifically, the feasibility study works like the well-known business plan model in its projection of cash flow, intended to demonstrate that the proposed project will remain solvent even with a reasonable assumption about vacancy rates, market rental rates, and seasonal variation. Both investors and

lenders will also be keenly interested in conclusions drawn concerning the cash flow impact of debt financing *and* the impact—positive or negative—of taxes.

- What risks are faced in investing in this project (for equity partners) or in lending money to finance this project (for lenders)? The range of risks may involve negative cash flow caused by high vacancies and unanticipated expenses, changes in the local economic climate, and reversal of current demographic trends; the feasibility study should raise all of these questions.

WHAT SHOULD A MARKET AND FEASIBILITY STUDY CONTAIN?

While there is no set format for the study document, the typical market analysis will contain the following items:

Cover page—The type of study, address of property, and names of the team members.

Letter of transmittal—Major findings, conclusions, and recommendations.

Table of contents—A list of all the sections.

Nature of the assignment—Description of the assignment, methodologies, and approaches used, and the scope of services undertaken.

Economic background—Establishes the market framework; discusses the larger market areas first (i.e., regions and/or cities) and the smaller market areas last (i.e. neighborhoods). Analysts should be sure to cover all the influences: physical, economic, governmental, and sociological.

Description of the property and proposed development—A description of the site and improvements should be provided separately. This section explains the physical and economic plan proposed for the site.

Competitive developments—While the economic background will include market data on the competitive supply, this section should include details on the development's most significant competition (existing, planned, and proposed). It should include rental rates and sale prices, vacancy rates, size of projects, and other information.

Market potential—Here the analyst establishes how well the proposed development will capture demand in light of the economic background and compared to the competitive developments. This is the place to quantify demand for the development. Where does the demand come from for the proposed plan? How is your proposed plan different or the same as the competition?

Conclusion of marketability—This section should not include any new data. This is the part dedicated to pure analysis. Everything included in the body of the report analysis so far is used to make a case for how the proposed development will compete in the marketplace.

A 10-year pro forma should be used, based on an assumed sale of the property at the end of year 10. The pro forma will require certain assumptions about rental rates, vacancy rates, absorption rates, and operating expenses. If the proposal is for a condominium development, the concept is the same, but an appropriately shorter holding period should be used.

Addendum—This section is used for any supporting documents such as site plans, maps, and material supporting other sections of the report.

Exhibits—In specific sections or as an appendix, include valuable additional items, including a map identifying the location of the subject, competitive developments, and the market area; photographs of the subject property, its block front and the block facing it; and schedules of competition (size, rent/sale price, and vacancy).

This format is meant only as a guideline. Actual format should be dictated by materials needed to make the case; the unique attributes of the proposal; and a mandate given to the analyst as part of the assignment.

The reporting format may include both market and feasibility study features. The distinctions between the two types of studies demonstrate that the range of requirements for thorough market analysis is comprehensive. An important difference to remember is that the market study may remain relevant for a considerable period of time, whereas a feasibility study is likely to evolve as financial realities change, including employment, construction and land costs, and other economic data (market rents for residential, lodging, office, and industrial properties, for example). The problem of reliability in a feasibility study in the lodging industry has been expressed by a market expert:

Are feasibility studies accurate? They probably are at the time they are performed. But hotel markets are highly dynamic, and unforeseen changes . . . can have a devastating effect on a hotel's future operating performance. With all these interrelated factors (positive and negative) occurring in a highly random pattern, predicting the future income and expense of a hotel is like determining the Dow Jones average three years from now.[8]

THE FIRST STEP IN THE MARKET STUDY: MARKET AREA

The market study is usually the result of thorough market analysis; but what form does this report take? In order to make this study useful to the reader (whether approval-granting agencies, equity partners, or lenders), the study should be organized in a logical manner, so that information presents a clear picture of the market in all of its meanings; so that important information can be easily located; and so that decisions can be made.

As with all well-organized reports, the body of the report should be in a narrative form, with supporting documentation within the report provided in graphic forms; and with detailed supporting documentation provided in appendix form. This format makes the report easy to read and digest; it keeps the body of the report fairly short (even when the supporting back matter is voluminous); and it highlights and explains four key areas of evaluation: overall market area, location-specific factors, demand factors, and supply of comparable properties.

These four aspects of the market analysis are designed to ask critical questions. In other words, if we are able to demonstrate that the market area, location, demand, and supply elements favor proceeding, then it would make sense to others as well. Equally important, if in the process of performing market analysis, we are unable to make a convincing case for the project, then why would anyone else want to proceed? The purpose to market analysis is to critically evaluate the underlying questions, and to determine whether or not the market is situated so that the project should proceed.

The starting point is a study of the *market area*. This is the range in which supply and demand operates. Traditionally, market area has been analyzed on the basis of studying the land physically. Today, however, new technology has expanded the potential of market area analysis, explained in one real estate book as being a new tool to assist market analysts in many ways:

Although analysts have traditionally been forced to approximate market areas by using census tracts, zip codes, or county boundaries because of data limitations, emerging geographic information systems (GIS) technology, or electronic mapping, is liberating real estate decision makers from relying on arbitrary boundaries.[9]

This new technology enables the analyst to look at geographical information from a truly big picture view. Artificial boundaries do, indeed, obscure the true market area in many instances. For example, a retail shopping center would be designed to serve a specific population and geographical market area, which also makes it possible to estimate the reasonable assumptions concerning traffic volume and potential sales. However, a careful study of the market area may point out that the results are not always as obvious as they may seem at first glance.

Everyone will agree that market area is an important starting point. You will want to identify the regional realities defining the potential

CASE STUDY: BELLIS FAIR, WASHINGTON STATE

In the typical market area analysis for a retail shopping center, we would study local population in order to determine whether a project is supported by the market. This does not always work, however; you also need to study the specific area to determine how market forces work. In Bellingham, Washington, the regional mall called Bellis Fair opened in 1988 on Interstate 5 in Whatcom County. At the time, many people criticized the plan for this development, arguing that the local population could not support the mall. Population at the time in the largely rural county was only about 120,000 (as of 2004, Whatcom County, Washington's population is 157,477). However, Bellis Fair has been a huge success.

Daily shopper traffic exceeds 35,000 people. The mall has 150 stores, with anchors of Bon-Macy's, J.C. Penney, Mervyn's, Sears, and Target. Overall, Bellis Fair has 768,906 square feet of leaseable store area on its single level, and 4,730 parking spaces.

How is it possible? The location—Bellingham—is the largest city, but its population is less than 70,000. The closest large city in Washington is Seattle, nearly two hours to the south. Bellis Fair is not a destination from that distance, so where is this market coming from? The answer: Canada. Bellis Fair is a mere 23 miles from the busiest border crossing, known as the Peace Arch. Here, U.S. Interstate 5

(Continued)

CASE STUDY: BELLIS FAIR, WASHINGTON STATE *(Continued)*

crosses into British Columbia. The metro Vancouver region (the area encompassing the border, north to the suburbs of Vancouver itself) has more than four million population. This is the dominant *market area* for Bellis Fair. A majority of shoppers in Bellis Fair come from Canada. The current exchange rate is 80 cents of Canadian to U.S. dollars, so Canadian shoppers enjoy a 20 percent discount by taking a short trip south. Given the added impact of high Canadian sales taxes, shoppers have even greater incentive to shop south of the border. British Columbia sales tax is 7.5 percent (as of 2004), plus federal taxes of 7.0 percent paid by all Canadians. So shopping at home costs 15.5 percent on top of the retail price, compared to a Washington State tax rate of about 8 percent.

Conclusion: Any *market area* study must look realistically at the effective market. The border between the United States and Canada (or between any two states) is artificial in terms of market area. It would be inaccurate for Kansas City, Kansas, to draw conclusions limited only to Kansas residents; obviously, the larger Kansas City, Missouri, market would dominate the market area. The same rationale applies in the case of Bellis Fair. The local population could not support a larger retail mall (daily traffic exceeds one-fourth of the county's population). The success of this mall has to be defined in terms of broader economic and demographic forces.

market itself. One modern tool worth using for the more complex market area studies is Geographic Information Systems (GIS). These systems may include any database with the ability to indicate a geographical location or spatial dimension for the variables in the database. . . .[10] Given the case history of Bellis Fair, it is clear that such regional factors are not always obvious. In any modern market area study, GIS would very likely uncover valuable insights for similar project studies. Additional market analyses may also be required beyond the geographic location of a perceived market. Some guidelines:

- Identify the region not only in geographical terms, but also in terms of where the market exists.
- The market area for tenants may be drawn from the immediate area as well as from other areas. For example, with residential projects this

could be related to the location of employment and ease of access to transit lines.

- Any project's analysis should include consideration for how the new project will affect existing projects. For example, meeting an assumed demand for residential housing may lead to higher vacancy rates in existing multi-unit developments.
- Be aware of the differences between artificial boundaries (county lines, state borders, etc.) and built boundaries like freeways that cut through neighbors, thus defining or restricting a market area.
- Be aware of historical patterns of development based on ethnic or cultural ties. These boundaries change and evolve over time, but they are remarkably persistent.
- Be cautious in making undocumented assumptions concerning the appropriate size of a development *or* the size of an existing market area. Initial assumptions should be studied critically and conclusions should be subjected to testing.

THE SECOND STEP IN MARKET ANALYSIS: SITE EVALUATION

Studying the market area enables us to take a broad view of the region. Clearly, the features of one area over another will vary considerably, and the factors are not always obvious. The features within an area affect the conclusions. For example, an interstate freeway, major border crossing, or employment trends in one city or region are going to significantly impact your conclusions about the market area. This leads into the second step, the more specific site evaluation.

A *site evaluation* should include comparative analysis—site to site—of physical properties such as topography, shape of the land, surrounding uses, and proximity to important features (such as transportation, for example). Comparative analysis helps you to assess a particular property or series of potential sites with features in mind. A shopping mall situated near a freeway exit would, naturally, have greater potential than one outside the city limits and away from the visibility of potential shoppers, the convenience of access via roads and transit stations, and the overall practicality of siting a shopping mall on well traveled routes. For residential property, local transit and access to conveniences such as schools and shopping, also play an important role in comparative site evaluation. While it may be obvious to some, it is important that the analyst walk the site. Sound real estate analysis cannot be done thoroughly from a desk or, for that matter, from behind the wheel of a car.

The question of zoning cannot be overlooked in site analysis, either. We cannot simply assume that, given the acquisition of land for a specific purpose, a rezone is automatically going to be granted. Lower-priced property may be so priced due to its current zoning, and local authorities (not to mention citizens living nearby) are likely to resist a rezone merely for the convenience (and profit) of development interests. On the other hand, in some cases approval for rezoning is relatively easy to obtain if the new project will benefit the community and local government through increased tax revenues. The potential problems of investing in land when zoning problems may arise is one risk factor in the site evaluation. You may need to compare overlooked but potentially profitable land with more obvious sites. The cost of already-zoned commercial land may be far higher, but the risk of antigrowth movements among citizens, or denial of rezone applications by local governments, is largely removed when zoning issues are not on the table.

The many questions that arise in site evaluation apply to every type of land use. The questions include whether a particular site is appropriate for the planned use; whether it is the best available property; whether there are amenities close by (public recreation, shopping, schools, etc.); and the larger question of whether citizens and local government would welcome your planned use.

Potential resistance to your proposal may exist even when zoning is in place. Those states that have enacted growth management legislation may impose restrictive growth limitations.

For example, a common principle in growth management laws is that a specifically identified urban growth area (UGA) should be in-filled before any new development is to be allowed outside its boundaries. While intended as a means for preventing urban sprawl, the actual result may be draconian density within the urban fringe with little or no growth on the outside.

For the purpose of site evaluation, it is crucial that you also check state

Valuable Resource

A web site linked to many of the state growth management sites, and identifying additional useful publications on the topics, is http://www.realtor .org/sg3.nsf/pages/landusezonegrowmgmt?OpenDocument and local laws beyond mere zoning. The zoning itself is meaningless if, due to GMA legislation, you will not be able to gain approval for your project because the site lies outside the UGA.

Growth management rules may further require that you *prove* the need for the development you propose as a precondition for approval. For example, you may need to evaluate a site within the context of a county's inventory of land sharing the same zoning. How much of that land is developed and under operation? Can you establish a demand for additional lands both zoned and developed in the same way? You may discover that opponents will use GMA rules to prevent new development, even when zoning is appropriate. While we may assume in most cases that properly zoned land is implied approval for your development, it is not necessarily so. You may win the point, but delays and legal fees could make it less feasible. In comparing one site to another in GMA states, you may need to limit your site evaluation to available land inside the existing urban fringe, or be prepared to prove the need for your development outside that boundary.

THE THIRD STEP IN MARKET ANALYSIS: DEMAND FACTORS

Closely related to the site evaluation and the practicality of developing a specific piece of land is the question of demand. Demand may be a factor of current zoning, inventory of lands zoned in that manner, and the boundaries of an urban area that has access to reasonably priced municipal services. It may not be limited to the widely understood definition of market demand.

Because *demand* does not necessarily mean the economic version of demand, we need to be cautious in interpreting statements made by others. For example, a local politician or antigrowth activist may state that "there is no demand for a project like this" in the area. What does that mean? In fact, it could mean that forces are at work to *prevent* such projects, whether market demand exists.

Economic demand is a form of demand in which consumers need and want more of a commodity or type of outlet (shopping center, apartments, houses, etc.) or, when that demand would be likely to follow if and when the development occurred. For example, a community may reside 60 miles from the closest large-scale regional mall. The lack of such a mall right in town does not prove that there is lack of demand; in fact, were such a development to be built, it is logical that shoppers would arrive almost immediately at that destination rather than traveling 60 miles.

So a study of demand should include an understanding and study of market forces and trends, but it is not necessarily so limited. We may face a more political definition of *demand* as well. At times, the real agenda may be to prevent change in any form; in that environment, appropriate zoning and municipal code provisions may not be enough to gain approval for your project. This is understandable; development is change, and change is often resisted for no other reason than because it is perceived as negative by some people. You may need to include as part of your demand analysis the local *political demand* for development. In some jurisdictions, political demand is at zero. From a development perspective, regardless of the economic demand, the project may simply not be feasible because of politics.

This problem is prevalent in many areas, but the range of problems associated with antigrowth sentiment in residential development (and most notably against low-income housing) is especially severe. As a matter of public policy, slow growth policies may ultimately prove the point that when government tries to control growth, it causes only badly planned growth but cannot truly prevent it. This problem is aptly described in one GMA-oriented web site, observing:

> *Jurisdictions are not accommodating growth because they either refuse to comply with the law, need political cover from NIMBY mentality, or lack the resources necessary to provide infrastructure, amenities and low income housing. During times of high demand, jurisdictions must do more to accommodate the need for housing. While the private sector determines the market for housing, each jurisdiction determines the availability of land to develop through comprehensive plans, zoning codes, permit requirements, fees, taxes, and other costs that may serve to encourage or inhibit growth.*[11]

THE FOURTH STEP IN MARKET ANALYSIS: EXISTING SUPPLY FACTORS

The concept of *supply* is as complex as that of demand in areas where legislation has been drafted in an attempt to control or even to prevent growth from occurring.

In an economic sense, *supply* is well understood. It is in reference to the available properties designated for a specific use. When economic supply is high, prices will soften because demand lags behind. When supply is short and demand is greater, prices are driven up. This basic economic concept is not complex, at least when viewed in its theoretical definition.

There are three specific kinds of real estate supply: already built, under construction, and proposed. Each of these has a different level of reliability, and the variables should be discounted by the analyst. For example, developers sometimes announce a project that they do not have tenants for, only as a way to scare off other developers or to try to attract a potential tenant in order to drive the development; most downtown office buildings cannot be built or financed without a committed tenant. So it is a common practice among developers to announce construction more as a marketing ploy than as a statement of fact.

In a written market study, the questions of supply and demand may be limited to a purely economic analysis. If a market study is undertaken to convince lenders of the viability and cash flow strength in a proposed project, those economic analyses are quite appropriate. The same is true when the study is designed to attract equity partners or to gain approval for tax credits in low-income housing, for example. However, if the purpose of a market study is to determine whether a project is viable both economically and politically, we need to look beyond the economic version of supply.

In residential developments, antigrowth conflict is often associated with questions of supply. Antigrowth forces may argue that there is an adequate supply of housing and it is not necessary to construct more. This argument is made even when economic demand is evident. However, the antigrowth argument continues: If we build more houses, more people will move here. That means more traffic, higher crime, the need for improved roads, larger schools, and other consequences of growth. So *supply* may come to mean *need* rather than a purely economic study of whether there are enough buyers available.

For commercial developments, the question of supply is equally complex. A market study would review buying trends, traffic patterns, logistics, and site-specific questions in order to convince the reader of the study that a mall, for example, would succeed at a specific site. Included in this study would be commercial vacancies, affected by shifting traffic and shopping trends, local and regional competition, and typical rental rates in the area.

Demand for either residential or commercial developments also needs to include a study of the trend in net absorption or, in the case of single-family homes, real estate sales trends in recent months.

Net absorption can be expressed as the square footage of *available* space over time, modified by vacancy levels. More specifically:

Net absorption = space occupied − space vacated + space demolished
− construction of new space

For example, in a particular city, residential vacancies have consistently run below 5 percent; however, in the past two years, several hundred new apartments have been added to inventory and today, vacancies range seasonally between 10 percent and 15 percent—a substantial increase. So net absorption has diminished. The question next becomes, How long will it take for the market to absorb the oversupply so that net absorption will improve? This estimate would have to be based on economic and demographic trends in the area.

In the case of properties for sale, demand is judged based on several forms of analysis. Checking with local lenders and Multiple Listing Service (MLS) offices, we find statistics concerning housing sales over the past one to three years. What is the trend in the inventory of properties? (*Inventory* is the number of homes available for sale, expressed in terms of the months of demand. For example, if 200 homes are sold per month and there are currently 600 homes on the market, then there is a three-month inventory.) The trend in inventory levels reveals the demand. If the inventory level is growing, then demand is falling. The trend reveals the health of the local housing market.

A related test is the *spread* between the asked price and the final sales price for properties. The wider the spread, the softer the demand. In markets where demand is exceptionally high, spread tends to be low. So again reviewing the trend, we would analyze demand in terms of whether the spread is expanding or contracting.

The third important test is time on the market. How long does it take properties to sell? In a high-demand market, well-priced properties sell very quickly and, of course, when demand is soft, even bargain-priced properties may remain on the market for many months. What is the trend? The answer reveals the level of demand and, more revealing, the trend in that demand.

Developers hiring outside firms to prepare market studies should ensure that the firm is qualified in the particular type of development being studied. The study should also identify specific factors given the market in question, rather than relying upon some generalized formula. For example, many studies are prepared based on markets defined via radius (three or five miles are common markets in such studies). But this method is not applicable in most areas. A real market may consist of people living along a highway as far out as 10 or 15 miles while few other potential buyers or consumers will be found within a mile-based proximity. The underlying assumptions of the study should be based on the geographical and local features rather than on a formula that almost certainly does *not* apply. For example, *drive time* is often a more reliable indicator of markets than actual physical distance.

One expert has noted that one significant error

is the failure to recognize that a new development will be able to capture only a share of the market, rather than the entire market. New projects do not necessarily create new demand. Many analysts incorrectly assume that if there is sufficient demand in the competitive market to absorb five lots per month, a new project will automatically capture all this demand.[12]

The same argument applies to economic modeling within the market study. Broad-based assumptions should be rejected and the market study based on the local realities and economic mix. This is essential if the study is to truly identify the market in terms of supply and demand. Such economic features cannot be formula-based because every region and municipality is unique in terms of its demographic and economic mix. The market study should analyze the area, rather than be designed to impose generalized assumptions on all areas. A competitive analysis within the market study should be prepared along similar lines: The market study should involve analysis of specific competitive forces rather than upon generalized observations about the nature of competition.

How can you determine whether a particular consulting firm uses boilerplate assumptions or actually goes into the field and studies the market? One effective method is to ask to see copies of recent market studies and to compare them. Since many such studies are publicly available and not proprietary (such as studies prepared for government program clients), a consulting firm should be willing and able to provide copies of recent market studies.

THE VALUE OF THE FEASIBILITY STUDY

The market study is intended to examine conditions of the local market and to demonstrate, by way of compelling supply and demand factors, that the development proposal is justified. In comparison, a feasibility study questions the financial aspects of the proposed development—tax features, cash flow, and likely profit or loss—in order to show potential lenders (or equity partners) that the numbers will work.

While the question of feasibility may be largely financial, it is more than an accounting exercise. The typical accounting revenue forecast, cost and expense budget, and cash flow projection is limited to documenting possible outcomes; the feasibility study, in fact, is far more. It is financial in nature, but it should be compelling beyond what the numbers reveal. A lender reviewing a feasibility study should be able to conclude that the *risk* of financing the project is acceptable. *Feasibility* should not translate to an attempt to show that there are no risks; a lender or potential equity partner would not accept such a premise, and, under any standards, such a claim would not be supportable. However, the question of risk is going to be on the minds of anyone approached by developers for financing or investment purposes.

Feasibility, in its most reasonable definition, is part budget and part disclosure document. It is properly treated as part of a test of the financial potential, risk, and financing required. All of this, which is part of the *due diligence* process, is aimed at testing the assumptions underlying the project. Part of that process—and a crucial part for the lender or the investor—is identifying risk. This risk may come not only in the most obvious forms of net loss or negative cash flow. In some instances, a far more troubling risk may be the possibility that initial financing will not be adequate to complete the project.

The feasibility study presents a pro-forma version of what is expected to occur during the acquisition, construction, completion, tenancy, and eventual sale of the project. What happens if initial financing or equity investment is not enough to complete these steps? Where will additional funding be acquired? Of course, the fact that the study attempts to show how currently known facts *might* look in the future—in other words, a forecast—should be accepted as one of many possible outcomes. We should be aware of an important distinction:

> *A forecast is not a prediction. Predictions require a leap in logic and are not necessarily based on known or knowable current information. A prediction does not attempt to show how the future relates to the present; it is stated as a fact, independent of and unrelated to what currently exists. A forecast, on the other hand, logically links current information with events that are expected to occur. In a forecast the future is not unrelated to the world as it currently exists or will exist; rather, current and future events are viewed as inexorably linked in some logical way.*[13]

The difference between these two is central to the theme. Consider, for example, the point of view of the people who are asked to bring money to the table—lenders or investors. Because the initial financing is the basis for identifying potential return to investors (or cash flow to lenders), if that financing is inadequate, it presents a very serious dilemma. More financing will be necessary if the initial lender or investor is to profit; however, the assumptions all change if and when additional funding will be needed. With this risk in mind, the feasibility study has to address the financial risk in very comprehensive terms.

As a planning document, the feasibility study serves as a risk disclosure summary within the due diligence process. It should follow the market study. Clearly, disclosure has to be based on market assumptions, so a feasibility study cannot precede a test of the market itself. In the market study, the big question is, Does it make sense in this market to proceed, given site attributes, supply and demand, and competitive realities? In comparison, the feasibility study should ask the questions, Can we *afford* to build the project as originally conceived, or do we need to examine costs with market and financial attributes in mind?

The market study indicates how the project should be completed in terms of improvement size and scope (thus, cost). So the assumptions that go into the feasibility study are based on the market study. That is the entire assumption base, in fact, for studying risks and determining whether or not a lender can reasonably expect timely payments or an investor can expect a return and, ultimately, a profit.

If a developer prepares an in-house market study and feasibility study and then goes forward to find financing, it would be normal for the picture to be optimistic. And many development firms do, in fact, prepare their market and business planning documents on their own. However, the real test of feasibility is achieved when an outside, independent consultant looks at the same questions objectively. As long as the developer pays the bill, we may expect a degree of bias and that is unavoidable. However, an outside consultant should adhere to certain standards and that is an important feature of the independent feasibility study. An appraisal firm may offer market and feasibility services but may lack the accounting skills to prepare a comprehensive cash flow analysis; their emphasis would likely be restricted to cost/value questions. An appraisal firm with a qualified real estate department that specializes in feasibility studies or a consulting firm with demonstrated experience in preparing feasibility studies, may be the best source for preparation of this feasibility study. A word of caution, however, is offered by a principal in one such organization:

> *Once you have identified qualified feasibility consultants, there are other factors that need to be weighed in making the selection. The most important factor is whether or not the chemistry is right and the match is a compatible one. This doesn't mean hiring a firm that will always agree with you. It means hiring people who have the integrity to tell the truth as they see it, and at the same time work with the people in your organization in a team effort that is not adversarial in nature. You must feel that you can trust the judgment of the feasibility consultant that you hire, without feeling that you can't challenge their interpretation of the data gathered.*[14]

The feasibility study is most effective when it includes three key features. First, the pro-forma number crunching has to be based on realistic underlying assumptions about financing, costs and rents, and these assumptions have to be critically examined to ensure that they are fair and accurate. Second, the assumptions used in the feasibility study must be an outgrowth of the market study. Why? Because "recommendations regarding overall project size, unit sizes and mix will drive the overall project cost as reflected in the development budget."[15] Third, a feasibility study should include a series of metrics so that the reader can better understand the cash flow statement. This could include time value of money calculations such as the Internal Rate of Return (IRR) or Present Value calculations. Other metrics that examine return for both investor and lender should be examined (such as cash-on-cash on both leveraged and unleveraged bases; loan-to-value; and debt service coverage ratios). Finally, a competent analyst will include sensitivity analyses that show how small changes in underlying variables (i.e., capitalization rate) may result in large changes in project value.

Feasibility cannot be studied in a vacuum but should serve as an outgrowth of competitive analysis as well as an understanding of supply and demand locally; if the market study shapes the development as it should, then the feasibility study shapes the financial questions in a meaningful way, including risk assessment as well as acquisition and development cost levels and cash flow.

One possible outcome of the feasibility study is the conclusion that, in fact, the project as originally conceived does not work out financially. If the investment cost is too high based on potential cash flow, the conclusion may be that the whole project will have to be scaled back. In the most extreme case, the idea may have to be abandoned and the land used for other projects (or if land has not yet been acquired, the whole project would be abandoned). In those instances, it is far less expensive to pay the cost of a market study and a feasibility study, than it would be to attempt to finance the project. The cost of proceeding when the numbers do not work would be far greater for all concerned.

WHO USES MARKET ANALYSIS?

Should market analysis be performed only as a means for obtaining financing? The market study and feasibility study are essential for raising money for a project, but is that the end of the process?

In fact, market analysis and the output obtained from it are valuable planning documents. These can and should be utilized throughout the project by architect, engineer, and the project planning team. In developing the raw material, the individual or firm preparing a study considers population, income, employment trends, commuting and traffic patterns, and more. But the market and feasibility studies should evolve beyond a summary of raw data if they are to be effective. Many ineffective reports end up gathering dust in the project manager's office, because they are not designed as action tools. Thus, the cost and effort that go into market analysis may be passively organized and presented, so that no meaningful use will be made of it. As an alternative, the document may be designed to provide vision and guidance to the many participants in making the project a reality.

A lot of emphasis is placed on *marketability analysis* of a project, either in terms of rental cash flow or—if the developed property is to be sold—how to maximize market value. But marketability analysis is only a small part of the larger concept of *market analysis*. The latter is effective when it includes the elements of the market study and feasibility study; but it becomes exceptionally effective when the information and conclusions are presented in a way that provides the project vision that is so important. Elements of that vision include community involvement along with planning at the municipal level; innovative design; sensitivity to local concerns; and the feasibility of the project in every way and not solely in terms of financial outcome.

The utilization of market analysis is so critical to a project's acceptance locally because no two projects are the same. Any attempt to use a cookie cutter method of developing projects is certain to meet with resistance. Variation in style, site planning, and price range should be based on a list of local attributes. These include citizen involvement and/or resistance to the development, local political mood, and the far more tangible site-specific attributes: topography, proximity to traffic patterns, and surrounding zoning, for example.

In considering the many diverse uses of market analysis, the most effective studies are those that meet the needs and answer the questions of each of the interested parties: lenders or equity partners (capital formation), developers or contractors (project generation), architects and designers (those responsible for creating aesthetic qualities as well as meeting local code requirements within the site), marketing interests or users (buyers or sellers, landowners and tenants, or consumers), and maintenance interests (property managers).

It is useful to review the end-user on a matrix of objectives, as shown in Table 1.1.

TABLE 1.1   Market Analysis Users and Their Objectives

Objectives	Lenders Partners	Developers Builders	Architects Designers	Buyers/ Sellers	Property Managers
Promotion and initial marketing efforts.		x			
Communication with local politicians and decision makers for project approval; outreach to land use and community groups.		x	x		
Employment and relocation of corporate tenants/buyers.		x	x	x	
Investment strategies or financing efforts.	x	x			
Project planning and design, long-term.	x	x	x		
Cash flow projections and financial analysis for investor profitability and lender risk assessment.	x	x	x	x	
Due diligence, multiple levels of review.	x	x	x	x	
Management of completed projects—tenant matters and maintenance.					x

THE GOOD AND THE BAD ON STUDIES

The analyst needs to remember who usually commissions the market study: the developer. Do not confuse the market study or feasibility study with the more independent and objective appraisal, for example. Some guidelines:

- *The analyst must remain objective.* There is nothing wrong with a study concluding that the site is not great and/or hard to build on.

- *Take caution if and when the developer's objectives are not clearly defined.* The analyst cannot be expected to know the purpose of the study without a clear definition.
- *The drive for profits by the consulting company blurs objectivity.* Be wary of the consultant that produces a glowing report promising high profits, but that glazes over the risk.
- *The study should be performed as a team.* No one person should be expected to produce an objective summary of all of the market and feasibility issues. The team not only assigns work to members based on expertise; it also provides a good checks and balances system ensuring overall objectivity.
- *Many projects suffer from fragmented development planning.* In all too many instances, the planning phase is finished before anyone figures out what the demand is. The process cannot be broken up and performed piecemeal. It has to move forward in an intelligent way. As the saying goes, Don't put the cart of desired results before the horse of as yet unknown demand.
- *Lack of strong personnel damages the process of market analysis.* A lot of damage can be done by a staff that is afraid to give the boss bad news, lose a profitable client, or fear sounding negative. Telling the truth based on a well-researched report and fully documented findings provides integrity to the process.

The analyst should also make note of 10 common weaknesses in the market study process:

1. *Inadequate analysis of indirect economic forces, such as environmental, social, and political.* It may be possible to build the project, but what is the community's stance on development? Research the political issues locally, in the early stages.
2. *Using best-case numbers.* It is far more valuable and realistic—from marketing as well as fiscal points of view—to use a range of possible outcomes: best, moderate, and worst-case.
3. *Ignoring the importance of sensitivity analysis.* Some numbers, if tweaked a little bit, can dramatically change the projections. Cap rate is a typical one. When dealing with highly sensitive numbers or exceptionally long-term projections, a sensitivity analysis is appropriate—a good place to insert a worst-case analysis.
4. *Underestimation of infrastructure cost.* Among the more expensive possible problems is the failure to realistically appraise the operational costs of the project. Remember, the devil is in the details. But the details are expensive.

5. *Inadequate analysis, particularly of cash flow.* To many analysts, cash flow is too elusive to fully document. This is an error. Carefully document all of your assumptions, so that if and when the numbers start to vary, you can go back and identify the cause. You will need to pin down the variance specifically: as related to market data, tax calculations, debt service, for example.

6. *Excessive use of statistics without any hard, realistic conclusions.* Numbers are great, but only to the extent that they lead you somewhere. Avoid the temptation to replace difficult conclusions with confusing numbers and test runs using estimates only.

7. *Failure to edit data property.* When reports depend on irrelevant data, how do we find the relevant parts? Market data is hard to get. So when you have limited data, be honest about it. The disclosure of these limitations is far more valuable than the use of numbers that simply do not help. At least then, the reader can ascertain what the situation is. A lack of clarity increases the risk; and if nothing else, the analyst's job is to highlight where those risks lie.

8. *Conclusions drawn on numbers but lacking consumer surveys.* Such surveys may be expensive and time-consuming, but they are often invaluable in what they reveal.

9. *Overvaluation of land.* The method you use to set value of land versus improvements will affect all subsequent ratios and financial tests—for lenders and investors, not to mention potential tenants or buyers. Depend on appraisal documents to set a fair value, and avoid the temptation to alter the numbers.

10. *A failure to critically assess management.* Who is the development team? What is their experience? Even the best market analysis is useless unless management knows how to make it work. This problem may be more relevant to the developer than to the analyst, who has no direct power to make changes. But as a part of the analysis, it does not hurt to emphasize the importance of professional management as a linchpin of a project's success.

In Chapter 2, we take these concepts to the next step and provide you with the means to put analysis to work to make the project succeed.

CHAPTER 2

Using Analysis Effectively

We may analyze markets using theories alone; however, we make these analyses powerful tools for decision-making only when we are able to express our findings in practical terms. This chapter provides an overview of the analytical process. It explains how analysis becomes an integral part of your business plan and its underlying assumptions; how the scientific method is applied to the study of real estate markets; and how to employ facts in the context of three distinct versions of real estate supply and demand.

The theory of market analysis is a starting point in our quest for information. However, once we have mastered the theories—meaning we at least know what questions need to be asked—a more challenging concept is how to make that information useful and practical.

How do we *convert* market analysis into forms of action?

FACTORS AFFECTING MARKET ANALYSIS— BEYOND THE NUMBERS

The market study and feasibility study may represent typical documents as reflections of a properly completed market analysis process. However, the mere presentation of fact is not enough. Just as accountants may present financial statements as rows and columns of numbers, those statements become most valuable when the accountant also explains what those numbers reveal. In real estate analysis, the same rule applies. There are several important differences, however, between specific real estate analysis and the more universal interpretation of financial results, including:

1. *Local market variables.* Real estate trends cannot be studied on a national or even regional basis. Local trends—those trends in the immediate vicinity—are all that really matter. Unlike most other forms of market and financial analysis, real estate analysis is, indeed, highly local in nature.

2. *Site-specific attributes.* The nature of a site itself also affects the methods you employ in translating market analysis. Two sites of identical size located next to each other may have vastly different potential due to attributes. For example, site A may be visible from an interstate, have a flat topography, and good drainage. Site B may be on a slope with a tendency for partial flooding and the need for improved drainage, and be invisible from the interstate or other well-traveled roads. Clearly, these two sites are *not* comparable in terms of market potential.

3. *Current market economic conditions.* If your market analysis was completed six months ago, the question of whether it remains accurate today must be raised. This is a chronic and recurring problem in real estate market analysis. Moving a development from concept to completion is a long-term venture, but current economic conditions will change during that process. This is one of many risk elements that have to be considered by developers and builders, lenders or investors, and end-users. If a robust market disappears by the time the project is completed, those anchor tenants who signed long-term leases, the lenders and venture capital investors, and the developer and builder, will all be faced with the unpleasant possibility that the project no longer passes the basic test of demand in the current market. Thus, any study of current market conditions needs not only to consider the current snapshot, but also to attempt to judge the longer-term trend.

4. *Ever-shifting demographics.* What happens to a residential development concept if the largest employer in town closes shop and moves elsewhere? What happens if an area suffering high unemployment suddenly finds itself the site of a major new employer? Clearly, these changes in employment would be among many possible factors that would change local demographic factors. People relocate to follow employment, perhaps more so than they move to escape high-crime areas. Today's demographic trends may shift unexpectedly if and when other factors—notably economic—change in significant ways.

5. *Developer/owner imposed restrictions.* Often overlooked in the market analysis is the developer's own restrictions. Some developers have

realized that investing in exceptional design, working closely with local citizens and government interests, and striving to *improve* local conditions provide great flexibility and creativity to the company or individual preparing market and feasibility studies. However, some other developers take a bare bones approach and are not willing to spend more up-front capital than required minimally. Their design tends to be flat and unimaginative; communication locally is poor and often leads to (and in some cases, creates) antidevelopment sentiment; and successful developers have to maintain at least an interest in social and public policy, if for no other reason than that it can boost profits.

6. *Financing limitations from lenders or equity partners.* Few projects are initiated with the mandate, "Money is no object." Invariably, lenders will not only specify a limited risk level they are willing to assume (and that is almost always less than 100 percent of the project's requirements). Lenders will also demand ongoing accountability in project completion and scheduling. Equity partners will impose similar restrictions, concerned not only with project costs and scheduling, but equally with cash flow and profitability after completion.

7. *Design elements and their influence on outcome.* The marketability of a project will depend to a significant degree on the design itself. A plain, minimally compliant design may pass government standards but will not add to the ambient nature of the surrounding area. Exceptional design is more than how buildings and roads are placed; it implies innovative architectural elements, heating and cooling systems, and environmental decisions as well. Investment in exceptional design can create dividends in future market value; thus, market analysis should take into account the design philosophy of the developer and architect. The key is to focus on architecture as not just making a building pretty, but rather to focus on how design can boost the operational efficiency of a building on behalf of its tenants.

8. *Local support of or opposition to a project.* The question of local attitudes toward new development cannot be ignored in the feasibility of a project. Because financial outcome depends on careful scheduling, it is critical to be aware of the effects of local opposition and the potential for project delays. Developers can take many steps to prevent or minimize opposition through preemptive steps like early communication. Most opposition movements thrive in information vacuums, so the key to reducing opposition is to make contact and maintain it with citizen groups, agencies, and elected officials. Other developers choose to take a silent approach and try to drive the process through quickly to minimize dissent.

THE ANALYTICAL PROCESS

There is an all too human tendency to begin with an assumed conclusion, and then to seek out facts that support that conclusion. However, this tendency can also serve as a trap. One possible way to view the analytical process is to seek the truth, even if the truth contradicts what we expect to find.

The *scientific method* is a process employed in analysis, with the purpose of finding an accurate and unbiased answer to a question or to a series of questions. The scientist, in testing an initial hypothesis, is satisfied with results because, at the very least, a negative outcome eliminates one possibility. When Thomas Edison stated that he had tried more than 2,000 ideas before finding a working carbonized filament for the light bulb, he was asked, "Does that mean you failed 2,000 times?" He replied, "No, it means that I found 2,000 ways to *not* make the light bulb work."

There are four specific steps to the scientific method, designed to not only test ideas but also to reliably eliminate possible outcomes that do not work. These steps are:

1. *Observation.* In the case of market analysis, an initial observation may be an apparent growth in the demand for market-rate housing.
2. *Hypothesis.* The developer may begin with the belief that it will be profitable to acquire land, build houses, and sell them at a profit.
3. *Prediction.* The developer hires experts to perform market and feasibility studies.
4. *Testing.* Objective tests are performed to ensure the validity of the previous three steps. For example, cash flow projections may prove that the idea has merit; it might also prove that the idea as conceived will not work.

Valuable Resource

For information about the scientific method, check the following web sites:

http://teacher.nsrl.rochester.edu/phy_labs/AppendixE/AppendixE.html
http://www.selu.edu/Academics/Education/EDF600/Mod3/
http://koning.ecsu.ctstateu.edu/Plants_Human/scimeth.html

In the performance of these steps, it is all too easy to derail the scientific method. If a developer views market analysis as a tool for obtaining financing—in other words, as a means to marketing the idea and nothing else—then the validity of conclusions may be in jeopardy. If the mandate given to the consultant is to prove a specific conclusion, then the outcome has been predetermined and will not be accurate.

You need to ensure that the hypothesis is valid and that the right types of tests are performed. Otherwise, the outcome will not be reliable. In the example of a market study for real estate, possible flaws in the hypothesis may emerge from the study, including:

- *An inaccurate picture of demand.* In a rental housing project such as apartment buildings, developers may proceed based on an analysis of waiting lists. However, these are not exclusively made up of people who lack housing; these lists may include people currently residing in other rental housing who desire to relocate. Thus, demand assumptions based on the existence of waiting lists could be highly inaccurate. The construction of new rental housing units may serve to increase vacancies in existing housing. In fact, real market demand could be far lower than the market study concludes. This is difficult to know because many agencies, such as local housing authorities, keep their waiting lists confidential; and location services often inflate both supply and demand sides to create the illusion of more activity on the market. Given these problems in quantifying the real level of supply and demand, it is impossible to discover how many people on those lists currently have housing and would simply move, versus the unknown number of people who want to relocate in the area or section of town, but cannot find apartments.
- *A less than accurate picture of the market area.* In the case of residential projects, the big question involves source of tenants. Where will residents come from and where do they live now? If, in order to justify the construction of additional units, the assumed market area is extended far from the site, it becomes increasingly unreliable.
- *Misunderstood employment statistics.* A study of local employment and trends in employment is easily misrepresented or misunderstood. For example, the major employer in an area may be downsizing, meaning that in the future there will be fewer jobs. So even though this employer provides a lot of jobs locally, the level of *new* jobs may be more dismal than an uninformed or biased study would reveal. Another reality that may affect results is seasonal employment. If an area depends on tourism during warmer months, what happens in the off-season? What may appear to be a robust

economy with low unemployment may, in practice, be that way only during half the year.

These possible areas affecting the reliability of the market study—and possibly other conclusions as well—demonstrate that the scientific method is a useful tool for avoiding inaccurate conclusions in the study of supply and demand. On this topic, one writer has cautioned that

> *It is easy sometimes to focus on supply, because you go out and count the trees—or homes or office buildings. But how does the supply of space in existence, under construction, planned, or otherwise expected to come on line correlate with historical, current, and forecast levels of demand? Are any apparent variables explainable? . . . it is easy to focus on supply. Demand is much more difficult to determine.*[1]

Assumptions or predictions based on artificial or misread demand for rental units leads to exaggeration on the demand side—one of the great problems in attempting to justify demand assumptions when, in fact, only the supply side has been identified and, of course, it also may have been exaggerated. Lacking strong assumptions on the demand side, it is all too easy to also misread local indicators.

The testing phase will be flawed if, in fact, the wrong data is tested. The developer and/or the consultant preparing the market study may interview the head of a housing authority for example, who confirms the premise that demand for new rental housing is high. Local politicians may voice similar beliefs. Ultimately, though, the testing will be flawed if supply is adequate for the real level of demand, and demand itself is inflated through (1) duplication of names on several lists, (2) names not removed when people find housing or move away, or (3) names on waiting lists of people occupying units who are part of the current supply. In cases where the developer wants a project to proceed, the incentive may be to maximize the demand for a particular project. As long as the developer is in control of how the market study is prepared and presented, the testing will be questioned.

The same problems with methodology would extend to the feasibility study. Any relatively skilled accountant can manipulate the numbers to make assumptions work out to reflect future positive cash flow. But again, if the underlying assumptions are not accurate, the financial projections will not be accurate, either.

A developer approaching potential lenders or equity partners—not to mention agencies granting tax credits, for example—may dispel suspicion by subjecting their proposal to a completely neutral consultant. By allowing a lender or equity partner to select a consulting firm that includes professional accounting and appraisers, the opportunity to create a desired outcome will be limited. While the majority of developers would be willing to subject a sound marketing idea to independent analysis, everyone will want to be aware that the minority may desire to use the system—including local planners and citizens, tax incentive programs, and, of course, lenders or investors—to create a desired outcome rather than to study the initial assumptions objectively.

MARKET ANALYSIS AND BUSINESS PLANNING

In some respects, the combined market and feasibility studies serve the same purpose as the more generalized *business plan*. However, there are important differences as well, notably when real estate is involved.

A business plan usually combines detailed budgets and financial assumptions with an extended-period marketing plan. This normally is found in business environments where the product or service is well-understood. In real estate, the market and feasibility studies begin with the following assumptions:

- *The market is well-understood.* The business plan usually is aimed at moving product or service to a well-understood market. A food manufacturer sells to grocery store chains and identifies the shopper as its primary market. Financial service firms target families needing investment and insurance advice. In the case of real estate, the market may be more elusive, but its elements remain constant. The end-user *and* the all-important physical location of that end-user will directly impact how a project is developed. We need to begin on an important basic theme:

> Assumption: *In real estate, we know who constitutes our market, and where that market is located.*

- *The product itself may also be a variable.* If we begin with a project concept, its very feasibility will be determined by the market study, followed by a test of the financial assumptions. We may discover, in fact, that the original concept needs modification, as a factor of market demand levels and costs. In the business plan, the product does not vary, but the market does. In the real estate market analysis process, both market *and* product have to be treated as potential variables. A second theme emerges:

> *Assumption: Our concept of the real estate product is determined not by the original idea as much as by the outcome of critical market and financial analysis.*

- *Market factors, either economic or demographic, may change.* In the business plan, a starting point often grows from a well-understood, unchanging economic and demographic data set. For example, a company that runs theme parks understands the demographic it serves: families with small children. It also knows that its own financial projections have to be based on national economic conditions. In comparison, the question of demographics is not specific in real estate developments. That depends on other *local* factors such as employment trends and housing costs. Economics also shift, at times during the project completion itself. Economic and demographic factors, by definition, are cyclical and trend-based and are not stationary. This is easily overlooked but an important distinction to keep in mind. The third important theme to remember in market analysis is:

> *Assumption: Market factors affecting both competitive and financial feasibility are always variables and have to be treated as cyclical phenomena.*

We cannot treat real estate market analysis in an identical manner as the business plan. Another way to make the distinction is from the developer's own perspective. The developer's market analysis is specific to a project and site, the local market and current trends, and the financing prospects and limitations. However, that developer's own business plan encompasses the entire business and marketing theme, objectives and standards, and profitability.

The business plan is an essential self-defining document for the business venture. The real estate marketing analysis refers to a specific project. The business plan defines (among other matters) the owner's objectives. For example, a particular developer, architect, or builder specializing in upper-income markets may establish a strong priority for creating projects of innovative design and exceptional artistic quality. Another firm might not even discuss the issue of quality, preferring to establish profit goals only. Low quality is acceptable if appropriate to a particular project. If a developer is building low-income housing units, the kitchens will not include marble countertops. While we do not suggest that the importance of business planning should be ignored, we emphasize that it is not the same as market analysis. The consideration of a specific site and its market potential is part of the specific job, just as a builder lays a foundation for a building, and just as a writer outlines chapters for a book and defines the potential reader as a starting point. Developers, architects, designers, builders, and lenders or investors, all need the exact level of definition for both markets and financial projections that are derived from market analysis.

THE KEYS TO MARKET ANALYSIS: SUPPLY AND DEMAND

At the heart of the business plan are budgets, goals, and market definitions. This is a well-understood concept, and the process of preparing and finalizing a business plan may invigorate management and employees. At the heart of market analysis is the dominant economic consideration: supply and demand

While the premise of supply and demand in a free economy is well-known as a basic premise, the application of these forces in real estate market analysis is more complex. In fact, market analysis needs to consider three different forms of supply and demand: These are in relation to the obvious market form (supply and demand for real estate); the associated rental supply and demand (tenant demand versus rental supply); and capital (financing and associated interest rates or equity capital from investors).

Real Estate Supply and Demand

The most apparent and best-known form of supply and demand is reflected in the market value of real estate. The theory is not complex. The higher the supply of properties on the market of a specific type (single-family residential, retail, or industrial, for example), the softer the demand; and the higher the number of buyers, the higher the demand. These factors and the trends they follow determine market value. When properties are in short supply—meaning there are more buyers than sellers—prices are forced upward. And when there are an excess of properties—meaning there are more sellers than buyers—prices level out and may even fall.

While most people may be aware of real estate supply and demand basics, they may not appreciate the *trends* that underlie and are reflected by these same forces. A lot of information is presented in the press and through industry associations on a national level; but in fact, all real estate trends are strictly local. We cannot judge the market in New York City by the same standards as the market in Sioux Falls, South Dakota. Every aspect of the market, attributes, economic and demographic trends, and competition are dissimilar so any attempt at comparison is invalid. However, if we review real estate supply and demand on a national level, we see only an average; such averages do not reveal any meaningful information about what is happening in a specific city or town or from one neighborhood to another.

Some analysts make the mistake of assuming that real estate trends can be tracked through a study of national averages, overlooking the local realities of real estate prices; or of trying to associate real estate valuation with inflation, as expressed by the Consumer Price Index (CPI). Housing, in fact, is not included in the CPI. "Price level changes for items such as tomatoes and video recorders have very little to do with changes in real estate prices," one analyst reminds us, and "price levels should not be viewed as independent of a specific market."[2]

It is fair to observe that real estate trends vary from one location to another, whether we are discussing towns, cities, counties, or metropolitan areas. But the local nature of real estate is even more specific. The price of a home on a busy street will differ from an identical home one block away on a quieter street. The location of a regional mall near an exit on Interstate 35 just north of Austin, Texas, will have attributes far different from those for a strip mall in the southern part of Sacramento, California. The attributes, specific location, age and quality, and other competitive factors make it impossible to compare two dissimilar properties when their areas have nothing in common.

Supply and demand in real estate—to the extent that investment value is affected—must be reviewed not on any national average basis, but on a local basis. Even checking the housing trends on a regional basis are less than revealing. For example, the Northeast encompasses areas including rural Pennsylvania as well as Manhattan's Upper East Side. The West includes the Yuma desert *and* downtown Phoenix, vastly dissimilar markets. The reports on these regional markets are merely regional averages; to judge your local market accurately, it is imperative that such averages not be used; the local market forces are all that matter. National and regional

Valuable Resources

The National Association of Realtors (www.realtor.org) compiles and publishes housing data based on regional studies. The regions as defined by the NAR include:

Northeast: Connecticut, Maine, Massachusetts, New Hampshire, New Jersey, New York, Pennsylvania, Rhode Island, and Vermont.

Midwest: Illinois, Indiana, Iowa, Kansas, Michigan, Minnesota, Missouri, Nebraska, North Dakota, Ohio, South Dakota, and Wisconsin.

South: Alabama, Arkansas, Delaware, District of Columbia, Florida, Georgia, Kentucky, Louisiana, Maryland, Mississippi, North Carolina, Oklahoma, South Carolina, Tennessee, Texas, Virginia, and West Virginia.

West: Alaska, Arizona, California, Colorado, Hawaii, Idaho, Montana, Nevada, New Mexico, Oregon, Utah, Washington, and Wyoming.

averages may be useful for comparative analysis between a specific site and those averages; but regional and national averages are not the market in any single city, town, county, or neighborhood.

Rental Supply and Demand

While the well-known market supply and demand dominates the attention of most investors, an equally important variation is the market for rentals. When the number of available rentals exceeds the number of renters, market rents decline; and when the number of renters exceeds available rentals, market rents rise.

This market is directly observed through trends in occupancy levels. When occupancy is consistently high—97 percent or 98 percent, for example—it indicates that the demand for rentals is high. When occupancy slips and begins to trend downward, it indicates that an excess of rentals has occurred. In some markets, these trends are seasonal and should be observed as such. For example, if a large portion of the local population consists of college students, of whom the majority are invariably renters, the supply and demand should be expected to reflect changes tied directly to the school schedule. If the school does not offer a complete summer curriculum, vacancies will rise and the market will see reduced demand for the season. However, once school begins anew, that trend will immediately turn around. As with all trend analysis, seasonal variation should be taken into account to ensure that the conclusions drawn are accurate.

Cause and effect in rental occupancy rates reflects trends in development. If the area experiences exceptionally high volume of apartment construction, the supply and demand interaction will be affected as soon as units become available. Historically, development tends to outpace demand, so the market is continually moving back and forth between supply and demand. Short-term trends are chaotic and it is often difficult to spot trends without a broader view. However, from a landlord's point of view, whether involved with residential or commercial properties, the direction of the trend often defines cash flow success or failure. In the course of market analysis, identifying the longer-term trend and anticipating the three- to five-year *likely* supply and demand realities is an important step.

It is also essential to recognize that real estate supply and demand (reflected in the prices of properties, the time they remain on the market, and comparisons between listed price and final sales price) is *not* always the same as the rental market's supply and demand. Much depends on the price level for properties and market rent levels. It is entirely possible that some markets will experience strong market demand but weak rental demand. For example, in a predominantly retirement-aged community, the majority of people may own their homes but, due to the lack of jobs, few younger individuals and families are likely to be found in the community. Conversely, it is also possible to witness a market with very strong rental demand and at the same time, a weakness in residential property prices. This may occur in areas with large student populations but relatively few jobs. Medium-sized cities in the Midwest may meet this definition. A large student population means higher than average rental demand for the population level, but at the same time there may be little requirement for owner-occupied housing.

This disparity further demonstrates why it is essential to study every local market individually. Formulas do not work everywhere. For example, if a market analysis were to conclude that shopping trends represent a specific factor *per capita*, how might that conclusion be different in dissimilar markets? A county located near the Canadian border may be inaccurately gauged based solely on local population. A largely student population is going to be vastly different from retirement-aged households. A city with 190,000 population in a primarily agricultural area of the country will not share the same demographic attributes (thus, rental demand requirements) as a city of the same size located within commute distance of a major metropolitan region. Consider the following population examples:[3]

City	Population (2004)
Des Moines, IA	193,333
Lincoln, NE	192,722
Greensboro, NC	191,591
Montgomery, AL	190,831
Madison, WI	190,816
Grand Rapids, MI	189,673
Yonkers, NY	188,185

Residents of Yonkers, New York, may easily commute to Manhattan, the largest city in the United States. However, those living in Lincoln, Nebraska, or Madison, Wisconsin, would experience far different employment prospects, not to mention property values, surrounding population trends, and other important considerations. All of these cities share approximately the same population indicator, but that is where the similarities end. We would further expect that the rental market supply and demand for these cities would not be comparable; this points out the necessity for reviewing a town or city individually, rather then employing formula-based conclusions. Ratio analysis works in accounting, where universally agreed upon standards apply. But in the rental market, there are no universal standards for market rates, trends, or relative health within the market.

Capital Supply and Demand

The third form of supply and demand is that for money, either debt or equity. Debt financing—from a variety of potential conventional or private lenders—is available at any time assuming that the developer is able and willing to pay the going interest rate. And of course, rates—like all supply and demand items—are cyclical. The span of these cycles may vary considerably. For example, over an 11-year period from 1994 through 2004, the prime rate changed only one percent (from 6.00 percent on January 1, 1994, to 5.00 percent on December 1, 2004). However, in the interim, rates were as high as 9.50 percent and as low as 4.00 percent, a considerable range. While real estate rates are normally tied not to prime, but to Treasury debt rates, we use this as an example. The prime rate tracks other rates and reflects changes from federal funds rates to Treasury securities, then to prime rate and above.

Table 2.1 summarizes the prime rate during this period as of the first of each month. Note the December 1 rate, for example. By the end of 1994, and through to the end of 2000, the prime rate was supported for the most part at about 8.00 percent and rose to 9.50 percent by 2000. However, in 2001, a shift began in the second quarter, with rates falling rapidly by the end of the year and remaining at about 5.00 percent for the two years following.

The 11-year cycle using prime rates as of December 1 for each of these years is summarized in Figure 2.1.

The concept that "money is always available" is only partially true. As long as you are willing to pay a going rate for mortgages, which of course, vary with changes in the long-term debt market such as U.S. Treasury bonds, it is certainly possible to find financing for a project. A more revealing question, though, is whether the debt service on financing is affordable. If a project's cash flow is not adequate to cover the debt service, then in effect, the debt financing is not available. If interest rates for mortgage financing rise, but market competitive forces do not, then cash flow is squeezed, perhaps to the point that the project is no longer feasible.

Within this same market—for capitalization—there may be equally important but far more subtle supply and demand forces at work for equity financing. Finding venture capital investors or limited partners depends partially on other available real estate investments and partially on tax benefits or restrictions. Until 1986 investors were able to invest in limited partnerships and reduce taxes considerably. With top federal rates at 50 percent, tax incentives were attractive and many tax shelters were designed to exploit the rules.

TABLE 2.1   Prime Rate History

Date	1994	1995	1996	1997	1998	1999	2000	2001	2002	2003	2004
Jan 1	6.00%	8.50%	8.50%	8.25%	8.50%	7.75%	8.50%	8.50%	4.75%	4.25%	4.00%
Feb 1	6.00	9.00	8.25	8.25	8.50	7.75	8.50	8.50	4.75	4.25	4.00
Mar 1	6.00	9.00	8.25	8.25	8.50	7.75	8.75	8.50	4.75	4.25	4.00
Apr 1	6.25%	9.00%	8.25%	8.50%	8.50%	7.75%	9.00%	8.00%	4.75%	4.25%	4.00%
May 1	6.75	9.00	8.25	8.50	8.50	7.75	9.00	7.50	4.75	4.25	4.00
Jun 1	7.25	9.00	8.25	8.50	8.50	7.75	9.50	7.00	4.75	4.25	4.00
Jul 1	7.25%	9.00%	8.25%	8.50%	8.50%	8.00%	9.50%	6.75%	4.75%	4.00%	4.25%
Aug 1	7.25	8.75	8.25	8.50	8.50	8.00	9.50	6.75	4.75	4.00	4.25
Sep 1	7.75	8.75	8.25	8.50	8.50	8.25	9.50	6.50	4.75	4.00	4.50
Oct 1	7.75%	8.75%	8.25%	8.50%	8.25%	8.25%	9.50%	6.00%	4.75%	4.00%	4.75%
Nov 1	7.75	8.75	8.25	8.50	8.00	8.25	9.50	5.50	4.75	4.00	4.75
Dec 1	8.50	8.75	8.25	8.50	7.75	8.50	9.50	5.00	4.25	4.00	5.00

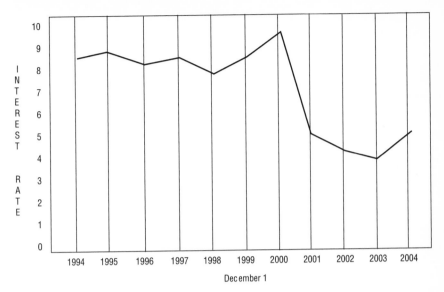

FIGURE 2.1   Eleven-Year Summary, December 1 Prime Rate

For example, a five-to-one limited partnership allowed an investor to claim deductions at five times the amount invested. So an individual paying taxes in the 50 percent bracket could invest $10,000 in a limited partnership and, by way of accelerated depreciation, claim a first-year tax loss of $50,000, or a loss equal to five times the amount invested. This tax loss reduced the individual's tax liability by $25,000 (in the 50 percent bracket). So for an investment of $10,000, liabilities were reduced by $25,000.

These shelter programs were closed down with the Tax Reform Act of 1986 (known as TRA). Now, investor deductions are limited to at-risk capital (investment plus recourse loans). Furthermore, in a passive investment such as a real estate limited partnership, while real estate professionals live with different rules, for most investors losses cannot be deducted but have to be carried forward and applied against future passive profits.

The current tax incentives for real estate investment are far less attractive than they were in the pretax reform days. However, equity investors may still be interested in placing money into real estate developments when the economic assumptions make sense. In the tax shelter days, the primary concern was for immediate tax benefits; now the numbers have to work in order to attract equity partners.

The competition for equity financing—other developments or pools such as real estate investment trusts (REITs) and mortgage pools, and similar programs—will appeal to investors as long as potential returns are higher or risks are lower. So in the supply and demand for equity capitalization, it is invariably a competitive environment.

THE NATURE OF ECONOMIC CONDITIONS

In any review of the real estate market—and remembering the three distinct forms of supply and demand—we need to remind ourselves that economic conditions are continually changing. This is easily overlooked. In the stock market, where shares are traded moment to moment, the liquidity is apparent. In real estate, where liquidity is completely lacking in most product forms (exceptions being certain publicly listed conduit investments like REITs), it is easy to forget that the condition of the market is in a state of change.

The tendency to consider current status of supply or demand as more or less permanent may be a fatal flaw in market analysis. If you listen to your local real estate broker, you will likely be told that this is the best time to buy; if you are a seller, the same broker is likely to opine that this is the best time to sell. When we work within a system where our experts are compensated by commissions, we are unlikely to ever be told that the market is weak. In fact, if we already know it is weak, the broker is likely to counterargue that the trend is beginning to turn around!

So when we see today's economic conditions as strong or as weak, we also need to be aware of some related facts, including:

- *The market is in a continual cycle of change.* Today's situation will not last forever; in fact, it may be different next month. Consider the changes in prime rate as demonstrated in Table 2.1. Rates remained at 8.25 percent for the 14 months from February 1, 1996, through March 1, 1997; and at 8.50 percent for 18 months from April 1, 1997, through September 1, 1998. But from the beginning of 2001 to 12 months later, the rate fell 56 percent from 8.50 percent to 4.75 percent. So there is no predictable pattern in supply and demand. The example has ramifications for the trend in Treasury bonds rate, thus the market for financing; but the same uncertainty applies equally to the market and rental versions of supply and demand as well.

- *Today's condition is never unmoving.* The tendency among investors and market analysts is to look at today's economic snapshot and to assume that this condition is permanent. Whether we explicitly believe this or not, the tendency is to draw conclusions on that basis. This is a tendency worth resisting, because the assumption that an economic condition is permanent may lead to errors in analytical assumptions.
- *We must keep the three supply and demand variations in mind.* Any market analysis should be undertaken with independent consideration given to the three forms of supply and demand: for market prices, for rental units, and for financing. If we ignore any of the components of this overall economic analysis, the conclusions will not be reliable. An analysis that finds all three conditions in agreement as to the feasibility of a project is encouraging. The three may act as confirmation points in an economic forecast. However, any opinion as to feasibility may be tempered when the three indicators are not in conformity with one another. The market analysis will be more reliable when the three different markets are critically analyzed together.
- *No one knows for certain the current cyclical direction or timing of the market.* In spite of what you may hear from experts, make a distinction between statements of fact and statements of opinion. Because opinion often is asserted as being factual, it is not always easy to distinguish between the two. But any forward-looking, predictive statement is only opinion. It may be based on experience, comprehensive analysis, and a deep understanding of the many facets of real estate economics; but even so, it is only an opinion. Just as you may rely on opinion only as a means for justifying your own estimates (versus attempting to *prove* that your estimates are correct), it is also important that anyone preparing a market study or a feasibility study makes clear distinctions between reporting between historical fact and projections. The factual record, including past financial history and trends, is most useful to support a premise included in a projection; but it should be made clear where the discussion moves from fact to opinion, if only because anyone reviewing the report may not make that shift automatically.
- *No investment decisions should ever be made under pressure.* If the source of information is a seller or a seller's broker, it is important to be aware of the bias. It is never advisable to make decisions (or to recommend a course of action) until all of the data is gathered, sorted, and studied; and until the analysis itself has been done.

■ *In listening to advice or opinion, we should always consider the source.*
Most sources of information have a bias. Anyone asking you to buy
property or to use services in the development or design of property,
has a self-interest in mind. This is human nature, and everyone is a
party to the interaction that is involved on the path from concept to
feasibility. However, let us not forget that, just as authors try to provide
value in order to sell books, the same is true of real estate brokers, designers and architects, engineers, city planners, neighborhood groups,
and an infinite line of experts we meet along the way.

CHAPTER 3

Valuation of Real Estate

What is a property worth, and why? This chapter presents the principles of valuation that determine market value; basics of appraisal science; and important economic and political trends affecting valuation. Finally, we demonstrate how valuation needs to be viewed on two levels: First, the basic principles of valuation need to be mastered and second, we need to evaluate how an investor actually enters the market with valuation questions in mind.

Market analysis is a process of sensible observation. By being aware of the factors that affect market value, it becomes possible to accurately identify how those principles apply to a specific property; a group of properties; or to properties sharing *similar* attributes (location, size, age, zoning, square feet, or neighborhood, for example).

Valuation is distinguished via attributes of properties and markets; further clarifications of value are based upon the priorities of the investor or owner, including cash flow and potential rental income tax benefits or limitations, and perceptions about future growth in market value. No one of these valuation criteria are exclusive; they are part of a larger overall analysis of a property's value. As with all market, *value* itself consists partly of what a property is worth today and partly what we believe it will be worth in the future. One definition acknowledges the broad range of meanings, but summarizes the meaning of value nicely:

> *The term "value" is often used inaccurately by non-qualified practitioners. It is an abstract word with many meanings . . . In an economic sense, market value has a specific definition—the present worth of future benefits realized from ownership.*[1]

PRINCIPLES OF REAL ESTATE VALUATION

We begin with a summary of the major principles that govern valuation. There are 10 primary concepts in this group:

1. *Progression*. This principle relates to one way in which market values rise. Expressed as a statement, progression tells us, "A property's value may increase due to the existence of similar properties in similar locations, containing greater quality." The idea that a rising tide lifts all ships applies here. In fact, progression is also expressed by the maxim that you profit in real estate by buying the worst house on a good block.

2. *Regression*. The opposite rule may work as well. A falling tide can lower all ships or, as the regression principle reveals, "A property's value may decrease due to the existence of similar properties in similar locations, containing lower quality." So an exceptional house may not appreciate as one would expect if and when other houses—even on the sale block—are outdated, obsolete, or poorly maintained. This concept is closely related to the third principle in real estate valuation, that of conformity.

3. *Conformity*. This concept is, "A property is most likely to appreciate in value along with other, similar properties in the same neighborhood." So if an investor spends a lot of money to upgrade a house, for example, conformity may limit the appreciation regardless of how the work is performed. This relates to construction materials, age of properties, number of rooms, and overall square footage and style. If the neighborhood consists of 2,000 square feet, three-bedroom, two-bath homes 10 years old, improving property above that standard may not be profitable. Converting a home by adding 500 square feet and changing the internal layout to four bedrooms and three baths could be money poorly spent, based on the principle of conformity.

4. *Substitution*. In real estate, comparison rules the way that valuation trends become established. Thus, progression, regression, and conformity are primary concepts. A variation on this theme is that of substitution. This principle is, "A property's greatest potential market value is limited by the market value of other, similar properties." Thus, it would not be realistic to judge market value in a vacuum. Without considering the market value of similar properties located in similar areas, we cannot accurately analyze market value of any property. This theory is easily observed. When two

similar properties are for sale, the lower-priced one will tend to sell first and, as a result, the market value of the remaining property may be lowered.

5. *Change*. This principle tells us, "No condition remains the same indefinitely; change is part of the economic cycle." Property values are affected by change in several ways. These include local economic and demographic trends, physical age and condition of the property and surrounding properties, character of a neighborhood or city, and natural events like disasters (hurricanes and earthquakes, for example).

6. *Anticipation*. Real estate investors—like those in all markets—are continually estimating the future value of properties. The principle of anticipation may be stated as: "Market value often is affected by expectations about future events." For example, if an investor believes that a particular area is likely to experience growth in coming years, that would mean property values would rise. The very expectation actually increases demand, and valuation rises as a result. The cause and effect can be more immediate than the time it takes for the cause to occur. If a proposed rezone is in the works, properties in the affected area could experience rise or fall in property value in anticipation of the change.

7. *Contribution*. This principle acknowledges a limitation on growth in market value, notably in the case of improvements. The additional market value one may expect from improving property is not equal to cost, but to the contribution those changes make to actual market value. Thus, in a low-demand market, an improvement may add only $2,000 to market value even though actual cost was $5,000. In the case of cosmetic repairs to properties in hot markets, the opposite effect may be seen as well. Contribution tells us, "Improvements add to market value as a factor of current supply and demand, and not necessarily on the basis of actual cost." The principle of contribution can also be defined as being controlled both by *increasing returns* and by *diminishing returns*. In other words, making improvements to property will cause growth in market value to an extent (increasing returns), but when improvements exceed that level, return on investment begins to fall (diminishing returns).

8. *Plottage*. This principle observes that consistency in ownership of land and zoning or usage, tends to maximize value. The principle states that, "Land values tend to increase when adjacent lots are combined into single ownership and put to a single zoning or use." This phenomenon is observed when a series of relatively small lots

remain under-developed and are eventually purchased by one person or company and subsequently developed. Each individual would be unable to organize such a development when many owners are involved.

9. *Highest and best use.* Closely related to plottage is the principle that "Real estate valuation is maximized when land is utilized in the best possible way." Thus, rich farm land should be used to grow crops and land located within sight of an interstate freeway is best used for highway commercial zoning. The same observations apply to all forms of zoning and usage. Real estate valuation is unusual in that sometimes 10 one-acre plots are worth more than one 10-acre plot. An analyst needs to compare land size to proposed land use, and be prepared to adjust valuation based on a site's variance from the idea.

This means looking at far more than just zoning and its obvious attributes. Zoning is only one aspect, one expert has observed:

> *How many times have we seen statements in reports that conclude that the highest and best use of a property is as zoned? Highest and best use, by definition, includes the legal, physical, and economic benefits of ownership, plus social commitments to a community at large."*[2]

10. *Competition.* The last primary principle of valuation is directly related to the broader concept of supply and demand. The principle of competition states, "Opportunities for profitable investment lead to competition." This has ramifications for valuation of all properties. A good idea is going to be imitated or duplicated. Thus, as long as demand remains unchanged, the emergence of competing properties will tend to dilute market value for all similar properties.

The 10 principles of valuation are summarized in Table 3.1.

MEASUREMENTS OF VALUATION

The principles of valuation are the guiding factors in market analysis; they define how and *why* value rises or falls. They are fundamental. However, an investment in real estate may be valued based on one of several different

TABLE 3.1   The Ten Principles of Valuation

Progression. A property's value may increase due to the existence of similar properties in similar locations, containing greater quality.

Regression. A property's value may decrease due to the existence of similar properties in similar locations, containing lower quality.

Conformity. A property is most likely to appreciate in value along with other, similar properties in the same neighborhood.

Substitution. A property's greatest potential market value is limited by the market value of other, similar properties.

Change. No condition remains the same indefinitely; change is part of the economic cycle.

Anticipation. Market value often is affected by expectations about future events.

Contribution. Improvements add to market value as a factor of current supply and demand, and not necessarily on the basis of actual cost.

Plottage. Land values tend to increase when adjacent lots are combined into single ownership and put to a single zoning or use.

Highest and best use. Real estate valuation is maximized when land is utilized in the best possible way.

Competition. Opportunities for profitable investment lead to competition.

measurements in addition to price. Four specific measurements of valuation are worth discussion. These are:

1. *Profitability.* The increase in market value is, of course, the most apparent method of measuring real estate value. In its basic form, real estate value—the price at which buyers and sellers reach a meeting of the minds—is at the core of this discussion. It is the primary means for distinguishing one property from another; from identifying the relative real estate value growing from different zoning and land use; and for spotting and quantifying trends in the market. Virtually everything centers around price and, more specifically, the *change* in price over time, or the price trend.

   Just as stock market investors follow market price of stocks, real estate investors also make a number of judgments concerning their market positions based on the all-important price trend. But is that enough? Perhaps emphasis on price alone is flawed because it ignores the equally important question of risk. In the stock market, a highly volatile stock may grow in value quite rapidly but present an exceptionally high risk as well. Investors saw this phenomenon—often too late—by investing in the dot.com fad a few years ago. Those who put a lot of investment capital in Enron, WorldCom, Tyco, and many other corporations whose bookkeeping practices were questionable, discovered the reality of risk too late, and many lost large sums of money. Does the same caveat apply to real estate?

The market prices of real estate cannot be observed day-to-day or hour-to-hour as they can in the stock market. They can be observed directly only through sales prices and indirectly through asked prices. Even so, the various risk factors unique to an area or a site should be viewed along with price trends. If those trends are surprising in any way, a skeptical interpretation of that may include a question of risk. If land is exceptionally cheap today, might there not be a reason?

Example: A study of local classified ads reveals that as a general rule, empty building lots average $75,000; however, a few ads offer building lots for about $20,000. Why? Upon investigation, it is revealed that the typical building lots have essential service hookups nearby, but the lower-priced lots could not be developed unless the owner were to pay to run those utilities. The cost of doing so would add $50,000 to $60,000 to the advertised price of the lots. The lower-priced land is not a bargain at all; to purchase land at the advertised price would include the risk that utilities might never be run close to the area.

Price is a good starting point in any market analysis. But valuation contains many additional elements of risk and reward; the current price of any real estate reflects a mix of factors, both advantageous and disadvantageous. It is unlikely that an exceptional bargain can be found without some offsetting factors.

2. *Cash flow.* To many investors, cash flow is more important than profits, at least in the immediate future. A simple analysis may reveal that even when growth trends are positive, cash flow may negate the advantage itself. Consider the following summary:

Price of real estate	$350,000
Down payment	$ 70,000
Monthly payment, 6.5%, interest only payments	$ 1,896
Rental income	$ 3,700
Less: Operating expenses	$ 2,800
Net operating income	$ 900
Cash flow after debt service and before taxes	$ -996
Annual growth in property value (est.)	3%

A basic analysis of this situation reveals that the overall invest-ment will not be profitable. If we accept the annual growth assumption of 3 percent per year, the $350,000 investment will appreciate by $10,500 in the first year. However, cash flow for the same full year will be $–11,952 ($996 × 12). An argument may be made that an invest-ment such as this is made for tax purposes. It is true that directly man-aged real estate provides unique tax advantages. But the after-tax cash flow does not work out.

Referring back to the same numbers, even if we assume that the entire monthly payment consists of interest and is deductible (ignoring the fact that principal would not be deductible), do the numbers on an after-tax basis continue to work? Let us also assume that depreciation (a noncash deductible expense) is $10,909 per month. This is based on a calculation involving residential property, which is depreciated over 27.5 years; and further, we assume that the land in this illustration is worth $50,000, so the remaining $300,000 is subject to depreciation (land cannot be depreciated). That would provide an annual deprecia-tion allowance of $10,909 ($300,000 ÷ 27.5), or $909 per month. Now the monthly numbers look like this:

Rental income	$ 3,700
Less: Operating expenses	–2,800
Net operating income	$ 900
Interest	–1,896
Depreciation	–909
Taxable income	$–1,905

If we assume that the effective total federal and state tax rate in this situation is 40 percent (assuming 33 percent federal plus 7 percent state), the monthly loss of $1,905 would create a reduction in income taxes of $762 ($1,905 × 40 percent). (Incidentally, these calculations may be fur-ther adjusted if and when the tax-based net loss exceeds the maximum allowed per year.) Now how does the after-tax cash flow look?

Net operating income	$ 900
Less: debt service	–1,896
Tax reduction	+ 762
Cash flow after operating expenses and taxes	$–234

We can conclude that this investment will produce after-tax nega-tive cash flow of $234 per month, or $2,808 per year. Returning to the original assumption that this property grows in value by 3 percent per year, or $10,500, our cash flow-based market analysis works out—but this analysis is highly optimistic. It assumes that, in fact, the 3 percent annual growth rate will continue to occur; that might not be accurate. It also assumes that the rents will be collected every month without any provision for vacancies. If growth estimates are correct, the compounded effect of 3 percent per year will be far greater than the basic $10,500 we have used. However, the point to be made here is that the investor needs to be able to afford the monthly outflow for the investment to work.

The study of cash flow as a method of valuation has two specific components. First is the question of whether an investor can *afford* the negative cash flow. Even if the numbers are promising, one would need to be able to continue spending more each month than was generated from rents. If, in fact, those funds are not going to be available, then the proposed investment simply lacks feasibility. The second component involves investment assumptions. If we accept the premise that the investor can afford the negative cash flow, is the net after-tax cash flow *higher* or *lower* than the assumed growth rate of the property? If that growth rate falls short of the after-tax negative cash flow, we again would conclude that the proposed investment lacks basic feasibility. We cannot reasonably expect to profit from investing funds, so why proceed? In general, the concept of buying a property that loses money year after year, but planning to make money in the long run through price appreciation, is unwise.

3. *Relative value of rental income.* A third measurement of valuation is related closely to the cash flow issue, but it involves an additional investment component. Rental income varies based not only on trends in demand for rental units, but also on the basis of location and property condition. The owner of an apartment building may be unwilling to perform routine maintenance, so conditions of the property are poor. As a result, turnover is high and vacancies become a chronic problem. This occurs even when demand is high, because the substandard conditions make the site unappealing. Those who can afford to pay market rates will prefer to do so, rather than live in a substandard apartment.

A buyer of such a property will recognize that the depreciated condition also affects value. Income properties are normally appraised using the *income method* (discussed later in this chapter). Essentially, value is derived from the income of the property. Clearly, an apartment complex with higher than normal vacancies, drawing less than market-rate rents, will appraise below market as well. The current owner may not understand that maintaining such a property is, in fact, a wise investment, or that the nominal savings accomplished by not spending money to maintain the property creates far lower market value. So the would-be buyer will recognize that the purchase price of such a property would be a smart investment. By upgrading the property, the new owner will be able to increase rents to market-rate levels, and also to reduce vacancies. After that transition is complete, a new appraisal would be likely to reflect a profitable change in market value.

4. *Tax incentives.* Real estate investors have historically acknowledged significant valuation based on tax incentives. In the days prior to the tax reforms enacted in 1986 (which effectively removed multiple write-offs and instituted at-risk rules; restricted passive loss deductions; and reformed depreciation), real estate was a favorite haven for tax avoidance, enabling those in top tax brackets to eliminate liabilities. Since these reforms, those investing in *passive* forms of real estate programs (limited partnerships, for example) can not claim loss deductions except to the extent that they offset passive gains. However, individuals who directly manage their rental income investments are provided benefits not available to other investors.

Those investors who are "actively involved" in management can deduct up to $25,000 in annual losses on real estate. Meeting this test is not difficult; an owner must be tied to selection of tenants, decisions to buy or sell properties, and maintenance. Even if a landlord hires a management company, meeting this test is a matter of staying in touch and putting in a minimum number of hours per month. To qualify, one also must own at least 10 percent of the property.

An exception applies for what the IRS calls a "real estate person." This is anyone who generates more than half of his or her business services in real estate; who performs more than 750 hours per year in real estate business; who materially participates in real estate business other than rental income; and who also materially participates in rental income activity.[3]

For the *real estate person*, real estate income is treated as nonpassive, meaning that the level of annual loss deductions is not limited to the $25,000 maximum otherwise allowed.

Even for those who are not real estate persons, the ability to write off up to $25,000 per year is significant. For many, the tax benefit spells the difference between positive and negative cash flow, when calculated on an after-tax basis. The deduction is restricted for those with adjusted gross income (AGI) above $100,000; once that level is reached, the allowable deduction is reduced by 50 cents for every dollar of adjusted gross income. For example, if an individual's AGI is $110,000, the allowable maximum is reduced to $20,000 ($25,000 – 50 percent of $10,000). Furthermore, the calculation of AGI for the purpose of this reduction is modified from the AGI reported on an individual tax return. However, for those with income below $100,000, the ability to reduce income by up to $25,000 is an important feature in valuation; the benefit—representing reduced overall tax liabilities—should be viewed as a tangible benefit of owning rental income.

Making this even more attractive, it is possible to have a positive cash flow from real estate investments and, at the same time, report a net loss for tax purposes. This is possible because real estate investors can deduct depreciation. This expense is a noncash expense, calculated based on the value of the improvements (which is roughly the purchase price minus value of land) and is allowed over a period of years (the recovery period). Depreciation is a complex topic beyond the scope of this book; however, it is an important feature in the calculation of cash flow and profits from real estate, as well as a feature in determining valuation.

A key point is that while depreciation is often confused with the economic life of an asset, it is not the same thing. Most real estate retains its market value long after its depreciable basis has fallen to zero.

Investment Features Affecting Valuation

In determining a broad-based conclusion of valuation for real estate, we must further consider the features of the investment. In any form of investment, it is not reliable to classify a particular selection as good or bad without further analyzing these important features. They are liquidity, leverage, risk, and marketability.

Liquidity   A comparison between two or more investments is accurate and reliable only when the attributes are comparative as well. Thus, comparing a highly liquid purchase of publicly exchanged stock, to an illiquid long-term real estate purchase, is not truly comparable. Thus, any calculation of return on investment, risk, or other important features would be similarly unreliable. We cannot judge real estate comparatively without being aware of liquidity issues. Direct ownership of real estate is illiquid under three distinct definitions.

Lack of Secondary Market   Some forms of real estate are illiquid because ownership cannot be easily transferred on an open, public exchange. The stock market is a highly liquid market, but units of limited partnerships, for example, can often be sold at a discount. The secondary market is lacking, because used partnership units are not appealing to new investors, as a general rule. As the maxim goes, "Limited partnership units are not bought, they are SOLD."

Potential for Low Demand in Public Markets A second form of illiquidity is found even when investors own real estate directly. If the market is soft in terms of demand, the property is illiquid with one of two consequences. First, it may take far longer to sell than the owner considers desirable. Second, it may be necessary to reduce the asked price in order to compete with other sellers. Owners also have to pay capital gains tax *and* tax on accumulated depreciation when they sell. This is a *huge* disincentive to selling. It can be compensated for, however, through the use of a 1031 exchange, also called a like-kind exchange. In that device, taxes on a current gains are deferred until a future sale of a replacement property.

Cost of Buying and Selling For directly owned real estate, it is expensive to buy and sell. Closing costs can easily absorb or even surpass a marginal profit, so in order to justify tying up capital, investors need to hold property long enough for its market value to season. The only alternative in dealing with this form of illiquidity is to refinance to remove appreciated equity, or to acquire a second mortgage or line of credit.

Leverage Most directly owned real estate is purchased with a down payment, often 30 percent or more for investment properties. The balance is financed. In this situation, an investor leverages the cash investment, controlling 100 percent with only 30 percent down. While many consider this a distinct advantage, notably when market values rise quickly, it is also a higher risk. The investor depends on consistent cash flow as a requirement for keeping up with debt service. A one-month vacancy may be serious, and a two- or three-month vacancy fatal if the investor has no cushion to make it through extended vacancy periods.

Risk The concept of risk is easily underestimated, especially by real estate investors. There is a tendency to dismiss risk on the argument that "it is easy to make money on real estate." However, a number of risks should be kept in mind. These include the all-important cash flow risk as well as less obvious risks: a slow market in which market value does not rise or even falls; catastrophic loss due to disasters not covered by insurance policies (including volcanic eruption, or earthquake, for example); the disastrous experience of having a tenant who does not pay rent and who refuses to vacate, and perhaps even one who destroys the property; and of course, the risk of a softening rental unit market. All of these risks should be understood as factors in real estate investing; for many, these risks reduce valuation to the point that it is not worthwhile.

Another form of risk involves spreading capital among markets with dissimilar features. Popularly called *diversification* or the avoidance of losing all invested capital in a single investment choice, the risk here is more accurately distinguished as *asset allocation*, or placing capital in entirely different markets. Diversification is best understood as placing funds in several different stocks or investing in mutual funds to spread risk; asset allocation is more closely associated with disparate market selection, such as stocks, savings, and real estate. Because real estate requires a large sum of investment capital, even in the form of a leveraged down payment, it is easy to forget or ignore the importance of asset allocation. Applying the concept of asset allocation is often difficult for investors of moderate means; it is difficult to diversify limited capital within the real estate asset class. The risk remains, however; if most of an individual's capital is placed in real estate, the asset allocation risk is very real. If real estate stagnates while stock market values become quite strong, the missed opportunities from poor allocation and planning affect overall profits.

Marketability The last of the four investment features is marketability. This is not the same as liquidity, although some of the same features apply. By marketability, we mean the existence of a ready buyer when a current owner wants to sell. Some real estate is going to lack marketability, for any number of reasons. For example, an individual who buys property financed by the seller may not realize that the property cannot be financed through conventional channels. In some areas, houses with post and beam foundations do not qualify for bank financing; only those with permanent foundations meet the criteria. So a seller-financed home may be marketable only through private financing. It is often true that what seems an attractive deal—seller will carry the loan—is in reality a situation in which the buyer takes on the seller's problems. In terms of financing, such a property is not marketable.

Marketability is also affected by obsolescence, the expense of outdated utilities, poor insulation, bad plumbing and electrical systems, or—in a general sense—the need for repairs that exceed the equity in the property. This last form of problem, one in which the property is essentially "totaled," is especially troubling to the inexperienced real estate purchaser, the individual who views the fixer-upper or landlording market as a method of building wealth in real estate. The concept of marketability refers to a range of issues that are not always apparent, which make an investment a poor choice.

Appraisal Methods

The final word on valuation is the appraisal. This is an analysis and report prepared by a professional appraiser. An appraisal may be performed for a lender as part of a loan application and review; by an attorney or escrow company during the closing of a sale; or as part of a procedure to establish current market value (closing of an estate, probate, or during a divorce, for example).

While it may be generally assumed that a property has a single, true value, reality demonstrates that this is not so. Based on the reason for the appraisal and the motivation of the individual or company paying for it, a range of reasonable estimates of current market value is possible. For example, a lender who favors granting a loan based on strong credit of the borrower needs primarily to ensure that the stated equity and value of property are within reason. An attorney representing one side in a divorce proceeding may be more interested in gaining verification that property value is *lower* than the adversary for the other side believes. While, in an ideal world, all appraisals would be entirely unbiased, these realities certainly affect how appraisals are performed. But no matter what that motivation, the appraiser is supposed to verify that the stated value is within reason. State licensing boards also exist to ensure that if an appraiser grossly abuses their position, they may have their license revoked.

Appraisers who work locally may be best qualified to render a solid opinion because they are familiar with area trends and values. They know where to locate comparable neighborhoods and properties; and they are connected with local real estate and lending professionals.

Appraisers use one of three methods, and the applicable method depends on the purpose of the appraisal as well as type of property. The three methods are cost, market or sales comparison, and income. Many appraisals of residential property compare the first two methods and then arrive at a reasonable estimate of current value based on that comparison. Commercial appraisers tend to rely on the third method.

Valuable Resources

To find a local appraiser, check qualifications, or to learn more about the science of appraisal, check the following web sites:

http://www.appraisalinstitute.org/
http://www.appraisalfoundation.org/
http://www.american-appraisal.com/

Cost Method   The cost method, or cost approach to appraisal calculates what it would cost to duplicate the existing improvements in today's dollars. A distinction has to be made between *cost* and *replacement*, especially for older structures with exceptional architectural or handwork features. A replacement of such attributes would be more expensive than merely replacing a structure of the same square footage and other internal features.

The cost method includes a calculation of construction costs, minus an estimate of depreciation and special site features, such as view, topography, or lot shape. The concept of *depreciation* for appraisal purposes is quite different from depreciation as defined for tax purposes. Tax-based depreciation involves writing off the value of improvements over a recovery period. Appraisal-based depreciation is an estimate of the difference between new construction (cost or replacement) and the current condition of property. So a run-down property will be given a higher allowance for depreciation than one that is newer and in better condition. A formula for arriving at value using the cost approach is:

Cost of construction – allowance for depreciation
+ added value based on site attributes = estimated value

The basic calculation using the cost value involves first figuring out the square feet and area of the building or buildings; and then multiplying the total feet by applicable cost figures (these vary by region). A useful summary of how to calculate cost factors is found at http://architecture.about .com/cs/buildyourhouse/a/costs.htm. However, the first step will be to compare local land and improvement values, based on data from a reputable and authoritative source.

Calculating a depreciation allowance to adjust for age and condition of the home is a process devised to define the *economic life* of a property, or a comparison between improvements and their contribution to overall value. An age/life method for calculating depreciation involves dividing 100 by the economic life to arrive at annual depreciation. For example, if the appraiser believes that the economic life of a property is 40 years, the depreciation calculation would begin with:

100 ÷ 40 = 2.5% depreciation per year

Next, the appraiser calculates the *effective age* of a property, which is the age of the property based on current condition of improvements (and not necessarily the true age). For example, if we assume that the appraiser believes a property's effective age is 15 years, the annual depreciation rate of 2.5 percent (in the preceding example) would be multiplied by five years:

$$2.5\% \times 5 \text{ years} = 12.5\%$$

The appraiser's estimate of cost to replace improvements would next be reduced by the depreciation factor. For example, if the current cost value of property is estimated at $300,000, the calculation would be:

Cost value of property	$300,000
Less depreciation, 12.5%	– 37,500
Net cost value	$262,500

Finally, the appraiser adds value for advantageous site features. By comparing the subject site to other sites in the area, the appraiser adds a factor to compensate for differences. For example, if the site is larger than other lots, the appraiser may add a percentage to the net cost value. In reviewing comparable lots, the appraiser may determine that it is reasonable to add 5 percent to the value of the property for site value:

Net cost value	$262,500
Plus: site value, 5%	+ 13,125
Adjusted value	$275,625

Applying these criteria to a subject property and three or more comparable properties, the appraiser is likely to make specific adjustments to arrive at fair market value; or to take an average among comparable properties to arrive at a base for calculations under the cost approach.

A cautionary note concerning the use of the cost method: When appraisal is performed for developers on larger-scale projects, selection of costs has to also take into account the practical marketing aspects, and not simply the cost of land and materials. It has been observed that

> *these costs are a function of the overall design of the project and the needs and desires of likely buyers of the finished lots. In forecasting site development costs, care should be taken to ensure that the forecast properly reflects not only the actual expenses, but also the timing of the expenditures. Often an appraiser is supplied with a cost estimate by the developer. The cost estimate should be cross-checked against the actual development costs of similar subdivisions and perhaps against cost service estimates.*[4]

The cost method is also often used for valuation of industrial properties that may have specialized equipment and do not have an easily observed rental market. As such, the cost method is more applicable than the income approach.

Market or Sales Comparison Method The second method is an exercise in comparison between the subject property and other, similar properties that were sold recently. These comparable sales are most valid if they occurred in the recent past. Thus, properties sold in the past three months would be more relevant than those that sold nine months ago. Recent sales reveal current market value and make a convincing argument in support of this appraisal method.

Adjustments are made to the comparable property sales totals to arrive at a true basis for comparison. For example, an appraiser may deduct a percentage of value from a comparable property because it was built a few years before the subject property. Or some value may be added to a comparable property with more square footage or a somewhat larger lot. So condition, lot size, square footage of improvements, and condition will all play a role in adjusting comparable sales so that, in the appraiser's opinion, the related sales are truly as comparable as possible.

The appraiser makes a judgment about how to equate comparable sales (after adjustments) to the subject property. However, more weight may be given to a property requiring the least amount of adjustment; or to a property whose neighborhood is most similar to the subject neighborhood. Is the decision about how to make an adjustment to be based on subjective or objective criteria? This appraisal approach is described by one expert as a paradox. He explains that some textbooks

> refer to the adjustment and final estimate of value process as more of an art form than one of mathematics. The appraiser is supposed to draw on his or her experience to aid in the adjustment process and rigid mathematical calculations should not dictate the amount of the adjustment. In actual fact, the opposite should occur. The valuation of any given piece of real estate should not be left to a process that relies on an artist's acuity, particularly when the outcome of value is deemed to have some type of mathematical significance.[5]

Income Method The third and most complex method for appraising property is based on rental income derived from properties. This method is used for both residential single-family or multi-unit buildings and for commercial properties.

For single-family properties appraised under the income method, a *gross rent multiplier* (GRM) often is used. This is a factor developed from a study of comparable sales prices of property and the monthly or annual income those properties generated.

For example, consider the case of five properties sold during the past six months. To compute the GRM on a monthly rent basis, the formula is:

$$\text{sales price} \div \text{gross monthly income} = \text{GRM}$$

Some typical numbers based on this formula for single-family residences:

Sales Price		Monthly Income		GRM
$125,000	÷	$ 950	=	131.58
132,500	÷	1,050	=	126.19
134,000	÷	1,000	=	134.00
141,500	÷	1,100	=	128.64
145,000	÷	1,125	=	128.89
Average			=	129.86

The same calculation can be made using annual rents:

Sales Price		Annual Income		GRM
$125,000	÷	$11,400	=	10.96
132,500	÷	12,600	=	10.52
134,000	÷	12,000	=	11.17
141,500	÷	13,200	=	10.72
145,000	÷	13,500	=	10.74
Average			=	10.82

An appraiser would conclude from this analysis of GRM for comparable properties, that a reliable estimate can be applied to be the subject property. More weight may be given to properties most comparable, so even these averages could be altered to make the appraiser's conclusions more accurate. For example if the appraiser uses the annual GRM method, it may be that the second and fourth properties are most comparable to the subject property. As a result, the appraiser may apply a factor of 10.62 (an average between GRM of 10.52 and 10.72) rather than the higher overall average.

Next, the appraiser would analyze annual rent derived from the subject property. If we assume, for example, that a single-family home has been rented out in recent years and currently generates gross rent of $12,000 per year, the annual GRM is used to estimate appraised value:

$$10.62 \times \$12,000 = \$127,440$$

Under this method, the appraiser would conclude that the property is worth $127,440. Factors affecting the selection of a GRM and making adjustments to comparable properties may include neighborhood condition, age and condition of the property, lot size and other amenities, and any other attributes the appraiser believes are significant (view, proximity to transportation or shopping, noise levels, topography, etc.).

For multi-unit properties, an appraiser uses a factor known as *capitalization rate*, or *cap rate*. The calculation of cap rate involves calculation of annual income and a comparison between the subject property and cap rates on comparable properties in the same area or similar areas. For example, in appraising an apartment complex with net operating income (rents less vacancy factor, taxes, insurance, management fees, repairs and utilities) of $52,800 per year, the current value of the complex can be calculated by comparison with other apartment complexes with a similar number of units, same or similar neighborhood, and similar condition and age. For example, checking five other properties, the appraiser may discover the following:

Net Operating Income		Sales Price		Cap Rate
$58,000	÷	$565,300	=	10.3
52,500	÷	522,800	=	10.0
57,000	÷	566,000	=	10.1
61,500	÷	605,400	=	10.2
55,000	÷	545,000	=	10.1
Average			=	10.1

The cap rates in these comparable sales are very close, so an appraiser may conclude that the 10.1 is a reasonable local rate. Thus, applying this rate against net operating income, market value may be appraised as:

$$\$52,800 \div 10.1 = \$522,772 \text{ (rounded to } \$522,800)$$

This method, also called *direct capitalization* of the subject property, is convincing when it conforms to market rates in comparable sales, when rents are at market rates, and when the properties are stabilized. Alternative calculations may be based on assumed available return on investment from other uses of capital, and the calculations are far more complex. For complex properties, such as office buildings or rehab properties with long-term lease tenants, the appraiser may find that rents are significantly above or below market rates. In these situations, appraisers will use a discounted cash flow over the entire life span of the investment by valuing earlier cash flow as worth more than future cash flow. The goal in this approach is to reduce the future value to present value or, put as a question, "What should you pay today for the future stream of cash flows?" Most appraisers will use specialized financial software tools such as ARGUS (www.argussoftware.com) to help with these calculations. This approach is complex and beyond the scope of this book.

The alternative cap rate calculations are troubling because comparisons between dissimilar investments are not always valid. Given different risk factors, return on investment is not as exact as market sales comparisons.

In appraising rental income property, appraisers may adjust their findings based on other factors, especially cash flow. The strength or weakness in projections of likely future cash flow is, perhaps, of more immediate concern to investors than profitability over the long term. As a question of feasibility, investors need to base valuation on the relative strength of cash flow adjustments. Three useful tests are used in appraisals for this purpose: debt coverage ratio, expense ratio, and loan-to-value ratio.

The appraiser may begin by questioning whether current net operating income will be strong enough to cover debt service on a mortgage loan. To determine this, the *debt coverage ratio* is used. To calculate, net operating income is divided by the amount of debt service to calculate the ratio. For example, when net operating income is $52,800 and annual debt service is $37,896, the debt coverage ratio is:

$$\$52,800 \div \$37,896 = 1.39 \text{ to } 1$$

This ratio provides a view of the net cash flow after expenses and debt service have been paid. How this compares to similar properties may reveal the relative strength of that cash flow and could affect the appraiser's conclusions concerning value.

A closely related calculation is a study of the *expense ratio* for an income property. In this calculation, operating expenses are divided by effective gross income (maximum rental income minus vacancy rate). For example, if effective gross income is $52,800 and annual operating expenses average $21,500, the expense ratio is:

$$\$21,500 \div \$52,800 = .41$$

This operating ratio is next compared to the operating ratio for similar properties to draw conclusions about whether cash flow conditions are strong or weak, in comparison.

A third calculation involving cash flow is the *loan-to-value ratio*. In this calculation, the mortgage amount is divided by the value of property. An investor purchasing a property for an assumed value of $522,800 may seek a loan of $400,000. In this example, the loan-to-value ratio will be:

$$\$400,000 \div \$522,800 = 76.5\%$$

These three ratios are most effectively used in comparative form, between alternative potential properties and between a subject property and comparable sales. Valuation is normally involved with identifying a reasonable sales/purchase price for buyers, sellers, lenders and investors; the three forms of cash flow analysis further identify valuation of properties based on comparative return, which may be of more immediate interest to buyers as well as to lenders. The question of affordability relates more to cash flow than to economic rent.

That being said, potential income value is also calculated based on a study of *economic rent*. This is an analysis of rent on the basis of rent per unit, per room, or per square feet (or all three). For example, if gross annual rent is being compared for five comparable properties, an economic rent analysis may reveal the following:

	Property #1	Property #2	Property #3	Property #4	Property #5
Annual rent	$11,400	$12,600	$12,600	$12,000	$13,500
Units	10	12	15	13	15
Rooms	32	37	48	41	45
Square feet	4,450	4,900	6,200	4,400	5,950
Annual rent per:					
unit	$1,140	$1,050	$840	$923	$900
room	$356	$341	$263	$293	$300
sq. feet	$2.56	$2.57	$2.03	$2.73	$2.27

These factors, like other appraisal steps, enable comparisons between comparable properties and the subject property, and may allow both appraiser and investors to draw conclusions about the efficiency, cash flow, return on investment, and other important questions. As a means for comparing the feasibility between two or more properties, the comparative analysis that is derived from appraisals is an integral part of market analysis and the overall study of property valuation.

Legislative Policy and Valuation

We have concentrated on market forces for the majority of our discussion on land valuation. However, we also need to be cognizant of how *artificial* forces may also affect land values. These forces—specifically consisting of local zoning, growth management and other legislative controls, and the government's right to exercise eminent domain—may significantly affect land values as well as the ability of the market to respond to forces of economic supply and demand.

The first U.S. zoning ordinance was passed in 1916 in New York City. It defined height and setback limitations on buildings and restricted incompatible land uses. The original purpose was to prevent industrial uses from moving gradually into Manhattan's office and shopping districts. Today, the three most common major land use divisions are residential, commercial, and industrial, with many potential subcategories as well.[6]

Local zoning is designed to control, limit, and regulate land use. One premise underlying zoning itself is to protect public health, safety, and welfare. The basis for this starting point is found in the Fifth Amendment to the U.S. Constitution, which reads in part, ". . . nor shall private property be taken for public use, without just compensation." An important landmark case heard before the Supreme Court clarified this principle with a ruling that zoning designed to protect the public health, safety, and welfare is Constitutional, but that when zoning is set for other purposes, it may be challenged.[7]

However, the issue of how and why municipalities enact specific zones may be challenged in some circumstances, notably when it can be shown that the purpose of zoning is to prevent certain types of development from occurring. This so-called *exclusionary zoning* is used improperly to keep out newcomers and to prevent growth, rather than to serve a legitimate purpose.

The city or county may employ zoning to provide exceptional design, encouraging developers to use innovative features such as cluster development, mixed use, and landscaping to add visual effects while also providing amenities (public areas, trails, sight and wind buffers, privacy, and common areas for residents, for example). A Planned Unit Development (PUD) is one device used by cities and counties to provide developers with exceptions to general zoning laws in exchange for innovative design.

The idea that a government can take land from citizens through zoning laws does not necessarily mean actually acquiring ownership of the property. A taking of land can be accomplished by reducing a property owner's rights to use of that land. So valuation of property can be determined by a change in zoning, for example.

Two U.S. Supreme Court cases set the rule that local governments can impose restrictions on land use only if there is what the Court called an "essential nexus" between conditions and regulatory objectives. The Court also ruled in these cases that there must be a balance between consideration of the public burden resulting from development, and a requirement placed upon a developer to fund the cost of infrastructure projects.[8]

So *takings* may be defined as limitations on development activity, changes in zoning that prevent an owner from using land as intended or desired, or the requirement by a city or county that in order to gain approval, a developer must pay for additional benefits or donate land. Of course, such requirements can be imposed, but they have to be measurable against the impact to the public of new development, and there must be what the Court called a "rough proportionality" between such conditions and the public burden caused by development.

The ability of a government to take property grows out of another concept, called *eminent domain*. This is a legal power granted to the government and found in the Fifth Amendment. It provides that the government (federal, state, or local) has the power to take private property for public use; upon exercise of that right, the landowner must be given adequate compensation (the proper or just value of property taken under eminent domain, usually market value). The exercise of eminent domain is most often called a *condemnation* or *expropriation*—nicer terms meaning the same thing as a taking of land.

Takings are allowed under law for the "public good." This means that when a freeway has to go through, or hospitals, jails, utility plants, and other *essential public facilities*, the government can override the private property rights of the current owner and buy the land, even when the owner does not want to sell.

Valuable Resource

To study current trends in takings legislation and zoning policy, check http://www.law.georgetown.edu/gelpi/takings/courts/.

Recent trends have demonstrated that in some cases, governments have used eminent domain to control development or to force through land uses that cannot be truly classified as belonging in the realm of the "public good." Condemning land so a new sports arena can be built might be advantageous to the community, but does it fit the definition of "public good" and does such a facility constitute an "essential public facility"? The controversy is ongoing. In other cases, governments have misused eminent domain as a way to prevent development from occurring, as a sort of institutionalized antigrowth movement, sanctioned by the local government. One possible risk associated with development, as exercise of eminent domain, would limit potential improvement in land values.

The trend in the courts shows that while some attempts have been made to abuse the power of eminent domain, those decisions are likely to be overturned. In two recent cases, state courts ruled that taking private property in order to resell it to other private owners was not legal.[9]

Real estate valuation may certainly be adversely affected by takings on the part of government. However, these occurrences are not common. In comparison, those states that have enacted so-called "growth management" laws have experienced a mix of outcomes, not all positive. Several states and some municipalities have enacted growth management legislation. Among the most controversial have been Virginia, California, Oregon, Florida, and Washington states. About one-fourth of Washington and Florida state increases in housing prices from 1995 to 2000 were due to restrictive terms in state growth management laws. Ironically, one stated purpose in growth legislation is to promote affordable housing. The record demonstrates that trying to artificially control market valuation through legislative tinkering is ineffective and, in fact, expensive.[10]

In such states, recent history has shown that the stated intention of Growth Management Act (GMA) types of laws has not worked and in the long-term, such plans will not be effective. In many states, notably the State of Washington, the GMA has been very controversial. Many of the decisions made by the Washington GMA boards have been overturned by the state's courts, fueling the debate. Growth management is intended to provide a means for public participation without needing attorneys; but in

Valuable Resource

To view recent court cases involving eminent domain, check the web site http://home.hiwaay.net/~becraft/recentcases.htm.

some GMA states, there has been an increased level of land-use litigation relating to GMA rules.

Methods of Entering the Market

The ramifications of growth management and other artificial impositions on market-based real estate valuation are serious for all real estate investors, lenders, and homeowners. However, the concern goes beyond the three most common forms of entry to the market: home ownership, single-family housing rental investments, and the fixer-upper (property flip) market.

These are the most common starting points for most people. However, questions of valuation are also on the minds of those who enter the market through other means. These include:

Individual Secondary Mortgage Lending Individuals can assume debt positions (lending money) as well as equity (owning property). These positions can involve significant risk as well. Granting individual second mortgages to property owners creates an income stream and higher than average interest rates. However, if and when such second mortgages are defaulted, the lender is entitled to get their principal returned only after the first mortgage has been paid. In cases where owners overborrow, second mortgage investors could be left with losses. The way to reduce risk is through careful screening and selection of borrowers with plenty of equity in their homes. Some companies specialize in placing money in second mortgages, notably through self-directed retirement plans or financial planning programs.

Mortgage Pools A relatively safe method of investing in debt is through what is called the *secondary market* for debt. Most conventional lenders sell their loans to one of the big government-sponsored programs, which include the Federal National Mortgage Association, or FNMA (http://www.fanniemae.com/index.jhtml) and the Government National Mortgage Association, or GNMA (http://www.ginniemae.gov). These organizations create mortgage pools of real estate loans and sell shares to investors. They are just like mutual funds, but portfolios consist of real estate loans instead of stocks and bonds. Investors can also enter into these positions indirectly by purchasing shares in mutual funds that in turn buy shares in mortgage pools.

REITs The Real Estate Investment Trust, or REIT, is a practical venue for acquiring equity in real estate. The big advantage of buying REIT shares is that they are traded on public exchanges, just like stocks. This liquidity makes the REIT a desirable and practical way to diversify an equity portfolio. The most popular type of REIT is called the *equity REIT*, in which investors buy shares of ownership in properties. Two other types are the *mortgage REIT*, in which invested funds are loaned out to builders and developers, current real estate project owners, or mortgage backed securities; and the *hybrid REIT*, which combines both equity and mortgage features.

About 96 percent of all REITs are classified as equity. About 1.6 percent are mortgage REITS, and just over 2 percent are hybrid. The REIT market is also interesting in terms of the types of property these programs select. The most popular choice (33.1%) is industrial and office; next are residential (21.0%); and retails (20.1%). These three classifications add up to about three-fourths of all REIT-based investments. The remaining equity goes to no real estate representing more than 10 percent of the total.[11]

Limited Partnerships Investors can also buy units in limited partnership programs. In the past, such programs were popularly called "tax shelters" because they were set up to provide big write-offs for investors, often exceeding the amount invested. Changes in tax laws essentially closed down the tax shelter industry. As part of the change, limited partnerships were classified as passive investments. This means that losses can only be deducted to the extent that they offset other passive gains. No longer can investors in limited partnerships claim large write-offs; and investors can never deduct more than the amount at risk (this is defined as the total of cash paid into the program plus recourse loans, or loans that must be repaid). One major problem with limited partnerships is their illiquidity.

ETFs A final category is also the newest. The Exchange Traded Fund, or ETF, is a type of mutual fund that is highly liquid. Shares are bought and sold on public exchanges rather directly through fund management companies. Traditional mutual funds were set up to emphasize a particular investment policy, such as "aggressive growth," "current income," or "conservative growth." In comparison, the ETF is set up to select a specific portfolio, such as stocks in an index or market average; stocks of a

Valuable Resources

A useful overview of REIT basics can be found at ReitnetOnline (http://www.reitnet.com/reits101) as well as at the National Association of Real Estate Investment Trusts (http://www.nareit.org).

Valuable Resource

The market for ETFs changes often as more investors discover the benefits and advantages of these funds. As of the writing of this book, four ETFs specializing in real estate were identified. While we do not endorse any of these funds, they are useful as a starting point to learn more about the ETF market:

Name	Trading Symbol
iShares Dow Jones US Real Estate	IYR
iShares Cohen & Steers Realty Majors	ICF
Vanguard REIT Index VIPERs	VNQ
street TRACKS Wilshire REIT fund	RWR

particular country or those that specialize in a precious metal; or funds with stocks in a specific industry or sector. An ETF may invest in real estate sector stocks, REITs, or both. Because the ETF portfolio is identified in advance, management fees are far lower than those for the old-style mutual fund. Finally, ETF owners often have the ability to break out segments of the fund, or to buy and sell options based on the ETF and its bundle of stocks. The ETF market is growing rapidly.

CHAPTER 4

Single-Family Home and Condo Analysis

Most people are familiar with residential real estate; however, this is itself a complex investment form. There are many different types of residential properties and analysis should be broken out and separated based on (1) location, (2) size, (3) local trends, and (4) other, special considerations (i.e., subsidies, rent controls, or tax credit incentives). We introduce these important issues in this chapter and also study the antidevelopment movement known as NIMBY (Not In My Back Yard), demonstrating how analysis in real estate is not merely economic; it may be political as well.

No particular property is necessarily easy to analyze. Some relatively inexperienced individual investors believe they understand the market valuation attributes of single-family homes because—like a majority of real estate investors—they own and live in a home themselves. This is a mistake.

The *investment* attributes of residential property are not the same as the features of owner-occupied homes, in four ways:

1. *The underlying premise for ownership is not the same.* An individual purchases a home partially as an investment, but also out of necessity. If that person does not own a home and make payments on a mortgage, the same money (in some instances, *more* money) has to be paid for rent, without the tax savings and long-term appreciation derived from home ownership. The premise for investing in rental property is entirely separate from the premise for buying a home. For anyone not yet a homeowner, the idea of ownership *is* the definition of the American Dream.

2. *Cash flow analysis is not the same thing as homeowner mortgage affordability.* It is not accurate to compare investment cash flow to the
   entirely separate question of a primary residence's affordability. Cash
   flow analysis is a study of risk as well as of affordability; many market
   and economic factors come into play when you are analyzing the feasibility of a particular property and given a specific market. The type of
   home an individual can afford is determined by income, down payment, and current interest rates. While an investor can simply decide
   to not proceed because the feasibility study is not encouraging, a
   would-be homeowner has more limited choices when the numbers do
   not work: Continue to pay rent or look for a home that does not cost
   as much. The homeowner seeks affordability, and the investor views
   cash flow issues as aspects of feasibility; these are not the same issue.
3. *Lenders have a far different risk profile for each type of real estate.* Individual real estate investors discover quickly that lenders are far more
   risk-conscious in the case of financing investment real estate than they
   are in the case of owner-occupied properties. When an individual fi-
   nances a home, good credit may lead to low-rate, low-down (or no
   down) financing, and fast approval. But investors traditionally are required to commit 30 percent or more to a down payment, and also
   may have to pay higher interest rates than homeowners.
4. *Tax benefits are vastly different.* Homeowners enjoy specific tax benefits, but these are also quite limited. They are allowed to deduct mortgage interest and property taxes on their primary residences, but
   nothing else that recurs from year to year. When a primary residence is
   sold, gains up to $500,000 are tax-free. This may be a good or a bad
   tax rule. If a married couple wants to move from their current home to
   a smaller one and their gain is less than $500,000 (and they qualify in
   every other way), the tax-free profit is a substantial benefit. However,
   in some regions of the country, properties purchased 20 years ago for
   less than $50,000 may be worth $1.2 million today. A sale may produce a profit of $1 million or more in these markets, and the maxi-
   mum tax-free profit is $500,000. In the past, gains could be deferred
   by buying another home, but under the tax-free rule, any excess more
   than the maximum of $500,000 for a married couple is taxed.

Investors are allowed to deduct as investment expenses their interest
and taxes, as well as other operating expenses: insurance, utilities, advertising, management fees, and auto or truck expenses, for example. Most
significantly, however, they can also deduct depreciation, which is a substantial benefit. Investors who actively participate in managing their own
properties can deduct up to $25,000 per year in tax losses. Upon sale of

investment properties, investors pay capital gains tax on the net difference between sales price and original purchase. They also have to pay taxes on the total of depreciation claimed over the period the property was owned.

If we move even further beyond the mere understanding associated with investment value, we begin to understand that for residential properties, analysis requires a comprehensive survey of market factors beyond value itself. One real estate book involving the necessity of the differences between financial and lifestyle (among other) issues affecting decisions people make, explains that:

> *much of the analysis for residential development must rely on a qualitative understanding of the market and its dynamics. Both the product and the consumer must be understood in terms of choices people make, evolving lifestyles, personal tastes, and many other considerations that cannot be quantified. Focus groups, buyer surveys, and other qualitative techniques augment the hard data of the market study. Understanding the lifestyles and other qualitative characteristics of consumers can help to appropriately define a residential product.*[1]

Therefore, it is wise to consider the nature of the end-user (homeowner) in an analysis of residential property and to accept the reality that those who buy homes may have a different series of assumptions, desires, and motivations from those who purchase warehouses and office buildings. Everyone is interested in value and cost. But homeowners are different enough and in significant ways that, in fact, when you attempt to identify valuation factors of residential properties—even using primarily financial and economic data—it is wise to also remember that the residential, homeowning consumer is unique and different from the commercial customer, the developer, or even the residential property investor.

HOME OR CONDO?

We make a distinction in this chapter between a single-family home and a condominium, and for good reason: The analytical and market attributes of each may be vastly different.

A single-family home is a stand-alone building and includes full ownership of the land and improvements. There are no shared common areas or expenses with other owners, except in those areas where covenants mandate—as part of the purchase agreement—that each property owner carries a responsibility for common ownership and liabilities of specific areas (such as park areas, trails, club house, sports facilities, exercise rooms, and meeting room areas, for example).

A multi-family directly owned unit is studied in the next chapter. However, its classification may properly belong here with single-family housing, as opposed to rentals as seen in apartments. Thus, duplex, triplex, and fourplex units are multiple units within a single building. They usually have separate entrances or access to units through a shared common area such as a lobby or hallway. Owners in multiple-unit buildings operate under the terms of an agreement for common-area maintenance, insurance, and ownership.

A condominium may come into existence in one of two ways. A development may be designed to create owner-occupied condo units, or an existing apartment building may "go condo," be converted to condominium ownership, in which case the purchaser buys an apartment. At the same time, the purchaser, together with the other unit owners, buys an "undivided interest" in the common elements of the building or development. Common elements generally include the land on which the building stands, the lobby, public halls, driveways, access roads and parking areas; and the electrical, mechanical, heating, and air-conditioning systems that service the building.

In a similar arrangement, the *cooperative*, or "co-op," a corporation is formed to take ownership of an entire project or building, and individual owners buy shares. In the condo, rather than owning shares in a cooperative, buyers own their individual units outright and receive deeds for them. Each of the unit owners is responsible for paying a proportionate share of the building's fuel costs, building employee salaries, and other expenses of operation. These are known as common charges. Additionally, each condominium owner pays real estate taxes, separately assessed against each unit, and the cost of any mortgage obtained to finance the original purchase. The condominium owner may deduct these tax payments and the payments of interest (but not principal) on the mortgage, from taxable income.

The condominium is governed by a board of managers elected by the unit owners. The board's authority to operate the building is explained in detail in the condominium declaration and bylaws, a copy of which is included in the offering plan. These provide rules and procedures for conducting the affairs of the condominium, and define the rights and obligations of unit owners. For example, the bylaws may restrict the right of unit owners to make certain kinds of alterations to their units or to lease or mortgage them.

In studying specific valuation factors, these distinctions should be kept in mind. The attributes of each ownership format may affect value. For example, the cost of a mortgage on a single-family home is not directly comparable to a mortgage on a condominium. Because condominium owners are obligated for additional fees, their relative cost-versus-benefit analysis should be made on the basis of total payment obligations.

Example: You are comparing the ownership of a three-bedroom, single-family home to a variety of condo units. The typical condo unit sells for $200,000 and on average additional monthly fees are $400. What is the equivalent cost to purchase a single-family home? Using an assumed mortgage rate of 6 percent and a 30-year term, the cost to the condo owner will be:

Mortgage payment, $150,000 mortgage	$ 899
Common area and other fees	$ 400
Total monthly obligation	$1,299

In looking at a book of mortgage amortization, a $1,299 monthly payment would apply on a $200,000 mortgage. So in theory (and assuming the same down payment) the monthly obligation for a $200,000 condominium would be the equivalent to the outright purchase of a $250,000 home.

This analysis is not entirely reliable. Some of the services provided within the monthly condo payments include expenses the homeowner would have to bear or pay separately—or pay for features the homeowner might not have. But even so, the brief example makes the point that in comparing costs, the analyst should consider not only the mortgage payment, but the condo (or co-op) contractual obligations as well.

VALUATION FACTORS UNIQUE TO RESIDENTIAL PROPERTY

In judging the market value of single-family homes, we need first to study the basic market characteristics and next to consider the supply and demand features for the property as well as site-specific attributes. The valuation factors should be broken down into three specific classifications.

Market Conditions in the Local Area

The "local area" in the case of single-family homes is, of course, both the immediate neighborhood and the city or town in which it is located. So we have to consider two versions of the local market in the analysis of a house. If the neighborhood is *in transition*, which way is it heading? As older owners move or pass away, younger families replace them and, as a general rule, tend to fix up outdated properties, adding value to the neighborhood. However, due to outside factors like high unemployment, some neighborhoods experience deterioration, high vacancies, increased crime, and other factors that reduce property values. While houses in such areas may be cheaper than market rates elsewhere in the same region, the negative transition is not a positive indicator.

Certain larger market areas—specifically towns, cities, or counties—also experience transitions. Growth is caused by factors such as employment, tourism, proximity to outside work centers, and other external influences. For example, if a city within a one-hour commute has a booming employment market, a relatively remote town could experience a rapid increase in demand as workers seek suburban "bedroom communities" nearby. Growth may also be artificially contained, controlled, or deferred through antigrowth sentiment locally or even through legislation. Growth management trends have demonstrated that attempts to slow down growth have resulted only in higher real estate prices (see the previous chapter). Such trends are anything but economic, and, time has shown, devices such as growth management, local building moratoria, and impact fees not only add to the cost of housing, they also do immediate damage to commercial and retail trends locally and may even cause growth rates to fall below desirable levels, and below levels required to sustain local jobs and trade. In one instance in North Carolina's Research Triangle area (Raleigh, Durham, and Cary) the consequences of impact fees included negative consequences. A 2003 story explains that

> *leaders in Cary . . . began to rethink their stratospheric impact fees after the town's growth rate plummeted below the goal of 4 percent to only 1.7 percent last year. Cary's impact fees are as much as four times higher than those in the city of Durham and six times higher than those in Raleigh.*[2]

Attempts to artificially control or prevent growth, or even schemes designed to create added revenues through impact or permit fees, invariably bring unintended consequences: unacceptably low growth rates, soaring real estate prices, and what can only be described as poor planning policy. Such artificial growth policies relate more to housing than to other types of property. A widespread belief that rapid growth in housing stock leads to higher crime, more traffic congestion, and deterioration in the quality of life may be based on some evidence, but the point remains that, in spite of efforts to the contrary, growth occurs in response to economic realities. It cannot be created where there is no demand, and it cannot be prevented when demand is high.

In fact, in spite of evidence that attempting to artificially control the market through imposition of growth management legislation has largely failed, many states continue to pursue the agenda of trying to determine what types of growth occur, both where and when, based on the notion that, somehow, such controls are good for the market. These so-called "planning intervention regimes" have universally had the opposite effect to the stated goals. As explained in one article, it has been demonstrated that:

> *local governments are unusually ineffective in achieving such over-arching public interest goals as preserving natural resources, containing urban sprawl, and mitigating losses from hazardous events. The reason is basic to decision making: individual, developers and local governments will act in their own self-interest.*[3]

The classic observation of how people act and react begs the question. In an economic sense, the theory of the "tragedy of the commons" prevails and motivates people, and this reality cannot be avoided.[4]

Economic Trends and Supply and Demand

A more ordered factor in the valuation of single-family housing is the collective basket of economic factors. Generally, this refers to supply and demand; however, there is more to the equation. Supply and demand markets may exist on several tiers (for housing, rental units, and financing), and the trends in those tiers of markets do not always move in the same direction.

Economic trends, of course, continue to rule, but the landscape itself has changed over history. The development of the automobile and mass transit have drastically changed not only how people work, but also where they live. We remain in the middle of a long-term trend of population movement away from traditional big cities and into suburbia. This new population center, dubbed Edge City by author Joel Garreau, is defined as a major change in U.S. demographic trends:

> *These new hearths of our civilization—in which the majority of metropolitan Americans now work and around which they live—look not at all like our old downtowns. . . . their landmark structure is the celebrated detached dwelling, the suburban home. . . . I have come to call these new urban centers Edge Cities.*[5]

CASE STUDY: ANTHEM, PHOENIX, AZ

One of the fastest-growing regions in the United States is the central Arizona Phoenix metro area. Much of the development is aimed at retirement or semiretirement age groups; one exception is the Anthem project, which began selling in 1999 and is planned for completion in 2007.

Developer Del Webb is well-known in the Southwest for its "lifestyle communities"—often gated, guarded neighborhoods. The Del Webb Corporation has built more than 100,000 homes since 1928 and is best known for its Sun City retirement communities. Anthem is the company's first nonage-restricted housing development and is described on its promotional web site—www.anthemarizona.com—as containing two sections. Anthem Country Club consists of "gate-guarded, resort-style living with two . . . 18-hole championship golf courses." The target resident market is described as professionals aged 40 to 60, preretirees and empty nesters. Anthem Parkside offers "real neighborhood living with activities and amenities tailored to fit the way your family lives, works and plays." This section markets to people aged 25 to 40 with children.

This self-contained approach to master-planning community design is typical of the Edge City trend. These are not small, either. By the time the project is completed, it will contain 12,000 homes—the size of a small city on its own. In fact, the project includes features one would expect to find in such a city: shops, restaurants, parks, open space, schools, commercial, industrial, and office space, and municipal services, for example. Because the area involved is both large and remote (5,760 acres 35 miles north of Phoenix) virtually all trips require the use of an automobile. And because the development is so large, it is also diverse, offering something for many different markets within the development itself. Even the recreational facilities are designed to appeal to all age groups.

A 43,000-square-foot community center is the hub of the community. It is next to the community park where the first K-8 school is also sited. The center includes after-school activities, a complete fitness center, tennis courts, dance studio, and a Big Splash Water Park. The Golf and Country Club, one of the few private clubs in Arizona, includes two full championship courses as well as swimming pools, tennis courts, fitness center, and a dining room.

The complex includes a 128,000-square-foot retail center called

CASE STUDY: ANTHEM, PHOENIX, AZ *(Continued)*

Anthem Marketplace. Included within are a Safeway store, drugstore, dry cleaner, restaurants, and a DVD rental store, among others. Business outlets are also located strategically at major intersections within the complex so that, conceivably, residents would never need to travel outside the immediate community. All of their schools, shops, and recreational facilities are available close by. Even a complete medical facility is planned in the near future.

What makes this large-scale project unique is that it is designed to respond to many different markets—semiretirement through families with young children. In many of the gated communities in the area, the predominant market is retirement-aged. In one of the dozens of communities in Chandler, Arizona, for example, a common complaint is lack of adequate healthcare facilities within the immediate area. The residents refer to the frequently heard EMS vans and ambulances as the "taxis to the hospital."

Anthem's design includes 36 percent of the total land area for open space and recreational use. This is a major selling point, especially for the younger age-group residents and their children. The site's design—the land was originally a remote rural desert setting—incorporated the natural terrain and desert vegetation into the community. Cacti that had to be removed for streets and houses were replanted, and an extensive system of trails provide for horse and foot traffic.

The Webb Corporation performed an extensive market analysis and, in the case of Anthem, this phase was more extensive than usual. The company spent $5 million on marketing before the project design was started. Research included a detailed survey of baby boomers and retirees. The Anthem design was based on the research, which included not only the survey, but also focus groups and interviews with potential buyers. Further research was conducted on existing residential communities in the area. The goal was to avoid mistakes and to develop a large-scale community that met the needs of the target markets.

The research paid off. More than 7,000 people attended a preview of the first phase and about 300 homes sold in the first week. With an estimated total cost at build-out of $1.7 billion, the mixed market approach may set a trend for large Edge City-type planned communities in the future. Rather than focusing on a single market, Anthem demonstrates that it is possible to appeal to a variety of different demographic groups.

The very concept of Edge City implies order and predictability, but when we consider the inefficiencies of the model, including the requirement that residents must drive virtually everywhere, we soon realize that as a planning device, the newly evolved Edge City, while part of a modern trend, may be as "unintelligible as in any dream."[6]

While Edge City-style planned communities represent an important trend, notably in areas like Phoenix, a parallel trend continues away from urban living to outlying suburbs. In some areas, this trend has been reversed as city centers go through renovation, but the widespread appeal of suburban living—whether in a planned community or an easy train ride to downtown—is undeniably continuing to occur. Additional economic forces, all of which affect supply and demand itself, include the following.

Local Development Trends   Some areas experience exceptionally high volume of growth in new houses, even when demand does not appear to support such trends. As a general observation, development does tend to perform in excess of demand and we see housing construction continue even as the supply and demand cycle peaks; just because the cycle turns, does not mean a slowdown in immediate construction. Construction takes time to finish; it is invariably better to finish and sell than to merely stop work.

The cause of the cyclical turn may also be attributable to financing incentives (cheap money and cheap land, for example), enabling builders to continue working and keep employees busy, due more to seasonal preferences than to actual demand for more homes. Of course, the whole cycle is driven by demand, but construction trends may rely equally on tax incentives (for affordable housing), financing, and favorable local growth policies.

The Local Job Market   As employers move into an area, people follow to obtain jobs. This tendency has characterized real estate and demographic trends since the post-Civil War era. Today, an equally important factor is that of proximity. People do not need to live where they work and, in fact, may find urban living far less desirable than buying a home in the suburbs. The emergence of this trend—purchasing homes outside of the city and commuting to work—is a dominant theme in residential real estate.

Local Amenities beyond Housing   We witness the growth of many areas based on economic factors beyond local job markets. For example, recreational amenities often *create* growth directly. When Six Flags Marine

World[7] opened its 136-acre park in Vallejo, California, years ago, the town was relatively small. While many factors have contributed to growth in the San Francisco Bay Area, Marine World's facility contributed significantly. Since 1970, the city's population has grown 70 percent and Marine World was the third largest employer in 2004, with 1,660 jobs (behind Kaiser Permanente Hospital and the local school district). Housing prices have followed suit; Vallejo made the CNN list of "hottest zip codes" for five-year growth in housing prices as of 2004; and the Vallejo/Fairfield metro area was in the top 10 regions on the Housing Price Index (HPI) that same year, showing a 21.8 percent increase in average home prices.[8]

Local Quality of Life Issues and Perceptions   Economic trends are also reflective of (and affected by) trends in other realities, such as safety, traffic, and crime levels. Every year, various cities and towns are rated in terms of the desirability or quality of life. Factors include jobs, housing prices, crime statistics, recreational amenities, climate, honesty or friendliness of residents (subjective to be sure, but an important test of quality of life), and similar perceptions about a city or region.

Attributes of the Site

Finally, we want to consider site-specific attributes. These are many and varied and include obvious as well as subtle features. For example, it has been observed that a house on a busy street will not experience increases in market value as much as an identical house on a quiet street—even when they are in the same neighborhood. Factors such as ongoing maintenance, age of the property, proximity to schools, shops and malls, recreation, and other desirable destinations, will also affect a property's value. A recreational facility, for example, may initially draw residents and lead to more housing construction due to new job creation, but ultimately the traffic congestion and higher prices may have a reverse effect on an area's quality of life. So the attributes of the site itself may be extremely negative or positive. The specific site has greater influence on market value than on the house's specific features. Thus, a property located at the end of a major airport's runway, for example, is unlikely to have as much market value as the same house on a quiet suburban hillside with a spectacular view of the bay.

Equally important in this comparison is a range of environmental issues. Among the greatest impacts is noise. While problems like flooding caused by poor grading can be mitigated, noise often cannot. It is more likely that measures will have to be taken to change the environment or accept lowered property values due to noise. The solution to noise problems can be summarized:

> There are only three ways to mitigate noise: (1) quiet the source, (2) put more distance between the source of the noise and the receptor, and (3) build or create a barrier to the noise. It is often infeasible for homeowners to have control over quieting the source . . . and it is equally impractical to move the house . . .[9]

Noise levels certainly affect property value and have to be considered in market analysis as well as feasibility phases. Some analysts believe that noise simply lowers property values and that eventually, current owners have to accept this and sell for less. However, if noise is severe enough, this may not be true. An "enticed population"—those willing to live in heavily impacted areas such as airport flight corridors—does so in exchange for property value discounts. However, the damage caused by noise and similar undesirable features of a property or area may make the potential buyer market so small that it must be discounted altogether. One appraiser explained:

> While some real estate analysts may initially believe that any potential buyer will purchase a damaged property if discounted enough, this is simply not true. To illustrate, consider a run down house in the middle of a heavy industrial area. Certainly a significant portion of the typical residential market will simply not purchase the property at any discount, as they simply will not live in such an area under any conditions and have no interest in buying, renting, or reselling such properties.[10]

TRADE AREA ANALYSIS

The analyst assesses trade area by determining the source of potential tenants, factors that determine the location, and the degree to which the study is merely blunt judgment. One worthy goal is to identify ways that analytical judgment can be made more accurate and objective.

Begin by looking at existing projects. The analysts will need to estimate how many people are here today, and how many will be there when the project opens. Then, calculate how many of those households can afford the subject project. Using census data for what you define as your trade area is key, whether based on tract number or by zip code.

On the supply side, begin by studying how many housing units are available now. Include a count of new competing projects that will be coming on line. There are more technical ways to establish trade area. For example, one author (Thrall) tells a case of determining the need for student housing. The analyst identified the address database for all 45,000 students and mapped it. The trade area was defined to be 80 percent of the students whose resident addresses were local. Next, supply was mapped by taking all apartments from lease guides for the county and building permit information.

Absorption predictions were made from looking at the way students would advance through the school, with the understanding that upperclass students would be more likely to live off campus.

The conclusion drew together all of the assumptions.

MARKET CHARACTERISTICS OF RESIDENTIAL PROPERTY

There is a tendency in some local real estate markets to consider market value in isolation, or based on outdated information. For example, if property values were rising quickly and houses were selling as soon as they were placed on the market last year, some market observers think those conditions are permanent. But since no economic cycles remain unchanged for long, in residential real estate, it is not realistic to base assumptions on past market conditions or on what is claimed by a real estate salesperson.

As with all other markets, residential real estate market value depends on many factors, both direct and indirect. The most apparent and best understood factors are demographic trends—the numbers of local residents and the growth in population in recent months and years. The market is easily observed in hindsight by examining the time properties that remain on the market; the differences between asked price and final sales price; and the local *inventory* of homes for sale. This is the number of properties on the market, compared to the monthly absorption on the market (average sales per month). For example, if a town experiences sales of 15 properties per month and there are currently 75 homes for sale, there is a five-month inventory.

These indicators are useful for spotting trends. However, today's statistics are not as revealing as they are as the latest entry in local trends. So if you see a spread between asked and sales prices shrinking, everlessening time on the market, and a shrinking inventory, these all are reliable indicators of a strong demand market. Because you are reviewing three specific indicators, when they all point in the same direction, they

CASE STUDY: SONOMA VILLERO, BOTHELL, WA

One might assume that siting a 240-unit development of condominiums near Microsoft Redmond, Washington headquarters would find a strong demand market, especially for affordably priced units. The high employment in the area is attributed to software development, Boeing, and the Bothell campus of the University of Washington. However, competition can cause a developer to change the entire strategy.

When the 160th Street Association developed Sonoma Villero in 1997, the need for flexible marketing became apparent immediately. Because a similar development was underway at the same time close by, the developer decided to rent out units initially, with the ability to convert to ownership later on. The fact that a 209-unit condo development was being built literally across the street led to community opposition to Sonoma Villero. Partly to deal with competition and partly to respond to the NIMBY sentiment, the developer literally shifted markets, at least initially. Instead of competing head-to-head for sales of condos, the developer changed original plans and went after a rental market. Demand for rentals was strong in the area, and market rate rents averaged $1,325 per month. Upon conversion to ownership, the condo units were affordable, especially by Seattle metro standards. One-bedroom units were about $120,000 and three-bedroom units were about $200,000.

With development costs through the year 2000 at just under $33 million, the developer learned from the experience that local opposition delayed the approval process, and the local market was affected by a directly competing project. The decision to shift to the rental market and gradually transition into sales was wise, given conditions at the time. However, the change in marketing strategies also made it difficult to decide which amenities should be included. For example, interior amenities and finishes (i.e., plumbing for washers and dryers) were excluded because of lack of demand in the leasing/rental market. However, including such amenities would have helped in the condo sales market when units were converted.

are reliable confirmation of the trend. Therefore, it is far less reliable to look at only one trend to draw a conclusion about the current health of the residential market.

The problems of changing markets during the development process aside, the need to shift due to competition in the immediate area was apparent to the developer in the case of Sonoma Villero. In analyzing the market for a condo, versus the market for rentals, this is one of many factors to bear in mind: The need to shift due to competition may change the entire development strategy. Because the analyst's point of view has to be based on a market-response strategy rather than that of a would-be buyer, the entire process is quite different. If analysis is premised on what an individual has experienced in purchasing a residence as owner-occupied housing, it is unreliable. There are vast differences in market characteristics between a residence and an investment property. We must consider mortgage affordability and adequacy of a *home* as well as location, type of neighborhood, and proximity to schools and shopping. But for rental properties, we also need to calculate after-tax cash flow, potential for growth in market value, and the supply and demand features of the local rental market, that is, occupancy rates.

When we expand beyond a single investment, the question of market characteristics has to be viewed with a broader perspective. When we look at only one property, cash flow requirements can be easily narrowed down and we can estimate the likely return on investment based solely on local rental market conditions. However, when we perform market analysis for subdivisions—especially those in highly specialized markets such as low-income housing—we also have to look at a larger supply and demand market.

In larger subdivision developments, we consider the same factors as those for solitary home purchases: household demographics, employment, and transitional trends locally. However, economic factors such as the number of people living below the poverty level also have to be considered when low-income housing developments are the subject of study. Because so many of these developments are constructed with taxpayer subsidies (via tax credits), there is a tendency to gloss over the realities of market demand, or to make assumptions in market and feasibility studies that are simply false.

The most serious among these is to believe that the entire perceived local demand will be absorbed entirely by the new development. Ignoring the realities of the competition is a mistake, but one that is made commonly. This is even more subtle than the obvious comparison: If two developers are building apartment buildings in the same market, it is not realistic for

CASE STUDY: EAST LAKE COMMONS, DECATUR, GA

Some developments are designed to appeal to specific, narrowly focused demographic markets. East Lake Commons is a high-density development of 67 townhouses near downtown Atlanta. It is a "co-housing" project.

Co-housing means just that: a sharing of responsibilities among residents. The market for this project included a diverse mixture of single people, retirees, families, and gay/lesbian couples. Residents work cooperatively through committees to manage affairs such as kitchen scheduling, financing, and neighborhood outreach programs. Meals are prepared and offered by community volunteers several times per week in the project's community building, and residents participate on a volunteer basis. No one is required to give time.

The developer originally purchased the 17-acre site to develop HUD Section 8 affordable housing. However, local civic leaders advised the developer that they preferred market-rate housing targeting working professionals on the site. The developer, Jack Morse, recognized a marketing opportunity and identified pent-up demand in the area for a residential development offering community-based amenities. This led to a revision of the original plan and, ultimately, to the design of East Lake Commons.

To help get the project moving, the developer presold 17 units to a group interested in setting up a co-housing community. The sale helped move the project forward, generating further interest in it. At a total cost of nearly $9.7 million, the project was completed in September 2000. It is an example of how design combines desirable features of urban living in a suburban setting.

either to assume that the entire local demand will come to their project. A realistic view may consider market share. However, a more subtle competitive view is required. A local planner, for example, who understands the market may further realize that local demand is not waiting only for newly developed housing. A portion—perhaps a majority—of those would-be tenants currently live in existing units, either other single-family homes being rented, or in other apartments. The latter tenant may want to move into a rented home because it is more desirable than remaining in an apartment. This reality indicates the real competitive condition in the market. In fact, new construction may create an oversupply and lead to higher than current level vacancies. In that case, the entire market (counting current as well as new real estate) will experience overall higher vacancies.

Judging the current supply and demand in single-family housing is not always a simple matter of studying occupancy/vacancy rates in rental property. Nor can the entire competitive condition of the market be judged based on market statistics for owner-occupied housing. The demographic and income mix of a region determines the subtle shifts in supply and demand. In evaluating the true competitive status of today's market, an analyst has to consider:

- *The obvious supply and demand attributes.* The obvious interpretation of supply and demand in the rental market is expressed in the study of occupancy and vacancy rates as well as trends. However, confusion may arise when we mix market analysis between the two major types of single-family residential property: owner-occupied and rental property. The local mix of population will determine whether newly constructed homes are likely to be put to use as owner-occupied or as investment properties. Thus, an analysis should include a study of local owner-occupied rates by neighborhood, the mix of population (for example, is the population aging or is it dominated by college students?), and income levels. All of these affect—and in fact, create—the type of demand locally.
- *The level of demand that currently has other housing.* Most important in a local study of supply and demand is the realistic analysis of the market. Whether you are dealing with subsidized housing or market-rate developments, the level of supply has to be understood properly. For example, if a developer plans to construct 100 market-rate homes, where will the buyers come from? If there is little available on today's housing market but the population is growing, then the demand is generated as *additional* demand above and beyond the current population. However, if buyers come from the existing homeowner population, this has ramifications for the competitive marketability of the homes. As current owners sell their homes to move into the newly built homes, the inventory on the local market remains unchanged (one home is exchanged for another). There is no *real* new demand, so prices are likely to flatten out or even fall. Performing a feasibility analysis of the new development raises the question of whether the estimated pricing of properties is correct. If the basic assumption is that there is a demand for housing (based on local sales trends), the indicator is false if, in practice, people will simply replace one home with another. In addition, the population is often distinguished by levels of

income in this type of analysis. It is one thing to say the population is growing, but in which economic levels?

- *The correlation between current population trends and existing real estate.* Is the local population growing above or below the rate of new housing construction? This basic indicator is often overlooked in favor of more myopic analyses. For example, if you were to consider statewide trends rather than local trends, the result is an average of a series of dissimilar markets rather than an indication of what is going on in town. Market demand is strong only when the local population of homebuyers is growing. This does not include college students or transient population groups such as migrant workers; it also does not include *existing* homeowners. If analysis includes any of these groups, then the real nature of competition on the market will be inflated beyond the real demand levels.

- *The influence of nearby markets in terms of rental demand, employment, and price.* Even though real estate trends are always local, it is essential that an analysis considers the scope of the local market realistically. For example, one small town may be largely rural in character and be more than 200 miles from the closest city. Another city of the same size in terms of population may be within 30 minutes commute time of a large city. These differences vastly change the supply and demand factors. The difference will be seen in the price of real estate, population trends, and basic supply and demand for new housing. So it is not realistic to base a market analysis on universal assumptions using ratios between population and market demand. These are meaningless. You need to study the actual nature and mix of supply and demand based on where people work, and on how the home-buying population is growing in response to local economic change.

- *The specific property design potential buyers seek.* Over time, desirability of interior design has to change as well. In the post-World War II era, families were happy with very small houses: small bedrooms and kitchens and, if any areas were expansive, it would likely have been the living room. This may have been based on how the young married person of 1945 grew up, with family activities focused around listening to the radio together. Today, the television generation has discovered that family size is smaller than in the past, orientation around family life has declined, and people do not necessarily gather together. As a result, couples prefer adult amenities. As fewer Americans are oriented toward cooking, for example, demand for larger kitchens is not as strong today. Most affluent Americans would rather have a wine cellar than a fourth bedroom, especially if they have only one child— or no children.

Valuable Resource

To get an idea of desirability in different housing features, check the matrix chart at http://www.davisandpartners.com/newsite/ammen.html.

CASH FLOW ANALYSIS OF RESIDENTIAL PROPERTIES

The development of a cash flow analysis is the essential part of a feasibility study. If the numbers do not work out, then the longer-term profitability estimates of a project are of no value. The question, however, has to be reviewed in terms of the specific type of project, influenced by many market and competitive factors, and studied in terms of all three supply and demand markets (for purchase of property, rentals, and financing).

We need to consider the cash flow question on several potential tiers of the residential market. These include:

- Single-family homes, as solitary investment possibilities for individuals.
- A development of many single-family homes at market rate or below market rate.
- A speculative investment in one or more homes, as fixer-upper properties.
- Investment in vacation homes or second homes.

Cash flow analysis in these different types of single-family home markets is going to be vastly different, so we need to approach the issue carefully. There is no single, universal rule for how cash flow analysis is to be performed. We analyze each of these markets separately.

Single Family Homes

The most popular entry into real estate investing is the purchase of single-family houses to be used for rentals. The concept is simple: Rents are supposed to cover the mortgage payment, insurance, taxes, utilities, repairs, and other expenses. In practice, the strength of cash flow depends on:

- *Dollar amount of down payment and, as a direct result, level of mortgage payment.* The higher the individual down payment, the lower the monthly payment on the financed portion of the purchase. The interest rate you pay also affects the mortgage aspect of cash flow. Real estate investors may be required to put 30 percent or more down payment into a property and may have to pay more to make the lender's cash flow analysis work.

- *Level of market rates compared to mortgage obligation.* The very basic first question individual investors have to ask is whether the *known* level of mortgage payment can be covered by market rates. This assumes full occupancy and no surprises such as unplanned-for repairs or maintenance. If the difference between rent and mortgage payment is marginal or negative, the cash flow will not work. Even when tax advantages are considered, the investor has to also plan for other expenses involved as well as with the prospect of vacancies.
- *Current occupancy rates and trend.* The health of the rental market should dictate the timing of real estate investments. The widespread belief that it is smart to invest in rental property should be questioned; if the current market demonstrates soft demand, that means higher than average vacancies and the possibility that rental income levels will trend downward from today's market rates.
- *Deferred and ongoing maintenance on the property.* If investors buy "bargain" properties—usually meaning those that have not been maintained—this also means it will be necessary to perform repairs. It may be that the demand for such repairs could offset any discount gained from seeking out bargain-priced properties, perhaps even making the feasibility negative as well.
- *Tax advantages involved.* An after-tax cash flow is the most reliable method for analyzing cash flow on individually purchased property. However, each individual is limited to annual deductions of $25,000 or less in losses from real estate, so as a tax shelter this offers value, but limited value. An exception: The real estate professional as defined by the tax rules is not limited to $25,000 in annual losses. But the point to remember for many first-time investors is that tax benefits may define the difference between feasible and nonfeasible investing, so these benefits cannot be ignored. The method used to value land influences the tax calculation, perhaps significantly. Land cannot be depreciated, so the value assigned to land also affects the annual depreciation deduction. An investor may prefer more depreciation to maximize tax benefits, or less depreciation because losses are limited and that extra deduction provides no annual benefit.

Allocation of value between improvements and land for the purpose of calculating depreciation is done in several ways. These include prorating on the basis of assessed value, insurance-based value, and appraisal-based value. All of these calculations have merit, but if an individual purchases more than one rental property, the same basis should be used in each case.

Developments of Single-Family Homes

Cash flow calculations for developments are, of course, far more complex than for single home investments. A developer has to consider design and engineering costs, approval and the possibility of legal fees involved in a challenge to the development, and construction costs of a project. These costs may include constructing new utilities, streets and sidewalks, landscaping, street lighting, traffic mitigation costs, environmental impact mitigation, and a range of other possible costs, all in addition to basic construction of new homes. The cash flow analysis for a development is complex because it involves so many possible levels of cost; furthermore, the financing of a development varies based on the type of property.

Cash Flow for Market-Rate Housing   The feasibility study for development of market-rate housing is often aimed at satisfying lender's questions. The lender must be convinced that the developer will be able to sell homes at an adequate profit to cover the mortgage obligation at the very least. A cushion of profits ensures that the development will be feasible, given the possibility that additional costs will arise beyond the known, estimated cost levels. When a developer runs out of money before completion, this presents a special problem for the lender. Refusing to loan more funds means that less will be recovered; however, giving the developer more money when the initial estimates were inaccurate could present even greater risks. So cash flow analysis for market-rate development has to include a demonstrated market demand, experience on the part of the developer in successfully completing similar projects, and the timing of completion that will ensure repayment of the construction loan before interest expenses absorb profits.

Cash Flow for Subsidized Housing   The cash flow analysis for low-income housing includes the same range of questions. However, a lender may be involved only in a limited way. Developers are more likely to use one of the many taxpayer-supported subsidized programs, with the idea of funding the large capital portions of the project (running new utilities, streets and sideways, street lighting, traffic signals) through selling of tax credits to investors. Approval of subsidized programs requires that housing be kept as low-income for many years, but developers rarely retain projects and manage them; they are more likely to sell off the properties as soon as final approval has been achieved. So among the possible costs of a subsidized housing development may be performance bonds a municipality will require with the likelihood that the developer will not be around during recurring maintenance cycles; the cost of finding likely buyers for projects;

and the possibility of having to absorb vacancies for a period of time if the local demand market is not strong enough to keep all units filled—an unlikely event, but still a possibility. (The developer in this situation may make a convincing case in the market study to show that demand is high, but when it comes time to rent out housing, the market realities may result in chronically high vacancy levels. This affects cash flow *and* the ability to sell the project for top dollar on the market.)

Fixer-Upper Properties

An interesting variation on single-family property investing is the purchase of run-down properties. The idea is to use *sweat equity*—the work performed in completing repairs—to bring the property's value up to market rates. This concept works when the cost of repairs is less than the appreciation in market value. Thus, cosmetic repairs—including painting and landscaping, for example—are easily completed at minimal cost but with the greatest potential for creating increased value.

The problem with the fixer-upper market is cash flow. If an investor holds onto a property for six months, the cash flow calculation is not limited to only the difference between discounted purchase price and market value, offset by the cost of repairs. The calculation also has to consider the six months' mortgage payment. When margins are thin or, when the improved property does not sell quickly enough, a minimal profit is easily wiped out.

Two alternatives many investors have tried are rental conversion and living in the property. In the rental conversion plan, repairs are done as quickly as possible after closing the deal, often in one month or less. The property is then rented out and held as a long-term investment. Because the property was purchased below market rates, the idea here is that cash flow will be healthy. Because the new owner charges market rates for rent, cash flow is positive and allows a cushion that would not otherwise be available. So the cash flow calculation in this instance is made as modified rental investment. The assumption here is that the repairs can be completed in a reasonable amount of time. Renovation projects are more prone to cost overruns than new construction.

The calculation is even easier when the investor moves into the property during a period of repairs. Because the individual has to pay either rent or a mortgage payment, this eliminates the duplication of negative cash flow. After repairs are completed, the house is sold or converted to a rental and the investor moves on. While this idea has merit on paper, it may prove stressful for other family members. Not only is a family expected to live in the middle of the chaos of repairs, they are also required to move frequently, as one project is completed and another begun. The idea solves the cash flow problem, but may not be practical for other reasons.

Vacation or Second Homes

A final type of investment requiring cash flow analysis is the second home. Many people purchase a cabin by the lake, a timeshare, or a house in a different clime. All of these ideas appeal to those who want to spend time on vacation, but the question of cost has to be considered as well.

A *second home*—defined as a part-year primary residence, for tax purposes—is partially subsidized through tax benefits. Individuals can deduct interest expenses and property taxes as itemized deductions on both their primary residence and a second home. This reduces the after-tax cash burden, but not entirely. The individual is still left with ongoing mortgage payments as well as taxes, insurance, and maintenance. One possible solution is to rent out a second home for that portion of the year it is not used as a second home. This provides a prorated tax benefit, because the property can be depreciated for the part of the year it serves as a rental. The owner can also deduct utilities, interest, insurance, taxes, and other expenses as investment expenses. So it is possible to create rental income to cover the costs of owning the second home for part of the year, and also to create a partial tax benefit at the same time. The problem with this plan is often one of timing. If the owner wants to vacation at the same time as everyone else, there is a good chance that the off-season will see low demand. One solution is to vacation at the second home during the off-season and get higher market-rate rents when everyone else wants to be at the beach, in the mountains, or at the Mexican resort.

LOCAL OPPOSITION AS A MARKET FACTOR

The phenomenon of organized land use opposition adds to the cost of development, often considerably. It is even possible that a group of local citizens can prevent certain types of development from taking place.

The Not In My Back Yard (NIMBY) movement has to be considered as a possible cost factor, notably for single-family housing aimed at low-income renters or buyers. Also called Locally Unwanted Land Use (LULU), Build Absolutely Nothing Anywhere, Not Anytime (BANANA), and Citizens Against Virtually Everything (CAVE), antigrowth forces often present ridiculous arguments against development. While such groups may oppose any form of development, rezone, or change in local land use policies, trends in recent years have been toward a focus on low-income housing. As one of the more important forms of development risk, organized NIMBY movements should not be overlooked. A survey of developers revealed that in terms of risk, "three common refrains were meeting governmental and utility regulations, dealing with neighbor complaints, and correcting unforeseen environmental problems."[11]

All of these risks can and should be anticipated and mitigated in advance. The NIMBY problem should not take a developer by surprise if the market survey is completed thoroughly—even when a project has real or perceived social impacts. The NIMBY movement has come about largely due to the increase in development trends aided by major changes in the tax law in the Tax Reform Act of 1986 (TRA), and through the creation of Low Income Housing Tax Credits (LIHTC). The greatest argument NIMBY groups make is that low-income housing reduces property values for surrounding properties. This argument has great appeal to local residents, and often leads to petition drives, letters to the editor and to the local public hearing file, and direct testimony. In some instances, local political approval may move the entire question to the courts, adding cost and delay to any development process.

Valuable Resource

Several studies support the argument that low-income housing does not adversely affect property values of nearby homes. Some examples can be found at:

> www.fhfund.org/educational_materials_reports.asp—*A Study of the Relationship Between Affordable Family Housing and Home Values in the Twin Cities*, Maxfield Research report.
>
> www.enterprisefoundation.org/—*Affordable Housing and Property Values*, The Enterprise Foundation.
>
> www.abag.ca.gov—*Myths and Facts About Affordable and High-Density Housing*, California Planning Roundtable.
>
> www.habitat.org *Why Affordable Housing Does Not Lower Property Values*, Center for Common Concerns.
>
> http://www.mcaws.gov.bc.ca/housing/housing.htm—*The Effects of Subsidized and Affordable Housing on Property Values: A Survey of Research*, State of California.
>
> www.uic.edu/aa/cdc *Affordable Housing Design Advisor*, University of Chicago.

As effective as the arguments are for protection of local property values, the facts reveal that low-income housing development does *not* reduce property values nearby. In fact, numerous studies have concluded that property values rise or, at the very least, remain unaffected, when low-income housing development occurs.

The concerns among NIMBY groups also go to increased traffic or crime, noise, loss of trees, and other amenities. In other words, NIMBY opposition grows from change. Such movements gain a lot of momentum from poorly designed development, from situations in which developers' actions do have adverse impacts locally, and when local planners do not enforce zoning laws, comprehensive plans, and other regulations.

The best way to deal with antidevelopment sentiment is by acting in a preemptive manner. The vast majority of momentum NIMBY groups achieve derives from lack of information. However, withholding plans from citizens is illogical. A developer's plans will be known soon enough, but if information is not available, all sorts of worrisome rumors find their way to neighborhood meetings. In one situation, plans for a large 200+ acre site were to build a truck-to-train intermodal facility. A well-organized local opposition group formed with limited initial success. However, when the group's leaders began spreading a rumor that developers planned to site a landfill on the property, the antidevelopment sentiment picked up speed, and financing. In that situation, the developer needed to get the land rezoned, and the rumor was based on a reading of the local code which, among other uses, allowed light industrial zoning, which included landfills.[12]

Developers who announce their lands in advance defuse much of the opposition that is likely to center around a project, especially in the environment where dependable information is not available.

CASE STUDY: SNOW HILL CITIZENS FOR DECENT HOUSING

In Worcester County, Maryland, this organization originally proposed a low-income housing project in 1995. It was defeated in a local referendum. In 2000, the group tried again, but first took steps to provide information about the proposed 24-unit housing plan.

The effort included brochures that were mailed out to residents; ads in the paper; and canvassing, both door-to-door and via telephone. The group also made the convincing argument that 42 percent of residents in the city of Snow Hill would qualify to live in the units based on income levels.[13]

Similar outcomes have been achieved in other places, largely due to an effort by developers or by organizations sponsoring low-income projects, to educate the public in advance or to hold community meetings to explain development plans. This is especially effective if people are invited to make suggestions to improve a project's amenities or design. In 2002, a nonprofit organization met virtually no opposition to building a 400-person homeless shelter in downtown Minneapolis. This was the result of community meetings early on and before the process began, in which a citizen suggestion for a design change in the building's façade was accepted.[14]

Rather than accept the alternative of extended battles, often involving expensive lawsuits and years of delay, including the possibility of rejection of plans for development, it makes far more sense to prevent such problems as an organized NIMBY movement, before it begins. Developers and market analysts also should keep in mind that even a ludicrous argument may prevail in a land use dispute. In one instance in Florida, opponents to allowing a homeless "safe zone" on 14 city parcels argued that allowing homeless people to have a safe zone would negatively impact sea life! The city's attempt to elicit comments from local residents included sending out 840 invitations to a public meeting concerning the issue. City officials were confronted by a hostile group they described as Not On My Island (NOMIs).[15]

It is also essential to test the mood politically in a community *before* coming forward with plans for a low-income housing project, or for that matter, any new project. That includes not only elected officials, but the heads of agencies, politically active citizens, and the person in charge of the planning department. All of these groups have an interest in planning and in land use issues. Advice to developers and builders worth heeding includes the observation that

> *while NIMBY opposition to affordable housing projects may be traditional, it isn't inevitable. Project sponsors can reduce or even avoid community resistance to affordable housing by taking a strategic, proactive approach to community relations.*[16]

Single-family housing is best-known to most people because they either own homes, or because they would like to buy a home one day. Those individuals who analyze investment properties—either solitary home investments or more complex subdivisions—need to realize that investment properties and developments have numerous market attributes that make this property vastly different from the market for owner-occupied homes.

CHAPTER 5

Multi-Unit Rental Property Analysis

Multi-unit developments compete not only with other developments, but also internally between units. Competition is driven by the amenities that a project offers, the size of the units, and the project's distance from retail, recreation, health care services, and places of work. In addition, there are specialty residential projects such as senior, disability, and low-income housing that compete both in the larger market and in their specialty submarkets. This chapter examines these complex issues and provides a context for analysis based on area-specific and developmental factors.

Analysis of multi-unit residential real estate is more complex than analysis for detached, single-family housing. The reasons for this include the variable of the demand market for apartments and similar multi-family units; and the complexity of analyzing actual demand locally, given the competitive market conditions and trends.

The market for apartments and other multi-unit projects is huge. The overall value of property (excluding single-family houses) in the United States, in 2004 was $5.275 trillion, of which 44 percent consisted of apartments.[1] The breakdown among apartments and other types of property is summarized in Figure 5.1.

There is a tendency to view the market inaccurately, in many ways. For example, it is popularly believed outside of New York City that virtually all apartments in the city are rent controlled. This myth is fostered in many venues, including a recurring gag line in TV sitcoms. Someone dies and, upon being informed, a friend's first question is, "Who is getting his apartment?"

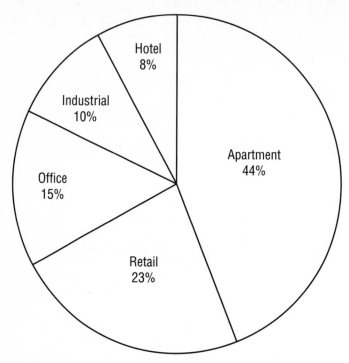

FIGURE 5.1   Real Estate by Property Type, 2004
Source: Society of Industrial and Office Realtors.

The truth is not as extreme, however. With more than 2 million rental units in New York, only 2.8 percent are rent controlled.[2] In fact, rent controls at any level are very rare outside of New York City.

Inaccuracies abound about many other urban markets. For specific projects, the analyst should remember that conclusions about market demand may be inaccurate, and it is a common error to base demand assumptions on the idea that a project will receive 100 percent of the current demand. Neither of these assumptions are accurate.

Current demand is the sum of all potential tenants currently seeking rentals in apartments or similar multi-family units (two, three, or fourplex projects, for example). One easy way to identify demand is by checking local waiting lists among existing apartments and housing agencies (Housing Authority, HUD Section 8 offices, and other agencies set up to seek and provide housing, especially for those individuals and families whose income is below local averages).

The problem with using such lists to identify demand is that any conclusions will be exaggerated. Many people on waiting lists currently occupy apartments locally. So this is not actual demand but would result in a shift between local units. This variety of demand results in additional vacancies somewhere in the same local market. Newer units are likely to generate interest especially if existing units cost about the same market rates; people like to move to newer units with better amenities. However, in larger perspective, demand identified from waiting lists is not reliable.

A more accurate measurement of demand forecasting should be based on local population trends, in comparison with new unit construction. For example, if the population has been growing by 5 percent per year and new apartment and housing starts have matched that increased demand, the market generates new demand that is easily quantified—assuming the analyst is also able to perform this study based not only on population growth, but also on growth by income levels. However, population alone does not necessarily justify an argument that a particular project is in demand, because we also have to understand that demand in the context of competing projects. How many competing apartment and housing projects are underway, and when will they be completed?

Market share is the degree of new demand a project will be likely to absorb. The tendency to assume that a new project will meet all of the new demand is simply unrealistic. If a study of recent population growth is supported by a healthy job market, we may identify a demand next year for 200 additional apartment units. However, if we build those 200 units, we cannot reasonably expect that *all* new demand will come to that project. If other builders are currently building 150 units, it may be reasonable to make an argument that our project will be justified by 25 percent of the demand (50 out of 200 new tenants, based on trends and forecast tenant growth).

A study of current demand and market share may not be entirely reliable, again based on the specific attributes of an area. It may be possible, through location selection, amenities, and design, to *expand* the local market and to attract tenants from outside of the apparent market area, that is, the geographical market.

THE LOW INCOME HOUSING MARKET

One important market in the rental industry is low-income housing. Congress, recognizing the importance of providing incentives to developers to include low-income units in larger programs *or* to willingly devote entire projects to this specialized market, enacted a Low Income Housing Tax Credit (LIHTC) program as part of the Tax Reform Act of 1986 (TRA).

CASE STUDY: THE YARDS, PORTLAND, OREGON

The riddle we answer here is: How do you attract markets from outside the area? In other words, why should someone move to a specific city or town and occupy units in a newly developed building?

The Yards is a community of about 600 affordable and market-rate apartments in the River District near Portland, Oregon's downtown. Portland is unique in the sense that specific neighborhoods retain their individual characteristics even though a part of a larger city. The River District is just north of downtown and—before redevelopment—was characterized by empty lots, vacant warehouses, and industrial sites like the large postal distribution center two blocks up from the water.

Complicating redevelopment, the site was contaminated with diesel and petroleum products as well as hydrocarbons, lead, and arsenic. Some of this contamination was found as deep as 10 feet. A total of 100,000 cubic yards of contaminated soil had to be treated or removed. Development was aided through a low-interest loan by the Portland Development Commission, augmented by the sale of tax-exempt bonds to provide construction and permanent debt. Further tax incentives are provided for the low-income aspect of the development through low-income housing tax credits (LIHTCs).

Fortunately, the neighboring Pearl District, which once was a primarily industrial area, also went through a transformation. Today this area includes art galleries, restaurants, and small boutiques as well as several developments of luxury condominiums. Demand in this and other areas of Portland with close proximity to downtown, has been high during recent years. Most of the project (four out of five phases) was finished by December 2002 and occupancy has remained steady at about 95 percent.

This project has demonstrated that proximity to a downtown area, consisting of affordable housing, can and does attract new market share from outside of the immediate and obvious existing market. Many people have relocated to The Yards, both from California and the Seattle areas to either semiretire or to change location while continuing to work. In this example, the combination of attractive location and price redefined the market. It enabled the developer to achieve a high occupancy rate by appealing to tenants beyond the immediate area.

As of 2004, this program has assisted in development of 1.6 million affordable apartment units to qualified families. Incentives for developers usually are provided in the form of tax credits, direct reductions in tax liabilities. Tax credits are transferable and can be used to finance the infrastructure of low-income housing projects, thus serving as a type of financing. On average, these tax credits finance 40 percent of total development costs.

The incentive has worked. Today, 40 percent of all multi-family developments include some level of qualified LIHTC units. The rules require one of two standards: Either 20 percent or more of apartments in a development must be occupied by tenants with incomes below 50 percent of median income; or at least 40 percent of units must be occupied by those whose incomes are at or below 60 percent.

The cost (measured in reduced tax revenues) is approximately $6 billion per year. Current issues being debated are one provision allowing states to allocate LIHTC resources to areas where they are most needed, and basing eligibility on statewide standards rather than on those standards in one area within the state. Objections to this proposal include concerns that states would possibly use LIHTC provisions to control where low-income housing could or would be built. Even so, the proposal is supported by many advocacy groups throughout the country.[3]

LIHTC incentives can induce developers to construct housing for low-income families while also helping cities and counties to encourage residents to move to new areas where affordable rental units are available, even in major metropolitan areas.

FACTORS AFFECTING MULTI-UNIT MARKET ANALYSIS

In studying the local market for multi-unit housing, the question of demand is central to identifying feasibility. How many units will be needed by the entire market? What portion of that demand should we expect to absorb? And *when* is that demand apparent in the local market?

These questions identify aspects of the *absorption analysis* process. Within market analysis, absorption refers to all forms of real estate; however, for multi-family housing in particular, absorption should involve a study of demand aspects. The most important among these is the expectation of occupancy level and timing. When do we expect to achieve maximum occupancy? This question should further take into mind the issue of *where* the market exists. So a market area study should include a realistic analysis of the real supply and demand market. Using strictly geographical miles-based arbitrary assumptions is not reliable. This analysis should include a study of traffic patterns relating to commute, location of regional and local jobs, transportation issues (public as well as auto-based transportation patterns), and the proximity from the site to schools, shopping, and other local amenities. So to simply identify the market area as existing in a ring of five miles from a site is rarely accurate. The shape of the market is not likely to be round, but is more likely to follow development and roadway factors, location of jobs, and the competitive factors—existence of competing or planned apartments within that realistic market area.

Absorption is an estimate of not only the occupancy level, but the timing as well. Certain events that delay completion of a project will direct affect the estimates, including complications in local approval of permits; labor strikes and other work-related problems; or unforeseen events that no one could possibly predict. In such instances, developers may need to find ways to give incentives to tenants through reduced rents, for example. One striking example of this was the first new development completed in lower Manhattan following the September 11, 2001, attacks on the World Trade Center.

CASE STUDY: THE SOLAIRE, NEW YORK

This development includes 293 apartments and contains 383,000 square feet in 27 stories. Total development costs were $120 million. Completed in 2003, this is the first "green" residential high-rise and the first project completed in the post-911 Zone I section of lower Manhattan, also called Battery Park City. The project is called "green" due to its innovative design incorporating energy-savings and environmental state-of-the-art features, marketed with the invitation to "live healthy, live green." Design and engineering translate to 35 percent less energy use and 67 percent reduction in electricity during the hottest summer months.

The unforeseen events of September 11 naturally lead to the question of whether the original feasibility assumptions concerning occupancy of these residential units remain valid. The site is only two blocks from the site of the World Trade Center. However, even with

CASE STUDY: THE SOLAIRE, NEW YORK *(Continued)*

this in mind, the complex is 90 percent occupied as of the end of 2004. Original projected rents were higher than the current levels between $2,200 and $6,700 per month. High occupancy was aided by grants provided by the Lower Manhattan Development Corporation, reducing rents by up to $12,000 (payable in increments of $500 per month) as incentive to sign leases by May 31, 2003. In spite of predictions concerning lowered market rents and high vacancies in lower Manhattan following the 2001 attacks, Solaire reports annual rents of $47 per square foot.

The developer, the Albanese Organization, Inc.—http://www.albaneseorg.com—is located in Garden City, New York. As part of the design, the building's tenants have access to an exercise room, aerobics room, children's playroom, a rooftop garden, and a green roof system to help insulate the building. Also provided: storage for up to 150 bicycles.

Recalling that this project's feasibility predated September 2001, it is not surprising that following the attacks, the lead construction lender withdrew from the project and new sources of financing were required. This was achieved in February 2002, when Congress approved the issue of tax-exempt Liberty Bonds. Developer Albanese was the first to receive funds through this program, in the amount of $120 million. The September 2001 disaster and changes in the financing structure of the project caused a nine-month delay in construction, adding $9 million to the total cost.

This project was completed successfully as measured by occupancy and rental rates. This has occurred in spite of the September 11 disaster and the building's proximity to Ground Zero. The combination of replacement financing and lease incentives offset the original concerns. Superior design certainly supports rental levels, which are not surprising by Manhattan standards; the incentives provided for signing leases further aided in completing the initial absorption for this property. Developers were faced with several initial problems: proximity to the World Trade Center, loss of original financing, and expensive delays in completion. Even so, they were able to revise their plans and create financing and lease incentives to offset what had been lost.

Any projections concerning occupancy in a project are going to be uncertain. The unknown elements in an extreme case—as we saw with The Solaire in New York—are certainly not typical. But even if a project is not sited two blocks from the World Trade Center, market analysts must expect some surprises.

One would use as a starting point the analysis of current supply. In beginning to approach the analysis of supply, be aware that there are specific kinds of supply: existing, under construction, and proposed (permitted). It is not adequate to merely count existing units in an area, because it may be that under construction and proposed units will drastically alter the supply, thus affecting the feasibility of the proposed new project. A skilled analyst should know how to weigh each of these as part of the study.

A realistic evaluation of the overall supply makes sense because, clearly, a comparison between existing supply and perceived demand, *should* reveal whether the project is feasible and whether occupancy assumptions are supported. However, it is equally important to remember that the issue of occupancy is not based solely on existing supply. Today's supply is a snapshot in time, but it will look far different when a project has been completed. We point once again to the extreme example of The Solaire to make this point. To some degree, it is important to allow for changes in the supply element. So if we are studying the feasibility for a project to be completed in one year, the completion issue will be far different from the same issue for a project planned for completion three years from now.

The ability to forecast supply and demand in three years is elusive in comparison to a one-year time frame. So the further away the estimated completion date, the less reliable the occupancy estimates. A one-year forecast period—at least for purposes of identifying emerging competition for the same market share—should not be difficult. However, because supply is more easily pinned down than demand, there is a tendency to place emphasis—perhaps too much emphasis—on the supply side, even in the short term. To elaborate:

> *In the short term, new supply is not (or should not be) a surprise. Even in cities with limited local construction, the quantity of new apartment completions in the next 12 to 18 months can be estimated closely enough to make informed decisions. And supply risk is tangible, readily visible just from driving by construction sites. Instead, the stealth forces—the factors that sneak up and surprise—lie on the demand side of the market equation.*[4]

While estimates should be as broadly inclusive as possible, the analysis should consider supply *and* demand with equal weight. Furthermore, it makes no sense to limit the analysis to only the obvious tenant market. For example, will a particular apartment complex be aimed at a market-rate tenant only? Or will some units be set aside for low-income, handicapped, or specialized markets? In urban centers, for example, many buildings generally geared toward family tenants also serve the growing corporate apartment market. The size of this business is considerable, according to the experts:

> *Corporate apartments [were] a $2.2 billion dollar industry in the United States in 2000. . . . This emerging segment is particularly interesting to multi-family housing owners and operators because 76 percent of corporate apartments are leased inside traditional multi-family complexes.*[5]

The need to accurately forecast is a basic problem in all forms of budgeting and forecasting. However, considering the maximum potential market area range is also crucial to accuracy in the forecast. Estimating future occupancy is easiest when we are looking at a short period of time and becomes increasingly unreliable as we look further into the future. At some point, the variables make the process little more than guesswork. So a market area with its economic and demographic trends is rarely exclusively reliable. We need to depend on a collection of many data to draw a *reasonable* conclusion concerning occupancy in the distant future. These include the trends in population, job market, transportation patterns, housing and rental prices, and other local statistics. While the demand for owner-occupied housing is entirely different from the demand for apartment units, the trends in housing may serve as a useful indicator in estimating future occupancy. If prices are flat and a large inventory of homes are for sale, we may assume that rental demand is also likely to be affected. As owners find they cannot get a desired price on the market, they may decide to wait until those market conditions change. In this situation, many of today's owner-occupied houses may be converted to rentals. And as an increased number of houses become available at market rates, there is an effect on apartment rentals as well. The overall market (for housing and, as an effect, for apartments as well) is affected more by current interest rates than by almost anything else. The various effects are not always indirect or obvious, because the demographic is not the same between ownership and rental markets, and neither are market rates. Many people living in apartments simply cannot afford to buy or rent a house; however, there is a segment of the market that is willing and able to afford to rent a house (or duplex, triplex, or fourplex unit) and prefers that over apartment living. As the volume of housing rentals increases, some level of demand for apartment units is reduced. Thus, absorption may require more time *and* occupancy levels may be lower as well. The timing, level, and *net rental demand* of the market ultimately determine and define feasibility in terms of occupancy levels one should expect. Net rental demand

> *means balancing the growth of rental households against the expansion of the rental stock. Although new rental communities may derive renters from existing communities through turnover, interpreting those moves as demand can lead to high vacancies in the overall market, which eventually will affect the subject project as well as the rest of the rental stock.*[6]

In attempting to identify likely occupancy timing and level, this is one of many factors worthy of consideration. It makes sense to include a reduction of total occupancy levels to allow for the competition from other apartments, multi-unit housing, and single-family housing.

Another factor making it difficult to project occupancy into the distant future is the unknown of competing apartment projects. Even in a market with very strong demand, competing developments are likely to be built to meet that demand. And units finished earlier than the subject project will get a share of the then-current demand, leaving less for later-completed projects. It is more likely that occupancy estimates will be made when a developer has a specific target date in mind. Supply analysis as well as demand analysis is usually limited to a one-year period, with the unknown quantities beyond 12 months a determining factor in how (and why) extended analysis is of little practical value—especially if the analysis is to be used to obtain current financing, determine appropriate design, and most importantly, to decide how many units to construct.

Some types of real estate can analyze supply and demand more easily because they are able to presell occupancy. Retail projects, notably malls, begin with long-term lease commitments from anchor tenants, and, once those commitments are in place, gaining additional leases is far easier. It is likely that lease commitments will be well in hand indicating at or near 100 percent occupancy, even before a developer closes the deal with lenders or investors. Thus, other aspects of the analysis, specifically cash flow, are more easily and more confidently estimated, even years in advance. The same benefit is not always possible in single-family residential real estate. It is unlikely that a future tenant will be willing to commit to a long-term lease a year in advance. It is unlikely that a majority of tenants will be able to make such commitments even a few months before move-in date; the majority of interested tenants will want to move into units as soon as possible. In comparison, both houses and condo units are often presold based on viewing models or other existing units.

CASH FLOW ANALYSIS FOR MULTI-UNIT HOUSING

Cash flow analysis depends upon occupancy assumptions, and this is where the uncertainty lies. The initial market and feasibility study—often performed at the planning stage—are based on current market conditions such as occupancy rates, market rent levels, and the current job market. We go forward assuming that those initial assumptions will be valid in the future; however, conditions may change. Once a project's completion is to occur within one year, cash flow analysis is far easier and more accurate.

It may be that neighboring markets will be built in response to development closer to city and town centers. As a result, today's potential tenant may find better prices further out, which also affects the market analysis. One writer has observed that this

> important intermarket relationship is often overlooked; the changes in market occur because of changes in the extent to which neighboring markets are built out. As a local market area gets an increase in units approaching the holding capacity . . . the price tends to rise, and buyers shift to the next outlying area.[7]

This predictable tendency—the movement of competitively priced units into ever-farther out locations—may lead an analyst to an inaccurate conclusion. Upon realizing that local rental rates have gone up, the analyst may conclude that this is good news in terms of cash flow analysis; in other words, more revenue will be earned. However, the flaw in this conclusion is that the initial analysis used a particular occupancy rate and presumed time for absorption, neither of which remains accurate. In addition to rates rising as tenants move farther out, a related trend occurs: the tendency toward lower overall occupancy, as a factor of competing market rates in other neighborhoods, where rents are lower.

Cash flow analysis has to consider issues beyond the initial assumptions concerning occupancy. Because the analysis involves dynamic rental markets, the analyst needs to not only anticipate the trend and its ramifications for the subject proposal, but also to identify the likely steps needed in response. These may include lower market rental rates, more attractive lease terms, or the addition of amenities that tenants will find desirable—all designed to bolster the occupancy rate to compete within the current trend.

While the identical market analysis problems apply to subdivisions, the apartment market is more subtle, because two different supply and demand markets are involved (market value *and* rental demand). In the typical cash flow analysis for subdivision housing, a form of "risk diversification" occurs because, upon completion, units can be sold individually on the market, or even presold when demand is high. Thus, a subdivision development is often able to finance its own cash flow without the need for gap financing. Presales usually pay off existing construction loans, and later sales are available for the developer's use. This eliminates the common risk of scheduling delays, causing higher interest expenses and debt service. In the case of apartments, which are *rental* units rather than buy-and-sell products, such advantages are not available in either case. They cannot be prerented, and there is no available after-market generated from sales (the exception, of course, is when a developer is able to presell an apartment development, which eliminates the typical interim cash flow risk). Some developers also have profitable relationships with REIT managers and other institutional investors who do not want to develop their own projects, but who have a voracious appetite for newly built projects.

The analysis should not be limited to rental gross income and occupancy, either. Basic real estate investment value is an important part of feasibility. Are land values reasonable today and, based on a study, what types of growth are likely to occur if the subject land is utilized for multi-unit development? Some analysts and appraisers assume that desirable location automatically translates to advantageous land profits when development occurs; this is not always the case. It may be flawed to merely assume that appropriate zoning (or a rezone) creates an automatic investment advantage. For example:

> *Zoning, as it translates to highest and best use, is the area where we see some of the major errors made by appraisers. When you have a diminishing asset (i.e., the availability of direct oceanfront properties), having a "multifamily" zoning designation may not translate automatically into the development at allowable density as the highest and best use.*[8]

Since both land values (and increases in such values) *and* rental income affect future appraised value, both have to be considered during the initial feasibility phase. With potentially higher than expected vacancies, disappointing changes in land values, or a longer absorption period in play, the cash flow issue becomes not only more complex but also more difficult to quantify. Thus, the analyst needs to manage the analysis by tracking the market during the development phase. If the cash flow assumption has been based upon market and feasibility studies, a concern develops on two fronts: the potential that the market has changed, as well as the potential that assumptions in the initial studies were flawed.

A *changed market* is likely if and when completion of the project runs over the initial schedule or if the market itself is moving through a rental demand cycle rapidly. We have provided one example, when rents in the immediate area rise due to scarcity, so the tenant market moves to adjoining locales, eliminating demand. It is ironic, in fact, that one motivating factor may be rising demand in the immediate area of the proposed apartment complex to be developed. In performing the cash flow analysis, it is important to be aware of how a predictable tenant base will act. The rising rents, in fact, are not positive indicators for cash flow; but there is a limit to its effect. Some tenants will not passively remain in the area and pay higher rents, but will move to more affordable markets. These may be only a few miles removed from the project site, but the market forces behind the migration are easily tracked: Higher rents lead to softened demand.

Flawed basic assumptions include a belief that the subject project is going to absorb all identified demand; that the demand is itself unchanging; and that the demand exists when it may not. These potential flaws in assumptions have been explained previously. However, putting together these three assumption-based problems may lead to a serious cash flow shortage. We may cast these three elements (inclusion of all demand, a static demand assumption, and softness in *real* demand itself) in another light, identifying three cause-and-effect aspects to the causes of flawed assumptions:

1. *Failure to understand the components of demand.* The market analyst who simply seeks out statistics in support of a premise that "there is a need" for a project, misses the point. Demand certainly may exist, but so does competition. In real estate, everyone gets the same good idea at the same time. If analysts cannot identify any potential competition, they are not looking hard enough . . . or it is not a good idea.
2. *Lack of recognition of the dynamic nature of supply and demand cycles.* When we say that a market is "cyclical," this means that it moves. More to the point, the market changes elusively. We cannot identify the timing by which a cycle strengthens or weakens, or reverses the current trend. While this is a troubling aspect of forecasting, it is also the most interesting. The key to effective cash flow management is being able to provide for "worst-case" outcomes in recognition of the uncertainties in cyclical timing, and at the same time devise a practical forecast that is useful to developer as well as to lender or investor.

3. *Failure to recognize that demand, in fact, does not really exist.* The most drastic error in the basic supply and demand analysis is to document the wrong factor. It is easy to prove that various apartment complexes, housing agencies, and governmental advocacy groups have waiting lists for housing. It may even be possible to document issues such as local homelessness, transient populations, or families living below the poverty level. None of this data is useful, however, in identifying the current level of demand. Because the population of potential tenants is itself complex, we cannot find it easily. When concert tickets go on sale, we can see a line disappearing around the corner, so we know that the concert will be sold out. When property is listed for sale and three offers are received on the first day, we know that demand is very high in that price range. However, we cannot assign the same visibility to demand for apartment units.

The fact that many people on waiting lists (1) live elsewhere, (2) have found living accommodations since adding their names to a list, or (3) have moved away complicates this entire question and makes list-watching the most unreliable method for defining current demand (not to mention identifying what demand may be a year from now). In recognizing that the list-watching method is not reliable, the astute market analyst will turn to recent housing and apartment starts, job creation, changes in population, and similar statistical data to estimate demand. Interest rates are valuable, too, as a tracking device. High interest rates mean more rental demand. As rates rise, more people substitute rental housing for owner-occupied housing. So a list alone does not tell the whole story; we also need to discover *why* a list is growing or shrinking. While lists are easier to find, we must also recognize that they are not reliable as indicators of actual demand. The combination of high occupancy in existing complexes, coupled with ever-present lists is one strong indicator of continuing demand; but that alone does not reveal the trend adequately to serve as a reliable, final answer.

Because the cash flow projection relies on the accuracy of a future occupancy level and absorption time, we need to utilize the local economic and demographic trend data, in addition to occupancy levels (and waiting lists). Clearly, if local apartment complexes have weak occupancy rates, no waiting lists, and declining markets for prospective tenants, there is no way to justify the feasibility of building more apartments. However, all this reveals is that low-demand markets are more easily recognizable than are high-demand markets.

Even when we *know* that demand exists, we cannot easily quantify the level of demand, the strength of the trend, or the level of competition; to discover the scope of these factors, our cash flow analysis has to be more inclusive of all the supply and demand factors at work in the existing market as well as within the trend.

THE OCCUPANCY ISSUE IN MULTI-UNIT CASH FLOW ANALYSIS

Cash flow and all of the assumptions that go into it rely upon accurate readings of the local real estate market. The analysis of cash flow and developing estimates of likely future occupancy levels is no easy matter. The chief economist of the National Multi Housing Council (Washington, DC) has observed that

> *knowing how a local economy is performing does not necessarily give a good indication of how the local apartment market, or any other property market, is performing. Differences in apartment-specific demand and supply conditions can weaken the link between the local economy and the local property market.*[9]

This observation has profound ramifications for the real estate analyst. If there is no direct connection (necessarily) between the local economy in general, and the local property market, how is a cash flow projection to be developed? What data can be used reliably to make the projection realistic, and to support that projection with rational assumptions?

In fact, estimating near-future occupancy and vacancy trends is more accurately done using performance data—indicating trends in market rent levels as well as in occupancy within a specific market. A correlation between these two trends—rent increases and vacancy rates—may provide the most reliable trend in estimating cash flow for an apartment project. Such information is useful only if applied within the same region as the project itself; because every region's trends are unique to that region, it makes no sense to use average rates involving the entire country or many regions. For example, an article in a Las Vegas newspaper compared one-year changes in average market rates and concluded that in many regions in Nevada and California, rates dropped (in California's San Francisco, Riverside, and San Bernardino counties, for example).[10]

While such regional data is of limited value and often outdated by time of publication, other local sources are useful for obtaining up-to-date information—not only on average rental rates, but also on occupancy trends. For estimating cash flow, the most reliable and meaningful analysis is a comparison between market rate trends and occupancy trends.

The two indicators do not necessarily confirm each other. In fact, rent increases and trends in occupancy/vacancy provide dissimilar types of market indicators. A popular theory states that in a strong demand market, we are likely to witness a combination of low vacancies and rising rental rates. This seems logical; however, long-term studies indicate that the pattern does not always come out according to this theory concerning the dynamics of supply and demand. In some cases, the highest average vacancy rates also report higher than average rent increases.[11]

Furthermore, the analyst should be sensitive to the likely correlation between the range of apartment costs and vacancy rates. There is a tendency for vacancies to increase as rental levels grow. For example, a trend in New York City demonstrates the consistency of this phenomenon. The lower the rent, the lower the vacancy rate, as shown in Figure 5.2.

The indicators causing rent increases are limited not only to response to local occupancy trends. While occupancy is one of the factors involved—recognizing that when demand exceeds supply, rates tend to rise—there are many others as well. For example, even a very localized study of a single metropolitan area may involve numerous dissimilar markets, based on income, rental levels, and amenities. We have already observed that as rents rise in the immediate area, tenants may move farther away. In the case of a large city, this move may consist of an additional bus or subway stop, an adjoining neighborhood, or the next suburb over, only two or

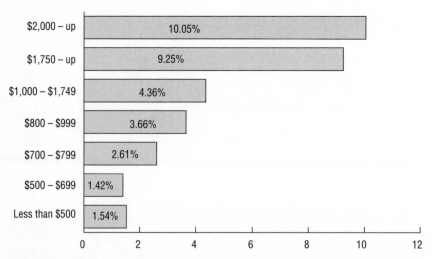

FIGURE 5.2   More Affordability = Lower Vacancy Rates
Source: New York City Housing and Vacancy Survey, 2002.

Valuable Resource

To find links to local information concerning MLS offices, occupancy rates in a particular area, and market rent trends, check http://www.mls.org/.

three miles away. In urban areas, the population is likely to be more dependent on public transportation than in more rural areas, so availability of transit sites may be more of a factor when residents use such amenities.

A study documented by Jack Goodman showed two large cities, Houston and Philadelphia, reporting high vacancy rates, but also reporting higher than average rent increases in the same markets.[12] This type of long-term data is valuable, as it includes information on both rent increases and vacancy rates. However, such studies also tend to be outdated by the time the analyst discovers them; and again, the data does not provide clear answers to the question of how cash flow estimates can be supported with current information.

More likely sources for current, local data would include regional landlord associations, lenders, real estate brokerage firms, and Multiple Listing Service (MLS) offices.

Amenities will also act as incentives in certain types of properties. This is especially true in the planned gated communities popular around Phoenix, Arizona, such as Scottsdale and Chandler; and in central Florida.

Today's tenant is willing to trade living space for specific and desirable amenities, such as nearby or on-site recreational outlets. While many

CASE STUDY: THE VILLAGES, FLORIDA

This central Florida development takes up 5.2 square miles. While the latest reported population was 11,828 (2000 Census), approximately 45,000 people live in the immediate area in owner-occupied or rented housing and multi-unit retirement and senior accommodations. This development combines gated communities with recreational facilities, notably a series of golf courses. However, with additional development *near* the villages, traffic congestion and travel distance to the courses are becoming a problem. The popularity of the closest golf

(Continued)

CASE STUDY: THE VILLAGES, FLORIDA *(Continued)*

course has made getting a tee time quite difficult, so additional courses are developed periodically, each one farther away than the last. It appears to the visitor that the majority of local residents use gas-powered golf carts rather than automobiles, to travel to and from the attractive central shopping area.

A visitor to The Villages notices at once the confusing array of apparently endless gated communities, acting as satellites around various golf courses. Because the courses cross roadways and local residents seem permanently attached to their gas-powered golf carts, this is a world apart from the more urban settings so familiar to most other Americans. In fact, there is a tendency among golf-playing residents to forget that some people continue to use the automobile. It is a common occurrence for golf carts to dart across roadways with their drivers oblivious to the danger afoot even in a 25-mile zone. Accidents are not uncommon, including car-to-cart as well as cart-to-cart mishaps.

The planned community continues to expand, even though road and golf course congestion have worsened over time. Located only 50 miles from Orlando and 75 miles from Tampa, The Villages is located in the very middle of Florida. Besides golf and local shopping, residents are within an easy drive of The Villages Regional Hospital and at least two medical centers, all within 20 miles. It is also about 50 miles to the Orlando or Gainesville airports. Web site: http://www.thevillages.com/

Described by a local travel guide site—http://www.city-data.com/city/The-Villages-Florida.html—as an "active 55+ adult community," recreational emphasis includes golf and other physical sports, health and fitness, and even bowling. The immediate area also boasts a staggering 153 Red Hat Society groups within The Villages (chapters of ladies aged 50 and over who meet monthly to plan events, web site http://www.redhatsociety.com/), which may be a record for a single area. This serves as a good indicator of semiretirement aged trends in this and similar planned communities.

The key feature of The Villages is the connection between active retirement and recreation. The median house value (as of 2000) was a relatively low $136,000, with median household income $42,542. This is an affluent mostly white (97.2%) population able to choose recreational amenities as close as possible to home, and that defines the development. One visitor observed that residents of The Villages were typically "a bunch of stressed-out senior citizens breaking their necks in pursuit of leisure."

people would consider high-density recreationally-oriented lifestyles to be unusually manic, they are nonetheless popular.

The Villages and its success demonstrate that amenities are, indeed, powerful incentives in certain populations. This is the case for the ever-growing semiretirement and retirement community. In Florida, the popularity of golf combined with low housing prices, have made The Villages an amenity-rich success story. However, it is also a double-edged sword. Its popularity—combined with roadway and golf course traffic problems—may ultimately change perceptions about just how desirable it is to be crowded into such a congested recreational area.

Many other considerations may enter into the analysis of residential property. The LIHTC program has become a major portion of modern developments. Similar tax abatement programs and other development incentives are used to encourage projects in specific areas. Even favorable financing may be available as further incentives to development of one type over another.

The next chapter moves away from residential property and examines the entirely different market for retail real estate. In many respects, analysis of residential versus retail are two entirely separate markets, and the analyst needs to use a different approach in judging markets and feasibility for retail development.

CHAPTER 6

Retail Real Estate Analysis

The retail and commercial sector is dissimilar to virtually all other real estate forms. Accordingly, analysis itself must be performed with completely different underlying assumptions. These assumptions include local economic and demographic issues as well as differences between urban and suburban valuation and current trends. As competitive factors affect how development occurs, valuation is also impacted by specialty target themes. This chapter provides guidelines for analysis of retail real estate with these questions in mind.

When we consider the *retail* sector of real estate, we are actually dealing with subtle variations; in some respects, the subsets of retail real estate may even be treated as distinct and separate, because the competitive, supply and demand, and locational attributes display so much variety.

In general, a retail market is defined by the existence of a customer. In owner-occupied housing, there is also a customer of sorts, more accurately called a buyer. And in the residential rental market, our customer is the tenant. These sources of demand are fairly easy to identify and to define. By studying migration trends to the extent that they follow the job market, the demographic mix of an area, and the existing supply of housing, we can quantify both supply and demand. In retail, the task is not as simple. The retail market and the customer it serves may be more elusive than the homebuyer or renter, and this requires that retail market analysis be approached and treated as highly specialized. This is also true for the appraiser who is asked to place a value on a retail property. By definition, the *valuation* of retail real estate depends on the elements of a customer base, both singularly and in comparison to competing retail areas.

AN OVERVIEW OF RETAIL MARKET ANALYSIS

Retail analysis is technically demanding. It involves as many intangible aspects as residential does, but some established methods of analysis may help. This is, in part, because retail was the first product to be analyzed in depth.

We begin with a review of general retail analysis theory.

Until the late 1800s, the location of retail was easy. Go downtown. With changes in transportation (foot, trolley, car, freeway), the ability to consume in different locations increased. Once location was chosen, the basic decision had to be made: freestanding store or part of a center.

Retail has many more forms than the other product types. In office analysis, we may define and distinguish building by conditional class: A, B, or C. Residential property is studied in terms of rental versus owner-occupied, and further by rent levels. Retail has entirely different forms. In the 1950s there were four basic sizes to retail properties: neighborhood, community, regional, and superregional. Now there are more as shopping and lifestyles have diversified. In the modern world of the shopping center, a *center* is increasingly defined by its tenant mix and not by its size.

In this culture of stores, a significant player is the *anchor* tenant. This is the key tenant that will draw customers to the mall, as well as other, smaller—inline—tenants. The inline tenants—those sandwiched along a row or line between outlying anchor stores—benefit by traffic volume drawn to the anchors. They both supply traffic of their own and benefit from the traffic drawn to the anchor.

Analysis in the modern retail tenant space involves (1) size of the tenant space, (2) type of tenant you hope to attract, and (3) attributes of the site (urban, suburban, rural).

Stages of Analysis

Retail analysis occurs by studying strata of market data. These include:

Stage 1: Pedestrian Era Count the number of people walking by. Aim for places with a lot of people. The cousin to the pedestrian analysis is the *signposting* approach. Retailers have realized that certain stores do well in certain locations. For example, in urban areas drugstores like to be on corners. They have discovered that a corner location is worth the extra cost. The corner location always costs more in rent because it provides higher visibility and more traffic.

Stage 2: Mapping and Cartography   With the rise of the automobile and post-World War II suburban growth, it was not enough to just put a store in downtown. Cities were becoming increasingly decentralized. Mapping provides useful intelligence on location of customer base and retail location (or potential location). This can be done from private data (i.e., store records of purchases).

Stage 3: Sales Potential and Predictive Modeling   Experience-based modeling identifies sales potential through the study of customer patterns. From the study of how people shop, it is possible to forecast and predict future predictive patterns.

Stage 4: Holistic View   The final stage is the aesthetic and subliminal effects of the space itself. This includes creation and maintenance of a corporate and store image; internal marketing such as location of high-volume products, number of checkout and registers, lighting, shelf placement, service level, and quality.

This scientific mix of analytical tools is part of a larger cultural trend toward the expansion of the shopping mall. These are found virtually everywhere, not only in large population centers, but even in and near small towns, at freeway exits, at the confluence of transportation routes, and even in the highest-density inner city.

An example of the expansive retail structure is the Mall of America—the ultimate mall in many respects. This mall is located in Bloomington, Minnesota, five minutes from the Minneapolis/Saint Paul International Airport, and 15 minutes from the downtown areas of Minneapolis and Saint Paul.

Some of the stats: Mall of America annually attracts more than 42.5 million visitors. Tourism from outside a 150-mile radius accounts for almost 40 percent of all traffic. The secondary trade area is beyond a 2.5-hour drive. These consumers are either visiting the site as a tourist destination or driving a large distance. To put this in perspective, The Mall's web site includes local hotel information.

International visitors account for approximately 6 percent or nearly 2.6 million of the Mall's annual traffic. How big is big? Some more facts:

Mall of America contains 4.2 million square feet.

It has more than 520 stores.

Visitors spend an average of three hours in the Mall, which is three times the national average for shopping malls.

Mall of America is one of the most visited destinations in the United States, attracting more visitors annually than Disney World, Graceland, and the Grand Canyon combined.

No need for extra heating systems; Mall of America's guests, along with miles of lights, provide enough warmth to keep the entire complex toasty warm even during the cold winter season (only the entrances from parking ramps are heated).

New construction will be about 5 million square feet, bigger than the Mall's original 4.2 million square-foot structure.

With malls on every corner, the only thing the retailers have left is to try to increase the level of customer service or boost the level of enjoyment you have while shopping. Being bigger is good, and being exciting is better. Like Mall of America, an increasing number of other sites are adding amenities beyond retail shops to add to the attractions. Thus, modern malls include entertainment and comfort as a key part of the shopping experience today. Whether with a Ferris wheel at the Mall of America, or natural lighting with skylights, today's mall aims to be a pleasant shopping experience.

Site selection in malled-up America works in the following manner:

1. *Identify an area for store expansion.* (This varies by corporation and by market. Starbucks went for a national presence in big markets and then worked down to urban centers with less than 100,000 people. Wal-Mart went for small overlooked communities and then worked their way up. Others will start with a regional presence and creep their way across.)
2. *Perform a geographical inventory.*
3. *Assess relative performance of store units.*
4. *Identify situation targets.*
5. *Assess market penetration.*
6. *Identify geographical market for expansion.*
7. *Make judgments concerning rate of growth, timing, and specific placement.*

FURTHER ANALYSIS FOR RETAIL SPACE

We will want to study retail space in terms of four types of analysis: market, economic, trade area, and purchasing power.

Market Analysis

Four steps are required to determine the amount of retail space justified by demand for goods and services—the essential task for the retail market analyst:

1. *Determination of the retail trade area for stores located on the property.*
2. *Analysis of the competitive environment in which the store or shopping center must operate.*
3. *Determination of the shoppers who currently use the stores on the property or who would use the stores if the property provided the retail they desired.*
4. Analysis of changes and establishment of forecasts for economic and demographic information developed in the first three steps.

Three major market categories will be distinguished in defining the market. These are:

1. *Generative business.* These properties offer such strong market appeal that the business becomes the destination. This can occur across all product types.
2. *Shared business.* In these properties, market appeal is based on working together and cross-marketing between different retailers.
3. *Suscipient business.* These retailers depend on a draw from other locations.

Economic Analysis

What level of demand is there for retail products or services? That is the big question. The driver, of course, is the identification of the number of consumers and their income levels.

A second level of economic analysis is site-specific. What is the demand for retail on the subject site? The analyst needs to quantity the level of purchasing power surrounding the site. Distance matters. While this is obvious, it is worth keeping in mind that those purchasing dollars are more desirable when found as close to the site as possible.

Trade Area Analysis

It is not difficult to find Census tract/zip code data, or block data. When defining trade area, two important questions should be foremost:

1. Where are the buying households? Is one side of the trade area heavily residential and the other side not?

2. Where are the different pockets of income groups? People tend to self-segregate by economic strata.

When the trade area analysis is being performed for a shopping center, three specific factors will affect the project:

1. Deliberate actions to increase customer traffic (ease of parking, provision of extra freeway off-ramps, signage).
2. Affinity relationships and the principle of compatibility.
3. Consumer perceptions of the shopping center's image.

Purchasing Power Analysis

Once the trade area has been defined, the next step is to find the purchasing power. Using the Census tract, the following information is required:

- Per capita income.
- Appropriate household income, both mean and median.
- Total population.
- Number of households.
- Age composition.
- Income composition of both population and household.
- Average size of the household.

The difference between the mean and the median will skew the purchasing power calculations. It is not accurate to simply multiply the mean by the total number of households. Depending on whether the median is higher or lower, true purchasing power must be arrived at by breaking out the different groups, finding the median within each subrange, and multiplying that by the number of households; then adding up the subtotals. That is the true purchasing power for the area.

FEATURES OF THE RETAIL AND SERVICE MARKET

The key to market analysis in the retail sector has to be the customer. However, we cannot simply conclude that a project is feasible because potential customers live in the area; nor can we conclude without further study that a low number of local residents will translate to lack of customer demand. In some instances, demand will appear because an outlet is sited. Of course, in order to draw such a conclusion, we need to develop sound facts and figures to prove that the belief is realistic.

We begin by making a distinction between *market area* and *trade area*. The concept of a market area is fairly well understood in a supply and demand context. It is the geographical area in which a proposed project will compete with other, similar projects. Thus, a retail mall proposed for construction would be analyzed not only in terms of demographics (distance of shopping customers, proximity to transportation, visibility) but also in terms of what other shopping outlets offering similar products will also gain market share.

The market area—and the assumptions used to study it—are based fairly consistently on population and geography. However, a trade area is more specific. It is "that area around your current or prospective sites that encompasses your largest concentration of customers."[1] In retail, identifying the trade area is important because it may be more expansive than the market area. A trade area includes the entire potential customer base when you are considering the type of project and its competition, but in a context of drive time, distance from population and competition, and supply and demand realities. In a previous chapter, we use an example of Bellis Fair located less than 30 miles from the Canadian border on Washington State's Interstate 5. Several trade area attributes of this site have to be considered when analyzing the retail market. Why? Because the local population is only about 120,000 people, but the mall experiences 35,000 shoppers per day. How is this possible? Several factors come into play. The mall is on a major interstate and easily accessible. The trade area is not limited to the immediate radius of population; it has to include metro Vancouver, British Columbia, where four million additional people live. Economically, we have to compare the Canadian federal and provincial sales taxes totaling 15 percent, to sales tax in Washington, about half that level. The discounted Canadian dollar also provides an incentive, making it economically feasible for Canadians to travel 30 miles to do their mall-based shopping.

In expanding the distinctions between market and trade areas, we further need to specify the *retail* market and trade areas, as these may be different—sometimes vastly so—from the market definitions for nonretail forms of real estate. A retail market area is almost always geographically defined. Thus, a retail center's retail market area would be articulated in terms of (1) distances to and from competing retail outlets, (2) potential for construction of additional competitors, (3) ease of access and proximity to transportation, and (4) immediate area population.

If we look only at the retail market area, we may not get the whole supply and demand picture. In the case of Bellis Fair, the whole Canadian shopping market—representing *most* of the mall's shoppers—would naturally be excluded. A 30-mile trip to go to the mall would not seem likely, especially if other malls are to be found closer to home. This ignores the economic factors related to the exchange rates and sales tax levels between British Columbia and Washington State. Thus, we need to check the retail trade area. The major distinction here is the location of actual and potential customers. In some instances, a customer base will be located much farther away than we would expect.

In a large metro area such as Dallas/Fort Worth, the retail market area and retail trade area will be formulated on drive time, competing retail outlets, and proximity to highways. There is no realistic consideration for extenuating circumstances that would justify moving away from that definition. But consider the case of a fairly remote location such as Bismarck, North Dakota. There, the retail market area *and* the retail trade area are narrowly defined to include the city itself and nearby Mandan. The population of these two areas (56,000 in Bismarck and 17,000 in Mandan) adds up to 73,000. This is approximately the same size as Wilson City, North Carolina. However, when we study the maps of these two states, we realize that the potential retail trade areas are significantly different. The Bismarck/Mandan area is far removed from potential population centers of any size; the surrounding region is entirely made up of sparsely populated farmland and small towns. However, Wilson is about 30 miles from the large Raleigh/Durham metro area and is surrounded by several customer bases within about 20 miles: Rocky Mount (49,000), Greenville (45,000), and Goldsboro (41,000).

While both Bismarck metro and Mandan have an *immediate* market area of about 73,000 people, the retail trade area is vastly different. The market analyst needs to study the differences in geography, access, and *nearby* population in order to better understand the customer base for a new retail project.

Adding to the complexity of this analysis, we need to also consider the type of retail outlet being offered. For example, one draw in the Mandan area is a large recreational park. The attraction serves as an attractive area amenity and, while not directly associated with the retail sector, it may enhance retail activity by drawing people from elsewhere, for vacation or a one-day visit. The promotion for the site reads:

> *Raging Rivers Waterpark and SpeedWorld Golf & Games is a family entertainment complex offering a full day of family fun featuring five major attractions . . . a water park, sprint car & grand prix go-cart tracks, mini-golf and video arcade, all lo-*

cated in a safe and friendly atmosphere. Raging Rivers Water-park and SpeedWorld Golf & Games are located off the Bismarck Expressway at the McKenzie Exit in Bismarck/Mandan, North Dakota.[2]

This brings us to a secondary feature in the analysis of retail trade area: amenities. These may be included within the retail space itself, or located nearby. Both serve as draws for a base of customers outside of the immediate retail market area. For example, many large malls include expansive recreational areas, restaurants, and an array of shops, all designed to draw people in and to then cross-market within a single mall or retail area.

CASE STUDY: LAS VEGAS HILTON, LAS VEGAS, NV

The obvious draw of a large hotel in Las Vegas is, of course, the casino. However, the LV Hilton is designed to draw business travelers, vacationers, and even families. This is part of a larger trend in the city to compete with "theme hotel" recreational facilities beyond the gaming tables.

The Las Vegas Convention Center, one of the largest in the world with 3.2 million square feet of convention space, is naturally a draw for the hotel based on its year-round convention business, often involving attendees in excess of 100,000—a volume most convention centers could never handle. The Hilton also has more than 2.5 million hotel guests per year. Amenities include 40,000 square feet of casino space offering virtually every game imaginable, including the Race & Sports SuperBook for sports betting. The hotel also offers a 1,600-seat live theater. Other specialized features: Star Trek: The Experience and museum, an array of restaurants (fast food, Italian, Japanese, steak house, seafood, Chinese, Mexican, sandwich shop, and even Pizza Hut. Other draws include rooftop tennis courts, swimming pools, several spas and steam rooms, and a fitness center. The lobby floor also offers dozens of specialized shops in a mall-like setting.

The combined array of recreational, dining, shopping, and convention-based amenities makes this far more than just another Las Vegas hotel and casino. The organization has expanded its facilities to appeal to as broad a market as possible.[3]

ANALYSIS OF RETAIL SUPPLY AND DEMAND

The relationship between supply and demand can never be overlooked. In retail, the concern we need to bring to our analysis includes local economic and demographic status and trends, notably the specific attributes of the site: proximity to nearby customer bases, convenience and visibility from freeways or widely traveled roadways, and the trends in population and economic growth. Beyond these starting points for analysis, we also need to study the competition in sufficient detail. The worst outcome of retail analysis is to overlook a source of competition, and to have to conclude, "We didn't realize we would face competition from there."

In an analysis of competing sites (both existing and planned) we need to consider location as a primary factor. We also need to understand the levels of competition between sites, based on amenities, scope of retail offerings (i.e., types of anchor tenants), structural features (i.e., enclosed indoor malls vs. exterior-access, types of parking, etc.), and finally, a determination of whether other retail areas are truly competitive. Some specifics:

- *Amenity comparisons.* A retail area may compete via amenities offered within the area or the site itself. This is especially the case with suburban malls. For example, many large malls include a game room. Such game rooms are frequently located near main entrances or adjacent to food courts—in primary strategic locations within a mall. While this may be a questionable use of space in terms of revenues generated per square foot (compared to other potential uses), there are good reasons. People who want to take time shopping drop their children off at the game room. This gives them more time to go to various stores. Translation: They are likely to spend more. Some malls have added to this concept by including a childcare center for younger children. So the teenagers are left off at the game room and the toddlers are deposited in the free childcare area—all services provided by mall management.

  Onsite amenities may also include attractive restaurants, cinemas, and even nightclubs. Some malls even provide live entertainment through lounge/restaurant outlets within the mall, including bands, stand-up comedy competitions, and other events meant to draw more people. A food court is a further important amenity, not only because onsite food services keep people in malls longer, but also because a range of good alternatives may also make the food court a destination in itself (further adding to the possibility of secondary shopping after the meal).

- *Scope of retail offerings.* Another feature that becomes crucial in determining who shops in a particular mall is the specific range of tenants and especially the identification of anchor tenants. Well-known and popular stores such as Wal-Mart or Target will bring a volume of people to the site. Including other anchors such as one of the large department chain outlets (Sears, J.C. Penney, etc.) attracts a different demographic but also a cross-market between groups. People will tend to visit a mall where they can accomplish all of their shopping needs, without having to go to a second location.

  In addition to anchor tenants, specific specialized stores add to the overall market share. Sports outlets, jewelry stores (or kiosks within aisles of stores, an increasingly popular alternative to the more expensive full store), discount outlets (cheap clothing stores, dollar stores, and similar offerings), and a wide range of other outlets (bookstores, toy stores, specialized food and gift outlets) all become important.

- *Structural features.* The science of mall design has become quite elaborate. The specific design of a mall should depend on climate, population density, and other local features. In extreme climate areas (i.e., Las Vegas) a temperature-controlled, fully enclosed mall is very appealing. More people are likely to visit an enclosed mall when the outside temperature is 115° F. In more moderate climates, exterior-access malls are popular and traffic visibility is more easily maximized. Thus, California malls tend to be either exterior-access with single-level parking, or a combination of exterior-access with internal enclosed or open walkways (variously named courts, aisles, concourses). In the larger cities, urban malls may be incorporated into high-rise building complexes. In New York City, a renovation of Grand Central Station in the 1990s included the addition of a retail mall and food court. The Shops at Columbus Center take up four floors of the Time Warner center. And Rockefeller Center includes 21 buildings and underground connecting tunnels, with dozens of shops and restaurants. All of these are examples of urban retail centers, coordinated with local office space, tourist attractions, and transportation hubs.

- *Competitive analysis.* Is it truly competitive? Perhaps the most interesting question an analyst can ask is, "Does a competing retail area really compete with the subject project?" It may be possible that two seemingly similar retail areas are not actually competitive for the same markets. For example, if we consider the differences between older downtown districts and outlying newer malls, we realize that there are several dissimilar attributes, including potentially the demographic of shoppers to these areas. In a large metropolitan area like Sacramento, a seemingly endless array of retail malls are found along major boulevards surrounding the city center. Some areas, such as the southern Florin Road area of the city, are characterized by a mix of less successful big-block malls but more active strip malls. And Old Sacramento, described as an "historic district," takes up 28 acres and contains about 140 shops and restaurants.[4] Although it is promoted as being historic, few of the shops meet that standard and, in fact, this is a packaged urban mall complete with its own mall-type amenities: parking garage, hotels, kite store, bars, and restaurants as well as several blocks of shops. The architecture is intended to look like Old Sacramento, but it is doubtful that the participants in the 1849 Gold Rush would recognize very much of what is there.

Does Old Sacramento truly compete with a Florin Road strip mall? This area is described in a lexicon found on an offbeat web site as:

Florin Road   *The south side of Sacramento falls off into heavy industry and run down suburbs. Running down the center of this area is Florin Road, an ugly strip flanked by large shopping centers, a somewhat run down mall, and a large number of car dealerships. The area has been hurt by the automallization of the dealerships, leaving large tracts of abandoned buildings and cracking asphalt that never are re-leased. Florin Road is often used to generalize this whole area.*[5]

We may also wonder whether Old Sac—as the locals call it—actually competes with another urban retail project, Arden Fair, an upscale site on the northern side of the city. Arden Fair is described on its web site:

Arden Fair *is the premier shopping destination in Sacramento, with over 1 million square feet of shopping! If that's not enough, soft seating areas, valet parking and year-round special events create the ideal atmosphere. The point is, there's no place like shopping than at Arden Fair.*[6]

These three urban examples—Old Sac, Florin Road, and Arden Fair— are vastly different, and not only geographically. It is fair to generalize that Old Sac is a tourist destination and only minimally used by locals as a shopping center; that Florin Road is a regional center, which most Sacramento residents rarely visit; and that Arden Fair is an upscale center serving as a regional destination, even though it is found within greater Sacramento.

IDENTIFYING THE *REAL* MARKET

The analytical study of a proposed site—as well as that of existing or competing sites—will be centered on valuation. The viability of a retail project rests with how many shoppers are likely to visit a retail area and on how much market share is likely to be captured by a new project. We have to expect the normal supply and demand rules to work.

For example—as retail establishments along Sacramento's Florin Road have discovered—building too many malls does not ensure success. One example is Florin Mall, an attempted traditional retail mall that has not competed well with the many strip malls and discount stores nearby. In 1996, the mall lost Weinstocks, one of its big anchor tenants; and in 2003, J.C. Penney also closed up shop. By 2004, many other stores in Florin Mall were also considering giving up on the underperforming location and moving out.[7]

With this in mind, the retail market analyst needs to be aware that while the new retail mall is often a great success story, it is necessary to analyze competitive forces carefully. Florin Mall was simply sited in the wrong place, where the market area preferred discount stores and strip mall shopping. Big department stores like J.C. Penney could not compete with local Goodwill stores and other discount clothiers. A market analysis failed to recognize a reality in this market area: *In some instances, the "competition" does not mean similar stores. It may be more accurately defined as shopping patterns and preferences.* However, in urban areas, retailers rarely have a choice. While such retailers serve a diverse population, their choices in site and in what they offer are more limited than in suburban mall settings, for example, where a greater variety of choices in site, cost, and market may be found.

For example, check the "You are where you live" link at www.claritas.com where you may enter any zip code to gain information about the types of retail outlets nearby. As the claritas.com web site explains:

> People living in the same neighborhoods tend to have similar lifestyles, proving the old adage that "birds of a feather flock together" still holds true. To a large extent, you are where you live![8]

One classic textbook on the topic of real estate appraisal discusses the importance of the "elements of comparison" in real estate.[9] Generally speaking, a discussion of this type would attempt to identify similarities between competing projects and a subject property. Thus, an analyst would find stores offering the same types of merchandise, in the same price range, and located within a geographical market area. But will these properties always serve as comparable properties? Using the appraisal standard, which for our purposes is somewhat limited, they are not. If we were studying a proposal for a Florin Mall-type of project, some possible conclusions might indicate the *lack* of similar stores in the area, indicating that anchors like J.C. Penney and Weinstocks would capture a significant market share. This would be an encouraging indication supporting feasibility—until we look further and realize that, in fact, the market of which the store may capture a large share may itself be quite limited. If the market area is to be defined as the Florin Road expanse (which is quite large) we also have to ask, "Where do people shop?" If these shoppers do *not* frequent J.C. Penney but prefer a different type of store, what is the point? Capturing 80 percent of a market share is worth little if the market itself is too small to support the retail store.

Yet another distinction between different markets may be seen in the attitudes among both customers and retail store employees. For example, in the previously cited example of Bellis Fair Mall—located less than 30 miles from the border of British Columbia—all of the stores accept Canadian funds without hesitation, and cash registers are set up to convert between U.S. and Canadian funds for sales totals and change. However, only 30 miles south of Bellis Fair, the Cascade Mall is a different story. In this mall, check-out registers in many stores include the sign: NO CANADIAN FUNDS.

Distinctions may also be seen in customer service attitudes. In Arden Fair, Sacramento, where customer service levels are attentive and high quality, customers are treated as welcome guests. In comparison to other sections of the same city, Arden Fair serves a distinct market. So does Florin Road, although that market is vastly different, as are the relative characteristics of the two neighborhoods. In other words, the same attitude is not experienced everywhere. A brief example follows.

As far as the traditional measurements of markets are concerned, it pays to question the assumption base with a degree of skepticism, especially given the chances for great diversity within a relatively small geographic change. Analysts have observed that shoppers will travel up to eight minutes to arrive at a neighborhood shopping center.[11] But is this always true? The retail analyst needs to exercise judgment, using this acknowledged rule of thumb as a starting point rather than as an absolute, conclusive fact. A *regional* shopping center and its market travel time indicate a tendency, but we also have to be aware that some formats are not going to find much of a market at all. Just as a large high-volume anchor tenant (such as Wal-Mart, Costco, or Home Depot, for example) will not succeed in an isolated rural community with a population of only a few

---

CONVERSATION WITH THE CASHIER AT THE STORE

Keep in mind I have a rather large piece of FURNITURE perched on top of my cart.

Cashier: Umm, you don't want to take that cart out to your car, do you?
Me: Well, actually that's exactly what I was intending to do with it.
Cashier: Oh. (pauses) Well, we're going to need a picture ID left at the counter.
Me: Why?
Cashier: To make sure you bring the cart back.

(The cart in question was actually swiped from a different store, but I grabbed it in the lot as I needed one and you take what you can get at this time of year.)

Me: But it's not even YOUR cart!
Cashier: Oh. (Longer pause) Well, you probably don't need to leave ID then. . . .[10]

---

hundred, big retail stores may be equally unsuccessful in markets with more subtle distinctions. One would think, based on population, traffic, and visibility statistics, that a large suburban-type mall with free parking, would succeed on Sacramento's Florin Road. This assumption would overlook the all-important shopping trend, or the *demand* for such stores. While a certain type of retail demand certainly exists in a densely populated area, it does not necessarily mean that a particular type of store will succeed there.

This example does not mean that the traditional approach to retail analysis should be abandoned. It does mean, however, that the historical methods have to be adjusted to take into account the unique features of a market area. One expert has identified five sequential tasks that analysts should use when studying a retail trade area. These are:

1. *Delineation of the retail trade area.* A locational analysis involves two primary elements: distance and "intercept" locations. A rule of

thumb indicates that retail customers will travel between one and one and one-half miles, or up to eight minutes, to reach a neighborhood shopping center—assuming there are choices within the market area. Location indications involve the relative site of a subject property and its competitor. The most critical issue here is whether a customer passes a competitor on the way to the subject property, or would need to travel in a different direction. The distinction affects the delineation directly.

2. *Estimation of total retail sales in the area.* A study of overall retail volume should include distinctions about potential competitors not only by location but also by type of site: neighborhood, community, or unanchored strip center. Additionally, the analyst will need to identify freestanding retail space within the market area in terms of sales volume, leaseable space, and sales volume *per* leaseable square foot. This level of detail becomes critical as a means for judging market area, assuming we first have narrowed down the locational intercepts and know how that affects potential market share.

3. *Estimation of local purchasing power.* The most reliable indicator of purchasing power is per capita income. Census data and area-specific studies by fee-based research organizations provide updated average income and population numbers. Multiplying the two provides overall purchasing power. This is a critical number for comparative purposes and if you are able to break down the demographic and income variables by a keenly focused market area (neighborhoods within cities, for example), then the value of those numbers is more useful than it would be for a broader greater metropolitan area of a city.

4. *Allocation of purchasing power to goods and services offered or proposed.* The total purchasing power is a gross number and it does not indicate where and how consumers spend money. The Department of Commerce publishes a report called Relative Importance of Components in the Consumer Price Index, which breaks down product categories for a specific area of the country. Search for the latest report for a specific area at http://www.ntis.gov/search/index.asp. The report provides common spending patterns and provides allocation weight for each and, to a degree, will help to narrow down buying and spending patterns. However, specific neighborhood allocation of spending patterns may require more in-depth analysis including the type and location of local merchants and their likely markets. (For example, one area may be characterized by high-end boutiques and gourmet food stores, while another may have a predominance of discount clothing and general stores.)

5. *Residual analysis.* The final step is simply a comparison of data accumulated in the four preceding steps. The purpose is to narrow down as finely as possible the actual effective local supply and demand factors at work. For example, your analysis may reveal the totals of retail sales as well as allocated purchasing power. The conclusions you would draw from a comparison of this data may be done on a current or a projected basis, depending on (1) the approach you take to analyzing the market, (2) the rate of anticipated growth and expansion in the area, and (3) the time required to construct the proposed subject property. It would be most revealing to compare total retail sales and allocated purchasing power for several areas, and to draw conclusions concerning the feasibility of a project. Generally speaking, if retail sales exceed allocated purchasing power, it implies that the market is overbuilt, and vice versa, when purchasing power is greater than total retail sales, it indicates that the market is underbuilt.[12]

Remember, however, that these are generalizations. When we look at specific market factors affecting retail, we may discover unique features that have to be considered. In an earlier chapter, for example we provided an example of Bellis Fair, a mall whose apparent local purchasing power would be quite lower than total retail sales, a puzzling relationship. However, when one would consider the actual state of the market, the reasons would be apparent. The vast majority of shoppers at Bellis Fair come from Canada, which is less than 30 miles to the north. Thus, available statistics regarding purchasing power and total retail sales could not be reliably translated from U.S. Census data or from Department of Commerce averages. The invisible line of the international border would make the approach invalid. This points out an important aspect to all forms of analysis: It is rarely safe or reliable to use rule-of-thumb data without also looking carefully and closely at the specific attributes of the project, the market, and the shopper.

This proposed sequence of steps supports our contention that markets have to be analyzed individually, and not using generalizations. Apparently, the significant points in the five-step approach were ignored or misread, including steps 3 (purchasing power) and 4 (allocation of purchasing power). These are the steps where an analyst should realize that customers in lower-range economic neighborhoods are likely to shop in vastly different patterns (i.e., Florin Road strip malls) from those in high-range economic neighborhoods (i.e., Arden Fair). So the combination of analytical study of the combined purchasing power and allocation of purchasing power, would tell the analysts whether or not the mall format (and specifically, the anchor tenants a developer has in mind) would even be appropriate for the neighborhood in question.

This works in both socioeconomic models. For example, in an upscale shopping center, there is likely to be less appeal for Ross Dress for Less, Goodwill, or Everything For a Dollar and other discount outlets—just as traditional retail department stores may fail in specific neighborhoods.

HIGHEST AND BEST USE AS A DISTINGUISHING ANALYTICAL POINT

The retail market analyst—like all other property analysts—needs to be aware of how the appraisal principle of *highest and best use* affects valuation. A retail center located in a disadvantageous place (via zoning, visibility, surrounding use, etc.) will not achieve total market value potential.

We tend to think of highest and best use in terms of maximizing land by the criteria just mentioned (zoning, visibility, surrounding use). However, the concept includes far more as well. A more subtle consideration is that the perceived or assumed use has to also be both reasonable and likely. A *reasonable* land use opens up the question of the potential variety of projects that could go on a site. The *likely* uses of land are limited in terms of local zoning laws, safety, and affordability. Even when zoning allows a retail use, it does not always make sense to build a retail project. For example, a retail-commercial zone may exist in a primarily residential neighborhood as an exception to allow daycare centers, convalescent facilities, and churches; this does not mean that a shopping center would also be appropriate in the same location.

The certainty of highest and best use is formulated in the understanding of market potential and valuation. Thus, highest and best use is an opinion based on study, and not on speculation. At the same time, this does not logically mean that there is always a single highest and best use for property; there may be more than one method for developing property for optimal profitability and future market value.

In analyzing property with this concept in mind, how can you define potentially multiple highest and/or best uses? If we accept the suggestion that within the definition of *highest and best use*, there may exist a *range* of possible development alternatives, then we need to select the criteria by which that range may be quantified. We should consider no less than four attributes in the identification of this highest and best use range:

1. *Physical attributes.* There may be a tendency to view projects in a two-dimensional way, namely by looking at a series of drawn plans. To

make the analysis realistic, a visit to the site is desirable if not essential. An analyst may not expect to be able to identify highest and best use if the physical attributes of the site have not been seen. For example, can a large retail mall be built on a sloping site? What limitations will that pose in terms of soil erosion and run-off, adaptability, traffic, and maximum build-out? The size of the land is equally as important; a rectangular or square site provides greater flexibility than odd-shaped sites, for example.

2. *Legal provisions and allowed uses.* There is little value in assigning a theoretical highest and best use if, in fact, that use is simply not allowed by zoning codes. We must further consider restrictions arising from environmental rules, fire and public safety limitations, and questions of title. (For example, if acquisition of a site requires local residents to agree to sell their land, a single holdout will defeat the entire project unless some accommodation can be made.)

3. *Correlation between perceived market and cost of the project.* Feasibility has to also be considered when analyzing a property's highest and best use. If, for any number of reasons, achieving what is perceived as the highest and best use would be cost-prohibitive, then it is not realistic to continue. Few retail projects are built as speculative ventures; in any retail project that includes an anchor tenant, the project will not go forward without a firm and binding commitment from that anchor. Finding that anchor and getting the commitment is invariably the first hurdle of feasibility that must be met.

4. *Markets and potential customer base (retail trade area).* The most important consideration in defining highest and best use is the market itself. In retail, emphasis is inevitably placed on identifying the potential customer and likely market share, given the competition. The question of value, of course, also rests with identifying appropriate sites that are physically, legally, and financially likely to address the perceived customer base. Expanding beyond the apparent customer, we also need to ensure that the retail trade area is thoroughly understood. Just as a specific type of retail project will not always work in a specific site (i.e., Florin Mall in Sacramento) because the customer base (retail trade area) was not interpreted accurately), highest and best use requires that a project be a good mix for the local market, meaning demand in a real sense.

The study of specific demographic and economic factors demonstrates that markets—or casting it somewhat differently, the *components* of markets—are vastly different. The people who shop on Florin Road and those who shop at Arden Fair are not the same market in terms of per capita income, neighborhood (housing prices), and other important qualifying tests. In a very real sense, Florin Road may be considered an urban area, whereas Arden Fair is suburban in nature. Even though both areas are within the same city, they are not at all the same in terms of retail trade area.

What would work on Florin Road? Apparently, the suburban-type mall does not work, at least not in comparison to the strip malls with which it competes. However, at the same time there is no identifiable city center for the Florin Road area, so the urban mall of the type seen in New York City or San Francisco—retail combined in with office space, transportation hubs, and tourist destinations—would not work in south Sacramento, where none of those attributes are present.

The question, "What would work on Florin Road?" is not the right question. The market analyst's job is not to renovate or justify an area's economic growth, but to identify whether an idea is sensible in terms of markets and cost. The right question would be, "Does either a suburban-type or urban-type mall work in the Florin Road area?"

If a market analysis included a question of highest and best use, the conclusion may be that alternative uses would work better on a site. Sacramento has attempted to bolster the area along with other lagging neighborhoods with a series of incentive programs: enterprise zones, tax credits, expedited permitting processes, tax credit programs, and workforce assistance programs.[13]

An analysis including the study of highest and best use would need to take such factors as local incentive allowances into account. Clearly, the conclusion will be affected significantly when government and business associations are spending money to improve an area's retail economy. In comparison, when there is little support for spending money to improve the retail sector, that fact may have an equally important detrimental effect on the overall analysis.

TRENDS IN RETAIL MALL DESIGN

The comparison among three malls in Sacramento, California—Arden Fair, Old Sac, and Florin Mall—demonstrates the reality that not all markets are the same. No single design formula is going to work everywhere. In fact, the Sacramento example also provides a good example of a trend described as "the mall meets the ghetto."

Florin Road, a high-crime area of Sacramento, is worlds apart from the area surrounding Arden Fair and Old Sac. It only makes sense that different formats and designs for shopping areas will work in these vastly dissimilar regions. Even in large metropolitan areas, the street-level store is gradually being replaced with the more efficient, more market-accessible mall. In New York City, the Fifth Avenue shops remain, of course, as landmarks. However, the new urban mall is gradually replacing the old-style shops in volume and popularity.

We may distinguish the market and study trends—and, of course, analyze a particular project—based on the type of shopping center proposed and its location. It is imperative that the design of a shopping mall or center be compatible with the neighborhood and market area it is intended to serve.

Several distinct design formats are emerging in the retail market for shopping centers and malls, including:

1. *Convenience centers.* These smallest formats of malls include a relatively narrow mix of products or services, and serve a limited market trade area. Some of these smaller shopping centers exist on a smaller scale design or expanded strip malls. A variety of shops may be offered, with perhaps a major grocery store serving as anchor. We often see a variety of stores such as hair care, drugstore, dry cleaners, travel agency, and beauty shop in such neighborhood centers—all designed to appeal to the auto traveler stopping for a carton of milk on the way home. The requirement for such centers, usually running no more than 150,000 square feet in total, is a market area no greater than three miles, and an adequate parking lot. The key word in this design is *convenience* for the customer—fast in, fast out, one or two store visits.

2. *Small-scale malls.* Above the shopping center is the community mall, usually sized between 100,000 and 300,000 square feet over 20 to 30 acres. This mall may have one or two anchors including a grocery store as well as a home improvement store, clothing outlet, or variety store (i.e., K-Mart). The market area will be between 3 and 10 miles, maximum. Some of these malls can also be defined as *off-price* malls, including or emphasizing low-cost or discount stores. An *open-air* mall generally consists of parallel rows of stores with unenclosed parking and walking areas. While canopies may protect shoppers from weather, there are no permanent, connected covers from one side to the other. In comparison, a *shopping mall* is similar in design but has an enclosed space between rows of shops. A *hybrid center* is any format including features of open-air and shopping malls, or mixing uses among retail, entertainment, lodging, and cultural stores.

3. *Regional centers.* Some of these are also called "power centers" or "regional malls." They tend to range in size between 250,000 and one

million square feet, and are characterized by at least three large anchor tenants (i.e., Wal-Mart, Home Depot, Sears, and other "big-box" types of stores). They also appeal to customers with onsite amenities such as cinema, food court, childcare centers, and game rooms. Valuation of the regional center

> *is dependent on the level of retail sales that it generates, and regional shopping center sales are dependent on consumer shopping behavior. Consumers shop at regional shopping centers for a variety of reasons; the three primary reasons are location, comparison shopping, and department store fashion image.*[14]

These reasons do not preclude shopping behavior based on consumer preferences. For example, many regional centers are designed to draw customers from larger malls nearby. (The example of Florin Center demonstrates that while a regional center may draw from larger malls, it is less likely that they will draw from neighborhood shopping areas and strip malls.)

4. *Larger malls.* The major malls tend to be sized between 750,000 and two million square feet, with three or more major anchor tenants and large stores, each with more than 100,000 square feet of retail space. They may take up as much as 100 acres or more. In an urban region, market area is 5 miles; suburban-based large malls may have a market area as large as a 10-mile radius. A *super-regional center* would have more anchor tenants and is more likely to have multiple shopping levels. The *theme center* or *cultural center* offers some unifying theme, setting it apart from more generalized shopping centers, often in terms of entertainment outlets, restaurants, or a mix of offerings within historic sites.

5. *Other design formats.* The preceding list by no means defines all retail design formats. We need to recognize that in some areas, strip malls or downtown shopping areas may be appropriate and even vibrant. The highest and best use of land invariably depends on the economic and demographic character of the area, and on the competition (the *real* competition, which will not necessarily consist of similar shopping areas, but more realistically, of areas where people actually shop—an important distinction). A *mixed-use* mall or center may include not only traditional retail stores, but expand to also offer a small hotel, offices, sports outlets, or cultural sites.

Some malls tend to be very narrowly focused. A good example is the increasingly popular outlet mall. These consist of a number of stores, including name brands, run directly by manufacturers and offering attractive discounts. In addition to discounts, stores may offer out-of-season merchandise or small-volume purchase of items normally available only in larger lots. For example, a dishware outlet store may allow customers to buy single pieces, whereas a particular pattern would otherwise be available only as a complete set. Distinguishing characteristics include open-air exterior design often visible from a freeway or highway; the lack of anchor tenants; and size usually less than 500,000 square feet.

The selection of anchor tenants is very interesting as a study in market value. The big department stores—Sears, J.C. Penney, and so on—may co-exist in a single mall and are favorites as draws for smaller satellite stores. In the process of market analysis, negotiations with potential anchors may produce variations in feasibility. For example, in some larger mall settings, anchors want to control the design of their store area and parking lot and may also insist on specific lease terms, including noncompete requirements for specific product types. Anchor tenants also pay significantly less than *inline* stores on the basis of lease costs per square foot. Many anchors prefer to purchase the land and part of the parking area in such arrangements. While this may curtail future rent revenues, such an arrangement may also reduce the need for interim financing and *improve* the feasibility of a mall project.

A visit to a series of larger retail malls demonstrates the variety of possible anchor tenants. But do the anchors necessarily dominate the market itself? While anchor tenants are, of course, a name-recognition draw, the shopping patterns shown by customers may be more mixed. Customers may *enter* the mall through the exterior doors going through a Sears or Target store, or through the food court; but shopping may take place at any number of smaller stores in the interior of the mall. Just as grocery stores always put milk at the rear of the store, mall design is consciously set to encourage shoppers to shop. In the case of the grocery store, milk is a common purchase, but to get to the dairy case, one has to pass through aisles of cereal, cookies, candy, and produce. In the mall, to get to the interior, the shopper has to pass through a food court or anchor tenant store space, which encourages *more* shopping. While some malls have major entrances directly into concourses, the shopper is immediately barraged with store entrances on all sides, so even in this situation, the direct promotion advantages of the mall design are apparent.

The many variations of anchor tenants, mall location, and design, and of course, the market area and retail trade area, make retail demand analysis elusive. However, it all comes down to the suggestion that the markets, competition, and population realities should be reviewed not on any presumed formula, but on a realistic basis. In studying economic trends such as per capita income, be sure to include a context. It is not enough to identify per capita income without also determining how consumers spend and where they are likely to shop. For example, a retiree with an annual income of $40,000 shops radically differently from a young family with two small children, even in the same income level.

The uncertainties of demand analysis may cause problems for the analyst in developing an objective, comprehensive outcome in their reports. The astute analyst may be wise to remember the advice offered by the experts, not only to give due attention to the demand side, but also to develop clear assumptions to support it:

> *Many market analyses focus excessively on the supply characteristics of a given market but neglect the demand forces that ultimately support rental rates, drive absorption, and create value. Analyzing demand can be a difficult, time-consuming, and imprecise process and, as a result, many appraisers give the topic only passing consideration in their reports. . . . When a demand analysis is well-founded, the assumptions are clearly stated and the conclusions are easy to understand. A weak demand analysis often requires the reader to take "leaps of faith" to come to the same conclusions as the analyst.*[15]

The same reality-based suggestions apply to supply analysis. In determining the level of competition, identify the types of design where the market area shops. In a region where most people go to neighborhood centers, small shops or strip malls, a large, upscale mall is not likely to work, for example. So if the starting point is the assumption that a specific mall design will work in an area—and competition analysis is simply a study of similar malls in the same area—then the conclusions will be unrealistic. A market analyst may be surprised to find that in a high-density area, there are no competing 200,000 square foot malls within the retail trade area. Does this mean the new project will capture 100 percent of the market? Or does it mean that the mall anticipated to be built there will not represent the highest and best use in that particular location?

Market analysis in the retail sector should never begin with a presumed understanding of either supply or demand. A realistic analysis of the market, using the scientific method, may indicate that a project is viable and may capture a portion of local demand; or it may conclude that, like the Florin Mall, the project will not work on that site. Florin Mall included high-visibility anchor stores, but even that did not change the realities of the local market. The same is true everywhere. When a project does not live up to expectations, local government and private interests may devise tax incentives and other means for boosting sales, but in the long term, a failed project reflects conditions in the market, and not the need for additional funding. It is more prudent to identify likely problems during the feasibility phase, by coming to understand the attributes of the local market—and that is less expensive as well.

CHAPTER 7

Office and Industrial Real Estate Analysis

Analysis of nonretail commercial space relies on certain attributes found in retail, but is not similar in every way. Industrial parks, for example, cannot be analyzed on the same underlying assumptions as a retail shopping center, because many of the determinant factors are entirely dissimilar. This chapter demonstrates those factors to be considered in office and industrial analysis, including economic trends, zoning, and a trend toward merging of office and light industrial zones.

Industrial and office real estate share many similarities and may often be analyzed using similar underlying assumptions. This is true regarding the most common type of industrial zoning and use, which is most often called *light industrial* zoning (also called *flex space*). This refers to low impact in terms of environmental, safety, noise, and other impacts. Typically, these uses include high-tech manufacturing, other clean manufacturing, warehousing (especially in port and intermodal sites), and laboratory and research uses.

The two are treated in a similar manner because these uses may overlap. For example, a commercial printing operation may be classified as a commercial office *or* light industrial use. A clean manufacturing operation (a pottery production plant, for example) would be clearly identified as industrial. However, these do not share the same attributes with the higher-impact forms of industrial use, most often called *heavy industrial*. These uses are highly specialized and not within the realm of most analysts' work. Included would be sites that produce significant amounts of toxic waste as a byproduct—railroad yards, mines, and quarries, for example. Analysis of the markets for heavy industrial land is most often performed by experts, government agencies, or specialists working for companies that own such lands (especially mining and railroad corporations).

Collectively, office and industrial property is the largest commercial property market in the United States. Of the different types of property, for the year 2002 office and industrial sales accounted for 62 percent of the entire market. Sales of office and industrial properties were $36.648 billion in 2002. Apartment sales were $13.248 billion; retail $8.095 billion; and lodging $1.474 billion. The total was $59.465 billion. The relationship between office/industrial and other markets—apartments, retail, and lodging—is shown in Figure 7.1.

Many office/industrial parks and complexes are specifically designed to facilitate both types of uses. It is a common design to place street-fronting offices, where signage is visible, and via access from a driveway, industrial bays are placed at the sides and rear of the building. Analysis

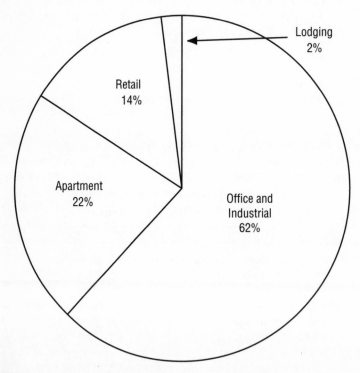

FIGURE 7.1   Real Estate Commercial Property Sales, 2002
Source: CoStar Market Report, 1st Quarter, 2003.

CASE STUDY: PIER 1, SAN FRANCISCO, CA

The original value of San Francisco's waterfront was tied to the Gold Rush in the 1850s. The harbor area, known as The Embarcadero, included an early version of an intermodal facility. A rail line on the street facilitated movement of goods to and from ships. However, the importance of this activity declined by the middle of the twentieth century, so that the entire harbor area on San Francisco Bay fell out of favor. Among the reasons was the emergence of the East Bay cargo sites in Oakland and Alameda, which also connected to rail lines directly, whereas San Francisco-based rail was limited by the Bay itself; the rather shallow bay which limited ship access; and the emergence of the city as a business center more than as an industrial and import site.

The destructive earthquake in 1989 further reduced the prominence of The Embarcadero as either an industrial or import center. The miles of piers centering on The Ferry Building at the foot of Market Street served more as historic landmarks than as any utilitarian centers for commerce. The Ferry Building itself had become nothing more than a terminal for ferry service north of the city.

In 1990, a seven-year project was begun, called the Waterfront Land Use Plan. As property values in the peninsula-type topography of San Francisco became increasingly higher, the city and the Port of San Francisco began seeking ways to redevelop the waterfront and generate interest in the buildings along The Embarcadero. The first phase was a restoration of The Ferry Building.

Immediately north of the Ferry Building is Pier 1. Originally built as a warehouse and storage facility in 1932 for C&H Sugar and later used as a ferry dock, Pier 1 eventually was converted to a parking garage in the 1960s, but otherwise was not used for any other purposes. Developer AMB Corporation (www.amb.com) won a bid with plans to include its own offices within the new site. Financed and organized as a REIT, Pier 1 was the first major adaptation of an old pier building. It provided needed expansion of the geographically limited San Francisco downtown area as well as valuable industrial space *near* the downtown neighborhood. The Port Authority leases 52,000 square feet through a long-term lease, which is 34 percent of the total leaseable area.

(Continued)

CASE STUDY: PIER 1, SAN FRANCISCO, CA *(Continued)*

Oddly, California state law forbids residential or commercial use of waterfront property, so the developer had to negotiate a compromise with the state. Public access is allowed to the building as a maritime resource, which also allowed the developer to gain historic preservation tax credits (equal to 20 percent of the construction cost via tax credits). Thus, the developer was able to arrive at an agreed-upon compromise with the state to expand tenant uses beyond maritime uses.

While the project represents the use of previously ignored space, it was necessary to expand the leaseable square footage to make the project feasible. As an historic preservation property, the developer was not allowed to change the outer appearance of the building; the same restrictions ruled out the addition of a second floor. The solution: construction of an innovative 50,000 square foot "floating mezzanine," taking advantage of high ceilings to create an additional space.

The project is a combination of historic space with industrial and office uses, working within a state mandate that 70 percent of the area had to remain "maritime" in nature. This was achieved partially through leases to the Port and partly by ensuring that all public areas met the requirements as well. Total development costs were just under $50 million, and the project was completed in 2001. The site is both historic and prestigious, located next to the famous Ferry Building and prominent to tourists as well as to locals.

of such properties should take into account the flexibility of potential uses and combinations of uses; design versus the requirements of potential tenants; and the possibility of including amenities to make the project more desirable (i.e., placement of restaurants, banks, gas stations, and other nonoffice and nonindustrial uses that will be convenient to employees as well as visitors).

The most basic measure of demand for office space is white collar job growth in the region. Pier 1 amenities include location and historic interest within the site itself. We cannot analyze this strictly on the basis of tenant expansion potential, given the restrictive waterfront tenant rules. However, space requirements for both office and industrial uses are a consideration, and should be. While office space is usually analyzed on the basis of square feet per employee, industrial structures are normally oriented toward the specific space requirements of the activity itself. Thus, the analyst faces an interesting requirement in recognition of the trend toward a merging of these uses: the need to allow for both per-employee and per-activity requirements of potential tenants. Given the added prohibitions involved when waterfront, historic preservation, and other limitations apply, these traditional analytical methods do not always work well.

The usual office-based analysis of a space may not apply in the emerging office and industrial park combined use. In comparison to the more

CASE STUDY: 4 TIMES SQUARE, NEW YORK, NY

This major high-rise contains 48 floors and 1.6 million square feet. One distinguishing characteristic is its "environmentally responsible" design. This includes systems and construction designed to minimize effects on occupant health, energy reduction; indoor air quality; recycling systems; and sustainable manufacturing processes.

Located at Forty-second and Broadway in Manhattan, 4 Times Square did not get off to an easy start. Construction began at a low point in the rental cycle and the developer, The Durst Organization (www.durst.org) was unable to obtain outside financing. The company put up its own funds to get the project started and soon found a major tenant, the Conde Nast Corporation. Part of a larger Forty-second Street Master Plan, this interesting "green" building has been called "a piece of urban theater."[1]

From a feasibility standpoint, questions included a nontangible, the developer's vision. While Durst's initial investment was high due to the environmentally-oriented design elements, long-term savings in utilities have been significant.[2]

Also called the Conde Nast Building, this project was the first speculative office project developed in Manhattan in more than 10 years. The locational amenity is a strong tenant draw, and the environmental design aspects are equally interesting, both to government and to potential tenants. This project makes the point that amenities and tenant-based value are not always limited to tangible benefits associated with a site. The amenity of *status* location and innovative design may be equally important and appealing.

traditional office building, the industrial park site may tend to consist of relatively small office spaces, a limited number of onsite employees, and a greater emphasis on industrial sites with a front office (as opposed to separate office and industrial tenants). It may be more common to find a concentration of employees in the production area of such combined facilities, with office space required only for reception/clerical employees and a few members of management. While this is a generalization, it is applicable in many situations. However, recognizing the advantages to flexibility in design, an office/industrial complex may be designed to respond to a variety of dissimilar tenant requirements, including specific design criteria for tenants able to commit to long-term leases.

The combined market and feasibility studies involved with office spaces often rely upon first finding a major tenant or, in the case of corporate offices, occupying a building as a headquarters or major divisional office. This is not always possible, however.

INDUSTRIAL AND SERVICE-ORIENTED REAL ESTATE ATTRIBUTES

The importance of the office and light industrial combined "park" development setting reflects a modern trend. Today, approximately one-fifth of *all* U.S. employees work in office buildings.[3] This may include urban high-rise offices, suburban complexes or office parks, and mixed-use (office and industrial) projects. Ownership, notably of larger projects, consists of approximately one-fifth owner-occupied buildings, with the remaining projects owned institutionally. For example, equity REITs or real estate partnerships may favor ownership of office and industrial parks as providing favorable cash flow as well as historically established long-term market appreciation.

The analysis of an office and/or industrial project would include consideration of five specific factors. These are:

The Class of Building or Project

An office building is usually defined in terms of its "class." Class A buildings are most attractive to investors, and are characterized by quality of materials, design, and amenities. Location may also be a factor; for example, a building located in a high-visibility, "status" address may improve marketability to investors (for example, Wall Street in New York, Wilshire Boulevard in Los Angeles, or The Embarcadero in San Francisco). This class attracts tenants who want to project an image of success and who benefit from the public relations value of the space. Class B buildings are often older, but functional. Rents will tend to be lower and design may be outdated. Tenants may include not-for-profit organizations, advertising firms, and other business service companies. Class C includes the oldest grouping of office buildings. Internal systems, heating and air conditioning, lighting, and amenities may be substandard.

Location of U.S. office space is, predictably, in the larger urban areas. The 10 largest office space markets are summarized in Figure 7.2.

The distinction between office and industrial may not be clearly discernible. For example, research and laboratory space may be classified as industrial, but be closer in characteristics to office space than to other industrial uses, such as unfinished warehouse or other manufacturing uses. Just as office space is defined by class, industrial space also is characterized by three broad categories. These are (1) manufacturing, (2) research and development, and (3) warehousing and distribution. About 60 percent of

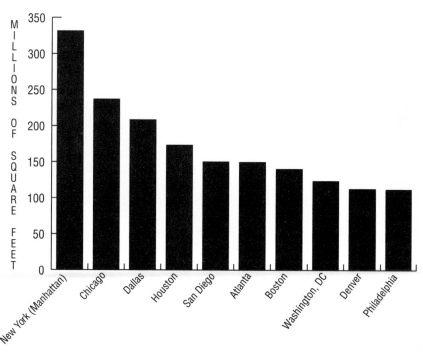

FIGURE 7.2 Ten Largest Office Markets, United States, 2004
Source: Society of Industrial and Office Realtors.

the nation's industrial space is dedicated to warehousing, and one-third to manufacturing.[4]

The three major industrial classifications may be defined in terms of their specific attributes. Bulk warehouse and distribution buildings average between 50,000 and 500,000 square feet; have 24 to 33 foot ceilings, and may include only 2 percent to 5 percent for office areas. Flex space—suitable for both office and industrial use—will be sized between 20,000 and 70,000 square feet, have 12 to 16 foot ceilings, and dedicate 20 percent or more of space to office use. These generalizations may be useful to the analyst in making distinctions among these classifications. For research and development space, onsite specialized equipment/services are to be the key factor in attracting tenants.

One difficulty in making distinctions within "office/industrial" is that there may be quite a lot of use crossover. Many office/industrial spaces are actually merged. It would not be realistic to attempt to separate the two spaces, as some uses—notably light manufacturing and research and development—share characteristics of both types of space.

The analyst's opinions and market conclusions may be affected by the amount of space locally, and by the size of the local industrial market. The 10 largest industrial space markets are summarized in Figure 7.3.

Location, Size, and Potential Uses

As with all real estate, the location of office and industrial space is a key consideration in both market and feasibility analysis. However, *size* can be deceptive. Many landlords will report a building as being physically larger than it actually is. The net rentable area is the reported size of the area available to the tenant; the gross square footage is traditionally the actual physical size of the entire building. Originally, when a landlord rented an office space, he would lease only the *tenant space* (the carpetable area), but also calculated a charge for the rest of the buildings (shared bathrooms, common areas, lobbies, stairways, and elevators, for example). Over time, some landlords discovered that it was advantageous to resize the building and claim that it was bigger than actual measurement. Tenants and their brokers became wise to this strategy, so that negotiations often involve not only rent levels, but also how to calculate the size of the space.

The analyst should try to confirm reported size independently and calculate actual size by reviewing floor plans, land maps, and other available tools. The analyst may even notice that two tenants on different floors occupy identical amounts of space but have different reported square footage.

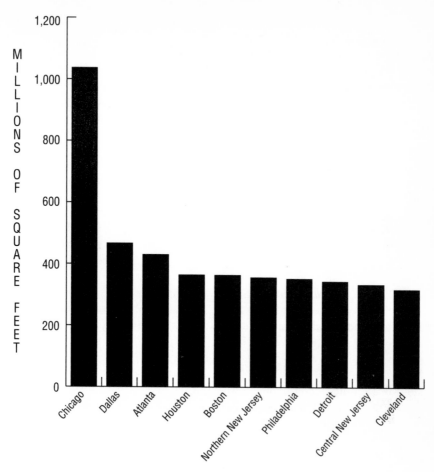

FIGURE 7.3 Ten Largest Industrial Markets, 2004
Source: Society of Office and Industrial Realtors.

Office space size classifications are quite varied, given the differences between high-rise buildings and stand-alone projects. However, even when larger buildings are involved, a second size consideration should be given a lot of attention, especially when an owner will be reviewing feasibility with tenants in mind: that of each floor's size. In a high-rise building, each floor may vary between 15,000 and 35,000 square feet, whereas smaller office buildings may have collectively larger space but more limited overall cash flow potential. If the floor area is too large, then distance from windows (thus, light source) and the building's core will be too great. If the floor area is too small, the space cannot be utilized efficiently. So the floor area may be critical to the specific use.

Location is another important feature for analysis. If an industrial space is in a relatively isolated location and is proposed for use with a lot of delivery and pick-up requirements, the analyst would have to factor in the added time and cost involved. If a similar space were located near a major freeway exchange, port, or railway terminal, it would be a considerable advantage. Clearly, these two properties would not be comparable because of the permanent differences in the cost of operation.

While the rules for judging feasibility, that is, reviews of cash flow projections, follow the same general guidelines no matter what sizes are involved, the analyst will need to review a project specifically by comparing square footage (overall *and* by floor) to perceived tenant mix, lease terms, and the flexibility in planning of space.

Amenities, Notable Features, and Division Among Uses

Does a building located in a large metropolitan area have its own parking garage? Will design include an onsite restaurant and other shops? How close is the building to transit terminals? Based on perceived tenant mix, how do planned amenities match? For example, prestige tenants like law and accounting firms may be attracted by the design elements in public areas; high-tech tenants may be far more interested in a site's internal systems and utility. Is the building perceived as primarily office or industrial space, or a combination? If a combination, how will the design facilitate (1) a separation between dissimilar tenant bases or (2) a coordinated need for both types of space? Individual floor planning may be required to achieve convenience as well as maximum flexibility. The design decisions made in the phase where likely tenants are to be identified, will ultimately determine which design elements will become most important.

Level of Obsolescence in Existing Space

Both office and industrial spaces will have to be designed to meet tenant (or owner) requirements based on the specific uses. An office space will need to be designed with a specific mix of tenants in mind and their design priorities. For example, will tenants need public areas (reception and waiting rooms), and if so, how important will appearance be to the clientele? Will the tenant be more interested in the systemic provisions within a space, and why? A problem at the design phase is to anticipate tenant requirements without knowing in advance what types of tenants are likely to sign leases.

To a degree, this problem can be offset by location of the site. If the building is located in an established urban business district, planners may know in advance the likely mix of tenants. If the project is a mixed office/industrial space located in a somewhat more remote area, the likely tenant requirements will be different. The likely tenant base can be most reliably identified by the characteristics of surrounding building use. But internal elements often define degrees of desirability. For example, the number of support columns within a large floor space and the distance between columns may be an issue. A column-free space is desirable but in older buildings, constructed before modern reinforcement methods, potential tenants may need to adjust internal design to minimize the effect of such features.

Conditions within the Rental Agreement

In analyzing a contract or lease for office rental space, it is not enough to merely determine the level of market rent being asked or offered. Other terms should be included in a negotiated commercial lease. These include:

Rent Abatements   A period of time during which the tenant does not pay any rent; the business logic here is that until the tenant is profitable, paying rent is a hardship. The landlord gives up rental income early in the term, and extracts it later through higher rents.

Leasing Commissions   Typically, these are paid by the landlord and are most often higher on new deals than on renewals.

Term Length   This is usually expressed as the number of years. Three to 10 years is typical, depending on location and tenant quality. Good tenants sign for longer terms.

Expense Reimbursements   Office tenants often are required to pay a share of building expenses. This can be significant and can represent a large component of total rent.

In the case of industrial space, internal design elements have to take into consideration the differences in modern design, compared to similar space design in the past. For example, modern warehousing activity today is coordinated with automated traffic and inventory systems. The size of a space is itself a determining factor in the type of tenant or, in the case of a long-term lease, the tenant may dictate the design elements. Warehousing space may further require space design beyond floor layout, including height design elements.

CASE STUDY: 25, ALBUQUERQUE, NM

When does an out-of-style building and amenities truly become obsolete? In the case of "25," an abandoned manufacturing plant was converted into a modernized, mixed-use office/industrial complex. Design elements effectively created a campus-style office park complete with amenities: retail shops, restaurants, and hotel sites.

Developer AGB Albuquerque took on the 200,000+ square foot plant that had been shut down since 1994 when Digital Equipment Corporation ended use of the facility to manufacture minicomputers. The site was a problem for future development. It is five miles from the city's central business district. However, the area saw growth in the form of restaurant chains and a movie theater. Zoned for industrial, the appeal of this site was high visibility from major intersections, with 134,000 daily car trips passing the site. Thus, while the *use* of the site had become obsolete, the visibility factor gave the location potential marketing advantages, offsetting the functional obsolescence of the old plant.

The name "25" is a reference to Interstate 25, which passes by the site, adding further visibility *and* accessibility. This project emphasizes the point that a piece of property should not be considered completely obsolete as long as potential remains, in terms of zoning, strategic positioning and access, and marketing possibilities. In the case of 25, the developer and design team exploited location. The buildings were gutted but roof, steel columns, and concrete floor left intact. Modernized design included large entrance lobbies at corners and midsections, breaking up the "industrial" appearance of the site. Glass and steel walls lightened up interiors, creating a very contemporary appearance overall. Original design was flexible as no lead tenant had been identified. Current tenants include Boeing-SVS and Intermec (r&d companies), ClientLogic and Uniprise (call centers), and Furr's Supermarkets' corporate offices. Leases range from 5 to 10 years.

The site is large enough so that 13 parcels of additional undeveloped land on 13 acres can be developed in the future. The development shows that even when existing design is considered obsolete, it does not exclude modernizing possibilities. For example, rather than viewing the existing high-bay, dark building as a disadvantage, the developer converted the space into innovative office and light industrial spaces. The developer also emphasized a coordination between design, marketing, and development rather than treating these aspects of the project as distinct from one another. The fact that this is a multi-functional office/industrial project on a large area—not to mention expansion possibilities on an additional 13 acres—25 is a good example of how an obsolete facility can be converted into a viable, modern investment.

Today, many industrial spaces are multi-functional, including the possible combination of light manufacturing, storage, and cross docking. So design for rail access as well as for truck turning requirements may also be a consideration in industrial design. A facility designed for docking transfers from ship to truck, truck to rail, or all three—so-called intermodal facilities—will need to be designed with a multitude of requirements on site. Depending on the specific mix of tenants and location, there may be a requirement for container storage, movement of large-scale container traffic, customs and security (for border crossing areas, where key import and export activity poses both design and security concerns), and even some manufacturing or assembly areas, especially when importing activity plays a major role. For example, some high-volume imports are manufactured overseas with final assembly occurring in the United States before shipment to a final destination. In these instances, assembly and minimal manufacturing may be desirable to site at the docking facility, which eliminates the need for one additional shipping and storage step. Designers of docking-related industrial spaces need to research these complex requirements and understand them as part of the overall design.

HEAVY INDUSTRIAL PROJECTS

One of the greatest problems for developers of *heavy industrial* projects is finding a suitable location. Suitability relates not only to available lands, but also to proper zoning and environmental concerns. Approval for certain types of heavy industrial sites exists not only locally, but also on the state and federal levels. Due to the nature of property uses involved, a high percentage of heavy industrial projects are owner-occupied. Three important aspects to such land use should be borne in mind by the analyst:

1. *Operational design.* The specific heavy industrial applications often are core to the company's primary business.
2. *Landlord risk.* Due to the risk of environmental contamination associated with heavy industrial use by definition, many landlords do not want to own such properties and be required to deal with long-term impact and mitigation issues.
3. *Equipment storage and use.* Many heavy industrial properties involve a lot of specialized equipment. Tenants will not want to move such equipment when relocating; it is easier and more economical to find a permanent home on the site.

A distinction has to be made between heavy industrial and light industrial; in the minds of many growth opponents, industrial uses are all undesirable. In fact, however, light industrial zoning is advantageous for numerous reasons. From an environmental point of view, light industrial by definition has little impact in terms of noise, pollution, safety, or destruction of local resources. In fact, light industrial uses have about the same impact as office zoning, and in most instances far less impact than retail uses. From an economic point of view, light industrial zoned uses tend to create decent-level wage jobs, while producing no traffic impact beyond employee activity.

In comparison, heavy industrial includes a wide range of private activities such as manufacturing, rail activity, landfill operations, and similar uses. In many states where growth management legislation has been passed, the difficulty in siting heavy industrial is acknowledged not only in zoning regulations, but also in defining essential public facilities. Not all of these would be considered heavy industrial; for example, hospitals and convalescent homes, prisons, and similar uses are *essential* but not industrial. Uses such as railroad storage yards, container removal and related intermodal activity, and other heavy uses *may* be considered light or heavy by local standards. Criteria will include noise and traffic levels, site impacts, environmental impact, and danger (i.e. storage of flammable or toxic materials). Thus, in some applications, uses like container storage may fit within the definition of *light* industrial while in others, depending on the materials involved, similar uses may be more properly defined as *heavy* industrial.

For the purpose of market analysis, these are critical considerations. Heavy industrial zones are properly well isolated from more benign uses of land; so land values will reflect zoning. However, access to strategically important amenities of interest to owners and developers of heavy industrial projects will vastly affect the potential market value of land as well as immediate value to tenants. These critical amenities include:

- *Access to major highways.* The nature of heavy industrial use often involves a volume of truck traffic. For example, movement of imported goods from a storage, import, or manufacturing area to the market rests with access to an interstate and other highways. The access affects land values; if it is a remote location, land will be cheaper but development will have to include construction of roadways between the site and highways. This invariably raises questions of traffic, noise, safety, and—for tenants—the ultimate cost of longer trips.
- *Proximity to rail lines or ports.* A second and related concern (and one that directly affects the value of a site to potential tenants) is proximity to major modes of shipping. This includes major ports in

cases where goods are imported or exported, and rail lines for domestic market distribution. An inland site used for heavy industrial such as manufacturing, will need to involve a study of how goods are moved between the plant and transportation routes. When comparing land values for various sites, it would make sense that better-located lands or advantageous strategic sites are worth more. Among the questions determining land values, the analyst should consider specific uses being proposed. If assembly or manufacturing will be part of the land use in addition to other uses (i.e., storage, intermodal activity, or customs inspections), the question of site may rest with whether or not the processes being undertaken add or subtract weight. Some finished goods are heavier than the raw materials going into them; others are lighter. Depending on which way the weight issue goes, a facility may be better sited closer to the end-user, or closer to the source of the raw materials. This is not a minor point; weight in small incremental levels may add up to large differences in per-unit profitability in high-volume operations.

When heavy industrial land use zoning is inactive, or requires re-zoning, the analyst will need to factor that in to valuation. If development has not occurred in the past due to environmental restrictions, local opposition, or regulation, the feasibility of a project must go beyond cost and investment value. It has to include consideration of a potential range of regulatory hurdles involving local, state and federal agencies.

■ *Access to and from the site as well as distances.* The question of access is a major consideration in the analysis and feasibility decisions concerning heavy industrial uses. However, having a practical route to transportation is only half of the question. Distance is the other. In the analysis of the cost of moving materials and products to and from a site, the market analyst will be concerned with the time involved; the potential problems involved with zoning and mix of property uses between the site and the freeway or rail line; and the likely problems the developer will encounter in overcoming those problems. For example, if a heavy industrial zoning area exists, but the closest interstate freeway is 30 miles away, what is going to be involved in running roadways? What zoning is found in existing land areas? What resistance will be encountered to running roads through existing commercial, rural or agricultural areas?

Market analysis in the case of heavy industrial property is especially difficult given the possibilities of resistance on many levels, as well as the need for environmental review processes involving separate governmental tiers. Approval may involve a matter of years rather than months, another factor making any feasibility study more complex. Likely tenants who would desire facilities today are not likely to be as interested if the unknown approval timeline is not certain. Thus, developers may be faced with the difficulty of needing to proceed without long-term leases and with no solid indications of interest from a tenant base.

CHAPTER 8

Lodging and Tourism Industry Real Estate

The market for hotels, recreation, and similar real estate are impacted directly by considerations such as seasonal trends, competition, and amenities offered. This market has undergone revolutionary trends in the past two decades and current trends demonstrate a continuing, emerging market that cannot be tracked based solely on history. This chapter explains how this market needs to be analyzed, and how this process cannot be performed in the same way as other sectors.

The variables involved in analysis of lodging and tourism properties include product type, location, season, amenities, markets, and competition. Analysis of hotels consists to a degree in defining the method by which one group should be distinguished from the other, as explained in one book:

> *The two principal methods of classifying hotels are by location (downtown, airport, resort) and by the market niches they serve. Hotels are probably more accurately described on the basis of markets served than by locations, which have blurred somewhat because of urban sprawl and evolving land use patterns.*[1]

While this observation is partially valid, we contend that analysis has to be all encompassing. No fewer than six features need to be analyzed in combination to truly compare values between one property (or site) and another. These six are:

1. *Property types.* We begin by distinguishing among five specific and separate properties types. These include downtown hotels, suburban hotels, highway/airport hotels, and resorts or convention facilities.
2. *Location.* The distinction between *types* of properties may also be made on the basis of location, as a specific locational decision also identifies a distinct market to be served. A downtown hotel is vastly different in terms of feasibility from a highway or airport hotel; and resort or convention facilities also are entirely different with respect to the methods of income generation, cash flow, typical guest, and seasonal factors.
3. *Markets.* The *market* ultimately guides the analyst in determining feasibility. An airport hotel will contain a different set of assumptions from a highway hotel; similarly, a downtown hotel will appeal on a different basis from a golf and country club-situated resort and convention center. The likely mix of guests—business traveler, family on vacation, convention attendee, or sportsperson—will determine whether feasibility works in terms of location and competition. But feasibility itself is complicated by the very fact that there are so many variables in lodging markets *and* in the mix of uses beyond lodging within sites themselves. "One of the least understood terms in the hotel/real estate business is 'feasibility.' What makes one proposed hotel feasible and another not feasible?"[2] That is the big question.
4. *Season.* The entire lodging and resort industry is seasonal. A specific travel season mandates the adjustment of pricing based on a volume of demand. Off-season prices reflect greater vacancies and even within the convention industry, specific locations offer greater appeal in specific seasons based on amenities, competition, and even the weather. Certain hotels also experience busy times based on local factors. For example, in many state capitals it is difficult to find a room while the state legislature is in session. Outside of those special situations, seasonality remains a significant point. Just the timeshare industry, a small part of the lodging classification, has grown since its inception in the 1960s to more than 5,000 sites worldwide only 40 years later. The United States alone has 1,200 resort sites and more than two million timeshare owners.[3]
5. *Amenities.* More and more, the lodging industry is characterized (and studied) on the basis of amenities offered. The entire tourism trade in Las Vegas is an example of this ongoing trend elsewhere. Once identified solely with casino gaming and related live shows, Las Vegas now

competes on the basis of many expanded amenities. In a less visible sense, the same amenity-based strategic approach to the lodging industry is a dominant force today.

6. *Competition*. Hotels and convention centers are highly competitive, because—as with all other free economy industries—specific types of facilities are desirable in similar places. So the convention site may offer vastly different amenities from a family vacation hotel; and a highway lodging may compete more on price and ease of access (as well as close proximity to restaurants, service stations, and other travelers' needs), while a convention center may need to offer sports outlets, live shows, superior restaurants, and other amenities many would call distractions—but that may ultimately determine whether a guest chooses one site over another. Hotels may physically survive long after their economic life is over. Because of this, hotel competition is notably fierce.

AN OVERVIEW OF THE INDUSTRY

The history of hotels is one of increasing segmentation. They have evolved from simple inns, to the hotel of the early 1800s (offering food, drink, shopping, retail, lodging, and consisting of up to 200 rooms, up to six floors), and the grand hotel of the late 1800s first in the great cities of Europe and then to New York City.

The hotel industry involves many intangibles and analytical variables. For example, a guest's "sense" of a hotel matters far more than the square feet of the room. This is most pronounced with "boutique hotels"—smaller facilities providing guest services, amenities, and atmosphere that justify an unusually high room rate.

These hotels were an early adopter of "supply induced demand." Basically, the theory behind this market approach is one of "build it and they will come." In the 1920s, motels began appearing along Route 66 East to West, and then on Highways 301 and 441 from the Northeast to Florida. In 1956 with the dawning of the Interstate Highway System, hotels tracked the growth of suburbia, and on a larger scale as air travel expanded, the airport hotel was not far behind.

The surprising aspect in this expansive history is that with each step, the old-style hotel has remained. It has been said the problem is not overdevelopment, but underdemolition. A suburban Holiday Inn has an economic life of 30 years; low-end budget sites have lives of 15 to 20 years.

ANALYSIS FOR THE LODGING INDUSTRY

For each of the specific property types—downtown hotels, suburban hotels, highway or airport hotels, and resorts or convention facilities—we begin by identifying the market area; demand level, both current and anticipated; demographic and economic drivers of that demand; and the competition.

The discussion of *lodging* as being entirely different from other types of property is usually valid; we are accustomed to the concept of hotels, convention centers, and resorts as standing apart from commercial or residential developments; however, all types of property may cross these lines. For example, many large convention hotels or urban office buildings contain entire shopping centers within their facilities. So the discussion of mar-

CASE STUDY: RITZ-CARLTON HOTEL, NEW YORK, NY

A lack of five-star accommodations in the southern area of Manhattan led Millennium Partners to create a mixed-use facility, a hotel-condo building. The neighborhood at the time this idea was hatched (1997) was in decline and part of the overall plan included reenergizing the area.

In the Battery Park neighborhood, the Ritz-Carlton is a 39-story complex offering 298 hotel guest rooms in addition to 113 condos. Views include the Statue of Liberty, the Hudson River, and the nearby park setting. The concept—coordination between lifestyle and guest amenities—has been successful. The building's lower 13 floors are hotel area, and the remaining, higher floors are devoted to condo units. Amenities, available to both hotel guests and permanent residents, include spa and fitness center, a restaurant, bar, conference and banquet areas and a rooftop terrace, and a Skyscraper Museum (http://www.skyscraper.org).

While the concept of combining hotel and residential living may seem complex from a management perspective, there is also a degree of economy in providing amenities to both markets within a single building. This adds market value *and* visual appeal. Additionally, the developer and design team invested in interior visual features to provide a nineteenth century touch in a modern building. This includes an art collection in the public areas, including the works of more than 100 local artists.

ket area, demand, demographic and economic drivers, and competition has to take into account the possibility that other uses may serve as important amenities within a project. Furthermore, lodging—unlike residential property—has an added feature affecting analysis: its going concern value. In appraising lodging property values, appraisers calculate the current and potential gross revenue and net profit. One appraiser makes the point that when calculating lodging property values, "it is generally considered that going concern value is inherent in the resulting conclusion."[4] As with other types of property, identifying the market area is a starting point; however, it would be a simple calculation if (1) all lodging produced similar profit scenarios and (2) all lodging could be evaluated as lodging only and nothing else. But these are impractical given the nature of the market—and as a consequence, the nature of defining market area itself.

Market Area

One difficulty with identifying a market area for the lodging industry is that we cannot limit the analysis to geography. It is more elusive than residential projects, for example. The draw of a convention center may be related to the city where it is located, that is, New Orleans or Las Vegas, where amenities of the city beyond the convention center itself may serve to create a less distinct market area.

The term itself—market area—implies a geographical distinction; and in the case of residential or retail, this is true. The analytical procedure for the lodging industry is going to be geographical as well, but only in part. To fairly estimate the market area, one needs to expand the usual definition. In some cases, a seemingly slight difference in geography may vastly alter the market area; this would not be the case in other real estate projects. For example, the difference between a convention center with its own casino and nightclub and one that is only a hotel is vast. It does not matter if the hotel offers competitive prices, larger rooms, or a finer restaurant; if the *draw* in that area is a casino and nightclub, that will be significant in defining market area, and in determining the feasibility of the project. A good example is a hotel in the Bahamas. Competition consists of other hotels on the island, but the *trend* is anywhere on the Eastern Seaboard. The key idea is that whereas with most other real estate, competitive supply is approximately the same, this is not the case for hotels. A hotel may compete with its neighbors but draw from around the world.

The same argument may apply to a highway hotel visible from the highway, versus a competitor one block away; or to a beachfront resort versus one a half-mile inland. A rule worth observing in the lodging industry: Location, amenities, and proximity to other services (nightlife, restaurants, transportation, and recreation) define the market area more than the traditional locational-only factors.

Identification of market area depends on locating the factors determining its true size and scope. (*Size*, for the purpose of lodging properties, has to be defined as a nongeographical market as well as a geographical one; for example, if one hotel can be booked online through one of the booking services, whereas another cannot, the market area for each will be quite different.) Research involves a thorough study of information from tourism bureaus and economic development agencies locally; convention centers and trends in local convention business; traffic studies and trends; strategic location of major transportation routes, especially interstate freeways; and trends in types of amenities that draw guest business to the region. Clearly, the type of draw depends on the region itself and the thematic reputation of that region (gaming in Las Vegas, Mardi Gras in New Orleans, seasonal activities like Super Bowl weekend, college homecoming at large state universities, or championship tournaments, political events, for example).

Siting of hotel properties, notably in new markets, may rely increasingly on the use of GIS-based siting. GIS

> *can integrate economic, social, and environmental data into the hotel-siting decision . . . [and is] well-suited to determining the appropriate location of hotel properties in emerging destinations, particularly those with fragile ecosystems. . . . As new hotels are being developed in environmentally sensitive zones, siting issues become increasingly complex. GIS analysis helps to identify both opportunities for and threats to development.[5]*

In such sensitive siting decisions, market area may itself be exceptionally complex. Additional factors determining market area will include:

- Actual location of hotels of the same type and in the same geographical area.
- Competition in terms of guests (families on vacation, business travelers via airlines or freeways, convention sites).
- Amenities offered by competitors versus proposed amenities at the site.
- Balance of proposed revenue sources (for example, some hotels depend on convention business as a primary source of revenue, while others rely on group travel packages; some hotels offer other draws such as live entertainment, recreational facilities onsite, or theme parks).
- Seasonal considerations, including market area and competitive strategies for off-season business.

■ Economic profile of guests and vulnerability in times of slower economic conditions.

Demand Level

Part of the market analysis rests with identifying a demand level or segment a new project may expect to win. A common error in demand analysis is to consider the entire current and anticipated market, and to proceed on the flawed assumption that the subject property will receive 100 percent of the market demand. This is unlikely. The analyst needs to consider not only the existing and proposed competitive projects, but a mix of amenities, location, pricing, and other features of the competition (and of the mix of demand). For example, it is not adequate to identify the number of hotel guests per year in a city. That does not reveal the specific lodging type. We need to break down the trend among the five major submarkets: downtown hotels, suburban hotels, highway or airport hotels, and resorts or convention facilities; and to then study demand trends based on those markets.

Just as it would be unreasonable to use apartment vacancy trends to justify a subdivision of market-rate, single-family homes (because these are different markets) the lodging market has to be broken down into these specific areas, and studied by attributes of demand.

In lodging, *demand* is defined by the type of guest; this includes identifying the trip purpose (vacation, travel stops or layovers, convention, resort, recreation); the time a guest will stay (highway hotel guests usually stay only one night, while convention guests are more likely to be onsite up to a full week); and single travelers versus families may also exhibit different guest patterns. All of these issues affect the quantification of demand itself. Based on an understanding of guest attributes, one can also identify the types of amenities the guest will require. Convention attendees prefer restaurants, live entertainment, and convenient recreational outlets. Business travelers, even those with relatively short stays, may require business centers, in-room Internet access, and free breakfast. All of the amenity requirements define the demand as well as the demand segment a particular lodging is likely to capture. While the modern tendency is to think in terms of a "package of demands," some facilities have been able to offer a single theme and attract a large market share. Examples such as the popularity of theme parks like Disney World,[6] for example, or Branson, Missouri[7]—billed as The Live Music Show Capital of the World—make this point. A number of similar outlets with a similar theme define a highly specialized amenity-based market.

CASE STUDY: OCEAN DOME AT THE SEAGAIA RESORT, MIYAZAKI, JAPAN

This facility is an example of a single-amenity hotel. In fact, it is the world's largest indoor water park according to the Guinness Book of World Records,[8] measuring just under 1,000 feet in length and just over 300 feet in width. This temperature-controlled amenity is about 85 degrees (F) year-round. Guests are ensured access to a pristine beach including artificial waves, a heated pool, children's pool, and three water slides. The large area also provides retail shops and a range of restaurants. The hotel also has golf courses and tennis courts.

The name combines "sea" and "Gaia" (Greek for "earth"), and this facility demonstrates how an amenity may define a facility. Traditionally, the idea of price competition and room features or hotel facilities (convention space, for example) dominated the choice of a facility. In the case of the Sheraton Grande Ocean Resort, the Ocean Dome is a primary draw.

This example makes the point that some hotel sites are a reflection of local culture. For example, "capsule" hotels in Japan or casino hotels in Las Vegas reflect local values more than any other products. In identifying demand trends, the analyst needs to understand that demand may be defined by a specific amenity. Whether that is the case or a more diverse offering of amenities is involved, the specific market must be studied, of which three broad types may be distinguished:

Business Travelers These include the *solitary business traveler*, whose primary concerns will be convenience to airports as well as transportation to local business districts; *corporate small groups* reserving blocks of rooms and seeking onsite meeting areas of limited size (day rooms, small meeting rooms); and *convention business*, requiring not only the full support for convention activities (including meal service for large groups, exhibit space technology and support, and a large number of rooms, hotel services, and nonconvention amenities such as restaurants, shops, and recreation). Convention hotels are typically located in downtown areas with 400 to 500 or more rooms, generous meeting and banquet space, large lobbies to handle big volumes of guest movement, and more than the average number of suites (for meetings and hospitality use).

Vacation and Leisure Travelers   This demographic includes individuals—often called free independent travelers or FITs—whose requirements are highly individualized and localized (for example, a leisure traveler may be interested in local museums, historical tours, or other specific local attractions); discount or wholesale travelers, often taking advantage of promotional prices as a primary reason for travel; charters and group travel, including secondary travel drawn from convention events (i.e., spouses of attendees), whose itinerary may be highly structured and organized; families (drawn to an area for its recreational offerings such as beaches, theme parks, or other amusements of appeal to adults and children alike); and various other specialized guests including long-term guests, including people who may live in a hotel for several months, for example.

A niche within this leisure market is the luxury hotel. These facilities have fewer than 300 rooms and a high employee-to-visitor ratio. They may be used for business meetings, anniversaries, weddings, and entertainment, or simply for an extravagant vacation.

Corporate Contracts   Many portions of this demand segment include the wholesale market, represented by a series on travel agencies and online travel web sites. Various providers commit large blocks of accommodations and offer them at discount to travelers, often combining hotel with air travel, car rental, and entertainment in a single package. Another form of corporate hotel use is the contractual guest arrangements, including room deals arranged for airline employees, representing a potentially large portion of business for airport hotels. Corporations whose employees may visit a home office frequently for conferences, training sessions, or other purposes, may also negotiate commitments with local facilities for room rates as well as conference facilities. Also fitting within this category are contracts with federal government agencies, the military, and other groups traveling on per diem allowances rather than more generous budgets.

The residence hotel is in a special class of its own, a hybrid between a lodging facility and an apartment. Rooms tend to be larger than 500 square feet, with kitchen or "kitchenette" included. This is a good market for corporate relocation or traveling professionals on extended projects. Increasingly, with a weaker hotel economy, some families are taking advantage of these long-term stay alternatives. The kitchen enables a family to vacation and not eat out every meal. These hotels are found in urban, suburban, and residential designs.

PRIORITIES IN HOTEL MARKET ANALYSIS

The overwhelming theme in hotel market analysis is increasing *market segmentation*. This carries over into trying to understand the trade area as well. For hotels, the market areas for supply and demand are entirely distinct.

For example, for convention hotels the market consists of the number of people who attend annual conventions; the attractiveness of the location; and the list of trade associations and other groups sponsoring such conventions. The "market area" is not geographical in one sense, because business professionals do travel to sites specifically to attend conventions. The "trade area" may be industry-specific as well, for example, accountants who attend financial conventions in one trade area within a larger market.

The market area for motels is in theory from anywhere along a traveler's route. However, the effective trade area will commonly be one-quarter mile from the interstate off-ramp. Secondary markets exist, as well. For example, a satellite of motels surrounding a high-population university may serve parents visiting their college-aged children.

While in most types of real estate (i.e., office and industrial) the analyst studies industries and employers to identify the market, in the hotel business the analyst reviews *demand segments*. These include the commercial market, tourist and leisure, long-term government or military clientele, or residential hotel guests, for example. Demand is elusive as well, in the sense the demand levels vary from one night to the next, as well as by season.

Hotel pricing works more like airline ticket costs than as a response to market forces. The competition is in advance sales and amenities—a supply inventory chasing after varying and elusive levels of demand. In fact, if hotels make a package attractive enough, it may even create the demand by affecting when people travel in addition to where they stay.

An outsider may be alarmed to realize that in an off-season a hotel may experience up to 70 percent vacancies—thus, the attractive reduction in room rates during the off-season (and even varying by day of the week). However, those seasonal losses are made up for by offsetting higher prices—reflecting greater demand—during high-travel periods. These variables are called *demand generators*. Business travelers—specifically seminar and convention organizers—are well aware of how convention hotels sweeten the deal by offering business-related demand generators (reduced meal costs, reduced block-reserved room rates, 5 percent to 10 percent complimentary rooms for large groups, transportation services, and extra amenities).

The competition in the hotel business cannot be limited to a study of room space alone. It is a starting point. For example, if there are 6,000 travelers per day in an area with 9,000 rooms approximately the same size, price, and location, competition will be fierce. Overall, one-third of those rooms will remain unoccupied.

As important as a rooms-versus-guests analysis is, in an efficient lodging market—one where levels of supply and demand float around the same levels—it is not the room that makes the difference; it is the amenities. Also, at the risk of pointing out the obvious, one of the best things about hotels is that you can inspect them yourself. Loitering at a hotel is not hard to do. If asked, one only has to reply that they are waiting for someone.

Further research is easily accomplished online, through published traveler assistance services, or through the use of a chain's own material. Room count can be established through visual inspection, hotel guides, phone calls, or a private data vendor service. If necessary, room counts can also be closely estimated by an analyst familiar with the chain and with the primary market it serves.

Room count is the easy part. Occupancy data is harder. Private data services are helpful for the analyst who spends a lot of time studying a particular real estate industry, but before drawing final conclusions, visual inspection and personal contacts are essential. To really get a handle on a site, the analyst should visit the market, speak with local chambers of commerce, financial institutions, local building permit inspectors, and hotel developers and managers.

Economic and Demographic Drivers

A primary factor in judging lodging properties is the season. Both vacation and convention-related guest activity tend to favor August as the highest-volume month (due to both weather and school schedules). October is the most popular month for those hotels in the convention market. December is the lowest-volume month for both vacation and business travel.

Both season and timing of promotional deals have to be factored in to a market analysis in the lodging industry. Furthermore, these variations have to also be varied based on the specific climate. Certainly, extremely cold weather during winter months will be of great concern in Buffalo, New York, but not as much in Phoenix, Arizona, for example. Some convention and recreation-oriented lodging sites are open only part of the year due to variations in weather. Examples include ski-oriented lodging or East Coast resorts are examples. In such cases, year-round profitable activity may depend on both discounting and expansion of amenities. For example, a ski-oriented area may attract year-round business by emphasizing summer-month convention activity.

Being aware of how seasons may affect demand levels and, ulti-mately, occupancy itself, a versatile lodging property—especially one far removed from population centers—may need to take ingenious measures to expand marketability of its facility. In measuring the level of demand, it is a mistake to limit the review to the specific seasonal activity, to only one type of guest, or—going in the other direction—to use the *entire* lodging market as a base when the specific site cannot possibly appeal to every type of traveler.

The Competition

Demand can never be reviewed on its own. One also has to consider how many similar facilities exist within the immediate geographic area. For ex-ample, it would be a mistake to estimate feasibility of a new hotel in a ma-jor metropolitan area, assuming the site would benefit from demand in all sectors—downtown hotels, suburban hotels, highway or airport hotels,

CASE STUDY: BURNHAM HOTEL, CHICAGO, IL

When the Reliance Building was used as an office space, its history was of little interest. The *amenity* was of no value to the office space.

That changed when the building was renovated and converted to a hotel. Located strategically at mid-Loop in downtown Chicago, the Reliance Building was constructed in 1890. Anticipating the modern skyscraper, the steel structure was dwarfed by later high-rise build-ings. Internal design was considered undesirable for office use until its changeover to the Burnham Hotel in 1999.

As a lodging facility, the Burnham provides history as a décor amenity. This includes cast-iron elevators, original mahogany wood doors, and opaque windows in guest rooms. The lobby and hallway areas include rich mosaic floors and marble walls. Rooms are deco-rated with half-canopy beds and chaise lounges. In this instance, his-torical design has also been an award winner, including the 2002 Urban Land Institute's Awards for Excellence, a National Preserva-tion Honor Award in 2001, and an Honor Award from the American Institute of Architects (AIA), also in 2001.

and resorts or convention facilities. It is highly unlikely that any facility would easily appeal to all of these groups.

Competition and its analysis often come down to the study of amenities offered within the facility itself, and other purely business-related competing factors. Hotels are more like operating businesses than other types of real estate. Thus, an analysis of the competition should include not only the physical issues such as number of rooms and other obvious comparative features, but also a model of business practice and philosophy, such as customer service levels.

Two directly competing hotels may be the same in terms of price ranges, location, room size, customer service, onsite restaurants, and other amenities. However, if one has a particular historic décor and interest, it may compete favorably with another hotel. It may also be interesting to note that hotel amenities may be more appealing than the same amenities in nonhotel buildings.

Amenities—like many of the other features that improve a facility's competitive position—may be subtle, and may also depend on the specific subgroup. For example, an internal décor serving as a historic amenity may be appealing in a downtown hotel, but of virtually no value in an airport or highway hotel. Hotels and resorts offer a broad range of amenities. Especially for resort and vacation sites, the type, quality, and number of amenities are what sell people on the hotels. In developing a project, the decision on which amenities to include should be based on four factors:

1. Whether the amenity can fit physically, economically, and thematically within the planned site.
2. The quantity that should be provided, given the market *and* the type of amenity being considered.
3. Timing for construction.
4. Cost justification (financial feasibility).

In the resort business, the big four amenities are: Golf, tennis, skiing, and marinas. However, the specific type of amenity is mandated not only by the desire to grab market share of a specific market, but also to improve real estate values and to augment marketing power. Amenities could be called loss leaders because, in the sense of market value, their cost is made profitable only when the property is sold. In the meantime, the right amenity will increase occupancy rates and make an image for a site. So often, though, it does not matter that guests do not actually use the amenity; it does matter that people know it is there.

Amenities are attractive to developers for marketing as well as ego-driven reasons. However, there are significant risks with amenities. These include:

- Potential market failure. If the cost of the amenity does not produce profits, it could end up losing the developer a lot of money.
- Amenities are often seasonal. The question comes up, "What do you do in the off-season?"
- Many amenity packages (the large ones like skiing) also bring up residual issues such as environmental impact.
- Amenities have a related cost to run. The site will require a qualified staff that knows what they are doing.

The market analyst may begin the task of identifying competitive forces—whether amenities are a factor or not—by first segmenting occupancy trends *and* available competitive trends on the basis of the four major subgroups (as opposed to a review of the whole market in the area). This may include not only a study of the number of rooms in what are perceived as directly competing facilities, but also on the basis of amenities, locational advantages, and price. A study of two specific factors—penetration and yield—is essential in furthering the study of competition (and how overall segment demand may work for a subject property).

Penetration is simply another word meaning demand share, expressed as the percentage of occupied rooms compared to total available rooms. Yield is average revenue per room for the subject property, expressed as a percentage of marketwide average revenue per room. The formula involves a series of calculations for both the subject property and the market as a whole in the same market. To make these calculations entirely accurate, the comparison to the overall market should be carefully defined: It is the directly competing facilities in the same market area, as defined earlier in the chapter. Thus, comparing *all* hotels in a geographical area will be inaccurate when the subject property is more accurately compared to the market area for the same guest population or, more accurately, true demand within that subgroup—the guest of the downtown hotel, highway, or airport hotel, suburban hotel, highway or airport hotel, or resort/convention facility.

The calculation begins with *occupancy rate*, which is the percentage of occupied rooms to total available rooms:

$$O \div A = R$$

In this formula, "O" is the number of rooms occupied; "A" is the total number of available rooms: and "R" is the occupancy rate.

The second step is to calculate penetration. The formula involves dividing occupancy rate for the subject property by occupancy rate for the market:

$$RS \div RM = P$$

.TABLE 8.1   Penetration and Yield Calculations

Examples:

| | Market | Subject Properties | | | |
		# 1	# 2	# 3	# 4
Available rooms	2,250	150	375	220	120
Occupied rooms	1,435	82	206	121	74
Average daily room rate	$ 175	$105	$123	$115	$142

| | Overall Market | Subject Properties | | | |
		#1	#2	#3	#4
Occupancy rate:					
$O \div A = R$	63.8%	54.5%	54.9%	55.0%	61.7%
Penetration:					
$RS \div RM = P$		85.4%	86.1%	86.2%	96.7%
Yield:					
1. RS × DS = IS		57.23	67.53	63.25	87.61
2. RM × DM = IM	111.65				
3. IS ÷ IM = Y		51.3%	60.5%	56.7%	78.5%

O = number of rooms occupied
A = total number of available rooms
R = occupancy rate
RS = occupancy rate for the subject property
RM = occupancy rate for the whole market
P = penetration percentage
DS = average daily room rate for the subject property
IS = revenue for the subject property
DM = average daily room rate for the market
IM = revenue for the overall market
Y = yield

In this formula, "RS" is the occupancy rate for the subject property; "RM" is the occupancy rate for the whole market; and "P" is the penetration percentage.

To calculate yield, we next perform a two-step calculation. First, we multiply the occupancy rate by the average daily room rate (for both the subject property and the market). Next, we divide the subject property yield by the market yield to find overall yield:

1. $RS \times DS = IS$
2. $RM \times DM = IM$
3. $IS \div IM = Y$

The symbol "RS" represents occupancy rate for the subject property; "DS" is the average daily room rate for the subject property; "IS" is the revenue for the subject property; "RM" is occupancy rate for the market; "DM" is the average daily room rate for the market; "IM" is the revenue for the overall market; and "Y" is yield, based on a comparison between subject and market.

The formulas for these calculations are summarized with examples in Table 8.1.

We may conclude from a review of this data that penetration and yield are revealing indicators. However, the conclusions to be drawn from this are only as accurate as the definitions of the overall market. Thus, it may be a wise exercise to divide the total, known market into subgroups for more reliable analysis. The market analyst needs only two groups: first is the identified direct competition within the known market area (i.e., for a convention center, one would identify the statistical information during the latest year for market-wide convention facilities); and second is "all other." By taking this step, the analyst ensures that the relevant penetration and yield analyses will be undertaken within the appropriate subgroup without overlap.

CHAPTER 9

Mixed-Use Real Estate Analysis

Planning trends have come full cycle. A century ago, neighborhoods naturally employed mixed uses. The interim "edge city" trend eschewed mixed use in favor of fully controlled neighborhoods that excluded mixed use. Today, innovative planning is returning to the older concepts, and modern planners have accepted mixed use as not only desirable, but practical as well. This chapter provides analytical guidelines based on examples and case histories, and studies the trend in various mixed-use forms.

The analysis of mixed-use projects is complex because added dimensions of markets are included; additionally, mixed use may have many varying aspects. In the mid-twentieth century era of development (notably since the 1970s) mixed use was the favored planning format in many towns and cities. Older urban areas had seen mixed use over many years. For example, in San Francisco residential neighborhoods of the 1950s and 1960s, it was not uncommon for a family to live above the store, or for service stations to coexist on the same block with schools and apartment buildings.

Mixed use includes numerous different property types, so the analyst needs to ensure that the comparisons made within the study are truly the *same* level of mixed-use projects. The first and most obvious definition of *mixed use* involves the zoning and utilization type of property. Second is the level of coordinated use; and third is the planning and design of a project. For example, one particular subdivision may include both residential and commercial uses as well as office rentals. However, is it really mixed if these uses merely reside side by side? In a truly mixed area, the varying uses will coexist in a specifically planned manner, and the uses themselves will serve as attributes of the project's plan. An example presented later in this chapter—Celebration, Florida—is an excellent one of how varying zoning types can be coordinated within a plan.

IMPORTANT GUIDELINES FOR MIXED-USE PROJECT ANALYSIS

Three critical points for mixed-use development are:

1. *There should be three or more significant uses.* More specifically, these uses should be mutually supportive. Simply having three different zoning types within one subdivision is not effective. However, when the use is harmoniously coordinated so that each owner or tenant benefits from the other, the plan will be more effective. Ideally, everyone in a mixed-use environment should profit. The homeowner enjoys the convenience of a retail center and may even go to work or access services in an industrial area, for example. A sporting center further enhances lifestyle for everyone. However, some types of mixed uses may not be money-makers but will serve an essential service enhancing the desirability (and thus, the market value) of other uses.
2. *Integration of components.* The specific use of land and uninterrupted pedestrian access define the mixed-use plan itself, notably for residentially-based mixed-use developments.
3. *A coherent plan.* The type and scale of uses and permitted densities make the project more marketable and boost absorption.

What does a mixed-use project look like? There are two models that represent the modern mixed-use trend: the urban and the suburban form. The urban mixed-use project may be found within a high-rise, for example. The AOL Time Warner Building includes a hotel, apartments, condos, a music facility, and a shopping center, as well as office space and a complete television studio. It would be difficult to imagine more mixed use, and the very complexity of these uses makes the urban mixed-use development a study in good planning.

The suburban model tends to concentrate on residential land uses first, with other land use features designed to serve the needs of residents. For example, The Villages in Florida is primarily a series of gated communities. But the numerous golf courses are what developers promote, clearly aimed at the leisure/retirement market. Additionally, a highly structured downtown area is in fact a shopping center designed to look like an old-fashioned town center. Typing together the residential, recreational, and retail aspects is a community identity that attempts to provide residents with a sense of belonging—not necessarily to the state or the county, but to the specific community itself.

MODERN PLANNING TRENDS

Planning industry restrictions on mixed-use came about as part of the massive housing boom following World War II. As suburban tracts were built, it made sense to builders and to planners alike to efficiently restrict commercial use in residential areas, and to create entirely segregated zoning in communities. This began to change in the 1970s when the idea of bottom-to-top city planning took hold. This included a number of important changes in planning and zoning, some of which had unforeseen negative consequences. Even while the strictly segregated planning mode continued, some planners began to realize that mixed use—if properly designed—would be a positive force.

The changes resulting from segregated zoning and the lack of mixed use, included:

- *Emergence of complete-planning schemes.* The idea that newly developed urban and suburban areas could be carefully planned and controlled was accompanied by an equally important belief: that dissimilar types of zoning should be completely segregated from one another. This led to the emergence of very sterile communities in which no mixed use was experienced; it was strictly forbidden. The planning community believed before the 1970s (and some continue to believe today) that segregated residential, commercial, and industrial areas are essential and represent "good planning." For the most part, planners embrace "new urbanism" now. Trends in urbanism and current thinking on the topic are one of many topics at http://www.cnu.org—web site for Congress for the New Urbanism. Mixed use, if properly structured, is a positive aspect of intelligent planning and actually aids in improving local environmental conditions (i.e., traffic) more so than in planning schemes where every trip away from home requires the use of a car.
- *Legislative changes and growth management laws.* As land use policy became mixed with the environmental movement, the two merged and legislation was passed in many states to strengthen the authority of

planners to restrict some types of land use. The result: Two good ideas were merged to create what often ended up as an ill-conceived series of public policies. For example, under most growth management acts, growth is restricted in cities and towns to an identified urban growth area. This is a border; growth may occur inside that border, but not outside it. Expanded growth can occur only when the urban growth area is completely in-filled. The *intention* of this plan was to prevent *urban sprawl*—the expansion of growth without any planning or fore-thought—but in practice, the restriction of growth has resulted in (1) congested urban centers coupled with underdeveloped and underuti-lized land areas around the UGA, (2) antagonism between citizens and planners, often leading to expensive court fights, and (3) higher costs of housing.

All of these consequences are specifically identified as outcomes that growth management wants to avoid. The good intentions be-hind GMA legislation meant to create sensible, well-planned growth, increase trust and public participation while opening up processes to people without lawyers, and reduce housing costs. It is ironic that the exact opposite occurs in growth management states with some consistency. This demonstrates that mixed use works well when it occurs in response to *market* forces rather than being cre-ated artificially and in response to political agendas. Whether growth management is solely to blame for these unintended con-sequences is debatable; a conclusive understanding of GMA impacts is not possible. Some believe that GMA policies do not have signifi-cant impacts.[1] However, statistical information does demonstrate a direct relationship between increases in housing prices and GMA regulation.[2]

- *A view of mixed use as a new idea.* New ideas are often nothing but a contradiction of what was believed in the past. A tendency to go in the other direction can often lead to unfortunate outcomes. As one ob-server noted, "Each generation of critics does nothing but take the op-posite of the truths accepted by their predecessors."[3]

As part of the emerging trend to treat zoning as a form of social control (versus its original intention to prevent incompatible land use in one area), communities began to develop comprehensive plans and to invite public participation. While the stated purpose of a compre-hensive planning system is to seek community input to planning, the truth often comes down to lip service only, and with planning depart-ments ignoring the stated goals and policies of the comprehensive plan. For example, even in areas where practical constraints make some types of mixed use impractical, comprehensive plans continue to include goals stating the "desirability" of mixed use—even when zoning specifically prevents such mixed-use developments from passing approval stages.

- *The desire to coordinate planning with environmental concerns.* Two opposing forces have been at work in planning since the 1970s. One side recognizes the value of mixed-use zoning, and the other continues to believe that the entire planning concept is useful as a means for social control over growth. The post-1970s era demonstrates how these two sides came into conflict. One of the most significant trends in the 1980s was a marriage between the planning community and the environmental movement. To some, *public welfare* is completely compatible with protecting the environment. However, as many court cases have demonstrated, the rules found in zoning ordinances and growth management laws, and the application of eminent domain, have often been misused by cities and counties to prevent growth. The line in the sand—a direct relationship between a regulation and the public good—has often been ignored. A public policy error has been to attempt to use environmental arguments to advance an antigrowth agenda.

- *Incompatibility between mixed use and practical constraints.* Even when communities determine that mixed use is a positive idea, it is not always practical. Often overlooked by activist citizens and planners alike is the reality that developers own their land and will propose projects that make sense to them, even when comprehensive plan goals do not agree. For example, a comprehensive plan may include statements encouraging mixed use, but it is not always possible. For those who remember the 1960s or 1950s, the traditional mixed-use neighborhood provided identity, good neighbor attitudes, and a natural sense of place. That same sense—knowing, for example, where the center of town is located—often does not exist in modern cities. Lacking a "downtown" or town center, the mall has become a de facto center of town in modern, isolated-zoning communities. To those who do not recall the days when town and city centers existed, mixed use is a new idea. Practical constraints found in the overly complex zoning ordinance and growth management rules may make it impossible to allow mixed use to occur without creating reforms in zoning or growth management restrictions.

For example, a comprehensive plan may encourage placing low-income housing in existing market-rate neighborhoods. But a developer may find it more efficient to create a new subdivision of housing, rather than buying up empty lots and building houses one at a time.

Even if it were desirable to construct low-income housing, tax credit incentive programs often encourage developers to view subdivisions as more practical. They may be able to fund the expensive initial infrastructure (utilities, roads, night lighting, grading) through selling tax credits to investors; this financial consideration makes it impractical to attempt mixed use even among housing types, not to mention inclusion of commercial properties within new neighborhoods. Even if the local planning department would allow it, the federal rules providing tax credits also prohibit funding any construction other than qualified low-income housing. The incentive itself works as a deterrent to meeting local planning goals.

KEYS TO ANALYSIS FOR MIXED USE

The major goal with mixed-use analysis is to answer one question: "Is there a premium to be gained from integrating dissimilar uses?" Integration is not easy and needs to be rewarded; otherwise why design for it? The big problem with figuring this out is the lack of comparables. The mixed-use development is not just another cookie-cutter shopping mall.

What makes mixed use attractive? Several features should be considered in the design, including:

- Higher density on the land due to different uses.
- Captive market advantage.
- Co-location, which leads to greater drawing power.
- Mixing uses may be the only feasible approach in blighted or empty areas.
- Faster development, the gain of efficiency that is possible.

Design should also be based on what works and how different uses are to be coordinated. Not every type of land use works well together.

What is critical mass of each use? With mixed use, the desire is to make an impact with each use. Each extra feature just makes the deal more complex. Complexity is bad.

Some specific points on each use:

Office: This should almost always be included in mix-use design. It is a no-brainer. Properly designed, the site offers office tenants unusual amenities that they will be willing to pay for. One possible problem is that mixed use does not provide the tenant with a trophy location. For those to whom corporate image is paramount, mixed use may not work.

Hotel: A quality hotel on site enhances the project's image. It attracts people all day and may serve as the focal point for entertainment and recreation. The hotel may also generate a lot of revenue from the point of view of taxing authorities.

Residential: While residential use serves as a centerpiece of many mixed-use projects, it is often difficult to make work. It may require coordination of urban density and lifestyle to suburbia, if an urban-type design is utilized. Developers will experience relatively low returns on residential, so it may be desirable to avoid including it in the mixed-use project.

Retail: This is often decided upon last. Retail is a function of the other uses as a lot of the demand might be generated on site (especially with convenience retail). This type of retail has three markets—onsite, primary, and secondary.

Other: Includes features such as a convention center, arena, trade mart, cultural outlet, or recreational facility, which may add great interest. But the analysis of these special features may be quite complex.

Design aside, an important caution about the marketability of mixed use should be remembered. First, people often assume that mixed-use projects will be self-supporting. This is not automatic. Farsighted design and planning—not only of where to plant hedges, but how to plan and lay out the entire site—are determinants in a mixed-use project's success. For example, mixed use today looks quite different from the old-style downtown mixed use, when merchants and their families literally lived above the store. Today mixed use is a more planned and controlled design and not just something that evolves naturally. To the contrary, traditional mixed use occurred due to practical constraints (such as a family owning the store but no car, for example) *and* a lack of zoning bans that disallowed such combinations. Today, the mixed-use site is carefully controlled in every aspect—not only where specific uses go, but where traffic flows, where people ride bicycles, what color they can paint their house, and even what kind of ornaments they can hang on the outside wall next to the garage. (In several mixed-use communities in the Greater Phoenix area, the residential covenants *require* that a decoration be hung on the outside wall, but it must be one of only four or five *approved* decorations—and as one might expect, these decorations can be purchased only from the homeowners association, the ultimate mixed-use Big Brother).

Many mixed-use projects include a carefully designed "town center." Good examples of this include the previously mentioned The Villages, where the "downtown" is actually a carefully designed series of streets with store fronts and well-placed massive parking areas behind—for cars, but with a predominance of spaces for the more popular golf carts that all residents appear to drive . . . with considerable abandon and recklessness, in some instances.

What purpose does the town center serve in the mixed-use development? Is it really necessary? Consider two points:

1. *People want to return to old-style downtown centers.* The actual trend toward mixed use is in part a reaction to the loss of identity, the replacement of downtown with the suburban mall. As more and more areas begin to look like Edge City, a reaction is to find the town center desirable as a form of "place making." The idea is that since we live with faceless suburbs, we can create a sense of place (and thereby community) by having town centers. Many people believe that we need new community gathering places.
2. *People want a place to gather together—and not always in the mall's food court.* Entertainment is often a driving force. People are looking for authentic experiences—and a sense of community. So local fairs, farmers markets, and celebrations take place in a town center. It is a lot nicer setting for these sorts of things when compared to holding them in a shopping mall parking lot.

ZONING SOLUTIONS FOR MIXED USE

The extensive planning and control exerted over mixed use—whether by local planners or owners and residents themselves—may prove to be a defining feature of mixed use. The legal and political complexities surrounding mixed-use zoning make this not only a complex topic, but a controversial one as well. The question of whether or not mixed use makes sense goes beyond the financial feasibility of a project; it also involves questions of *how* a community-wide planning effort should go forward. In many communities, allowing mixed-use development solves a number of problems, including the desire for affordable housing, siting of small retail establishments, and traffic congestion.

The analysis of mixed use is further complicated by an inconsistency in the definition itself. To some, *mixed use* means any combination of dissimilar density, that is, single-family, market-rate housing and multi-unit, low-income housing in the same neighborhood. In fact, those opposed to such mixed use often assign a negative definition to the term. It is also quite inaccurate. Some definitions specify that these uses must be revenue-producing; include physical and functional integration of project components; and conform to a specific type of plan format.[4] However, mixed use does not have to include such specific attributes, nor is the term necessarily restricted to income properties. The most universal definition is the combination of different types of zoning—residential, commercial, industrial—within a single neighborhood or area. It may be somewhat accurate to distinguish between housing densities and separate residential zoning as a form of mixed use; but for practical purposes, it makes more sense to review the analysis and feasibility of mixed use on the basis of broad zoning classifications.

If we view zoning as serving a restrictive role—the prevention of

CASE STUDY: AOL TIME WARNER BUILDING, NEW YORK, NY

Columbus Circle has gone though many transformations in its long history. Following the mega-merger of Time Warner and America Online (AOL) in 2000, the newly formed $84 billion capitalization company built its New York headquarters at Columbus Circle, to serve several different markets.

It is architecturally interesting as well as multi-functional. The 880-foot double-tower project has residential, office, entertainment, hotel, and retail sections, all within one double-tower project. The left tower is topped with condominiums (ranging in price between $1.5 and $36 million), then floors of office space and Time Warner's own floors; beneath this are several floors for CNN's television studios. The right tower has residential floors at the top (66 units starting at $3.6 million), and then the Mandarin Oriental Hotel (251 guest rooms, restaurant and bar, 7,000-foot meeting space, spa, pool), office space, additional Time Warner floors, and a section of entertainment floors called Jazz at Lincoln Center (an educational and performance organization including a 12,500-foot concert hall). Along the entire street level and expanding four stories up is a large area of shops and restaurants.

Completed in 2004, this urban mixed-use project is clearly "upscale" in terms of cost. Many people associate mixed use with affordability, especially for residential units. This is not the case for the AOL Time Warner Building, where prices are about four times the average cost of property in Manhattan.[5]

infringing land uses between dissimilar zones—then mixed use has to be carefully managed and arranged, often requiring exceptions to current zoning laws or development of mixed use within the confines of PUD zoning. Cooperation between developers and planning authorities is certainly a requirement in such instances, unless the local zoning code provides for specific commercial/residential mixed-use zones.

Defining a project as mixed use should include some degree of coordination, however. Simply proposing that a corner store should be allowed in an otherwise residential area is simply providing an exception; it does not rise to the level of *coordinated* mixed use. In a truly mixed-use area, we would expect to see substantial coexistence and planning of different types of use. The successful model of the office/industrial park is an excellent example. The impact of these zoning land uses is similar (when "industrial" is limited to light industrial and does not allow heavy industrial tenants), so that the mixed use in such professional parks makes sense. Separating light industrial from commercial office use would not make sense. Many office/industrial parks also include retail outlets of various types, further expanding the application of mixed use. So banks, service stations, restaurants, insurance offices, and other retail outlets are a sensible fit in such zoning projects.

In urban settings, we see an even more complex form of mixed use. In some respects, the limited availability of land—requiring high-rise development in place of geographically separated zones—has led to some creative mixed-use projects. Some urban mixed-use projects have been very successful and have become local as well as tourist destinations. Some examples include Peachtree Plaza in Atlanta, the Embarcadero Ferry Building in San Francisco, and Rockefeller Center in New York.

The AOL Time Warner Building would never be described as an *affordable* mixed-use project. As such, it does not meet the popular definition of mixed use as a way to create low-cost housing or retail space. Even by New York standards, the residential and hotel rates are on the high side. The Mandarin Oriental chain, a self-described *premium* hotel group with properties in about 20 cities worldwide, has summer room rates between $500 and $900 per night.[6]

This example makes the point about the complexity of analyzing mixed-use projects: There are many varieties. In some communities, mixed use is specifically aimed at revitalizing depressed areas and providing affordable housing—perhaps a more common issue the analyst is likely to encounter.

The analyst should remember in studying such projects that it is more expensive to plan mixed-use projects than single-use projects. The key

CASE STUDY: THE COMMONS AT GRANT, COLUMBUS, OH

In 2001 the City of Columbus approved a project aimed at improving its downtown area. The mayor and city council set up a $5 million Downtown Incentive Housing Fund to aid in developing housing in the city core.

The Commons at Grant included facilities for the homeless and for those with incomes below $24,000 per year. However, the location was next to a historic neighborhood and residents were concerned about the effect of the low-income housing on their property values. This is typical in residential mixed-use situations; resistance to development involves property value concerns as well as higher crime, traffic congestion, lack of jobs, and public service accessibility.

Local opposition was overcome through voluntary agreements concerning property maintenance and appearance, safety, and monitoring of residents. The project's apartments coexist with market rate housing in the downtown core with the additional management provisions. In this example, mixed use provided needed affordable housing in an existing neighborhood.[7]

question becomes "Does the synergy arising from the specific mixed use justify the added expense or investment?" The Commons at Grant and similar mixed-use projects may be more typical than the AOL Time Warner Building. The comparison between these two demonstrates the complexity and range of the idea, not to mention the cost; there is no one model that defines mixed use exclusively.

Furthermore, location of mixed-use projects may be diverse. Such projects are not found exclusively in city centers or business districts. A trend in combining residential, commercial, and recreational uses is growing in popularity, notably in Florida and Arizona.

Be aware that the trend in mixed-use development is aimed toward two primary models or types: the urban model (such as AOL Time Warner, Rockefeller Center, and other similar projects; and in other settings, the Planned Unit Development (PUD) such as Celebration, Florida, and Miami Lakes, Florida, for example. For the analytical point of view, mixed use may create a community where one did not exist before—rather than

CASE STUDY: CELEBRATION, FL

If breaking residential sales records is a test of a project's success, Celebration, Florida, would probably win. Annual sales above $120 million for three years running demonstrates the popularity and success of this mixed-use complex. It is home to more than 8,000 residents in 2,300 homes and 1,200 apartments. The complex also has a 1.8 million-square-foot commercial building and a 110-acre Class A commercial district; office and office complex sites; and a hotel conference center. Commercial tenants include Walt Disney Imagineering, Bank of America, SunTrust Bank, a post office, a cinema, and a town hall.

Located just south of Walt Disney World on Florida's Interstate 4, Celebration has many of the amenities and features found elsewhere in Florida and in the projects popular in the greater Phoenix area. Celebration may be the epitome of the nonurban mixed-use complex, with a notable addition: Residences are affordable compared to mixed-use projects in the big cities. Home styles include eight model types. On the low end are Terrace Homes with prices beginning in the $170s. Prices increase as model types become larger and closer to amenities such as golf course and green belt. The top of the line, Estate Homes, start in the $800s. Residential style and price are broad enough to fit many budgets.

People accustomed to thinking of mixed use as a combination of densities in residential style may look down on mixed use as problematical—but not so in Celebration, Florida. Here the combined variation of home styles *and* commercial, industrial, and office space make this community complex livable. The carefully planned and designed community includes community parks, playgrounds, walking and bicycle paths, fitness center with 60,000 square feet, golf and tennis, community swimming pool, and adult education (instruction in classical music and languages, for example). The complex also has a full hospital on a *health campus* as well as a range of medical specialists.[8]

merely putting up buildings and then selling or leasing them. The Miami Lakes project, for example, eventually incorporated itself as a new city. If a mixed-use parcel is laid out like a city and not only as a neighborhood, it may become so given enough time.

Many successful variations of mixed use via planned unit developments and self-contained communities like those in Florida and Arizona, augment the efficiency of projects in urban centers and further shows that varying income levels and cost of housing can be planned without having a negative impact on market values; and that in cities like New York City, multi-use buildings are not only possible, but efficient and practical as well.

LOCAL PLANNING AND ITS EFFECT ON MARKET ANALYSIS

Mixed use, planned properly, can provide a project with a captive audience. Residential feeds retail and makes the whole package more attractive to the whole mix of users. Market analysts working with developers of mixed-use projects will need to understand both the local zoning code and its restrictions, and the political mood in the community. The local planning department will be more flexible in considering mixed-use proposals (i.e., within its PUD zoning ordinance) when they want to encourage growth. In communities where the political mood is antigrowth, the same ordinances can be used to deny permission for developers to devise creative mixed-use plans.

Good planning—on the part of developers as well as on planning departments—can and does increase value of the project. This is an important point to bear in mind as part of the feasibility analysis of a proposed project. Especially in a mixed-use project, creative and exceptional design adds to the overall desirability and value of the project and is also a requirement in most communities. To quality as a PUD, the element of "exceptional design" or "innovative design" is likely to be built into the language of the zoning ordinance.

In Arvada, Colorado, the definition of a PUD is typical:

The Planned Unit Development zoning district allows projects of innovative design and layout that would not be permitted under the Land Development Code because of the strict application of each zoning district or general development standards. The PUD

District encourages innovative land planning and site design concepts that achieve a high level of environmental sensitivity, energy efficiency, aesthetics, high quality development, and other community goals.[9]

The need for exceptions in zoning codes is clear; most communities tie in the mixed-use concept via PUD-type developments with innovation. At Iowa State University Extension, a *Land Use Series* report explained that:

Traditional zoning can be rather rigid and result in a "sameness" to the look of neighborhoods. In some situations, an intermixing of land uses may make a community or neighborhood more appealing. . . . Probably the best known of the innovative zoning techniques is the Planned Unit Development (PUD). Under this approach, the zoning ordinance allows flexibility in the development of large areas . . ."[10]

Even more specific are the design criteria specified in zoning codes. Under these, developers are provided with an exchange: Exceptions to an otherwise exact series of zoning requirements (including density and setback exceptions, for example) in exchange for innovative design *and* preservation of environmental features of the land. In Marshalltown, Iowa, the zoning code is quite specific for PUDs:

Design Criteria

The following objectives are sought:

- A maximum choice of living environments by allowing a variety of housing and building types, by permitting an increased density per acre and by reducing dimensions, yards, and building setbacks.
- A more useful pattern of open space and recreation areas and, if permitted as part of the project, more convenience in the location of accessory commercial uses and services.
- A development pattern which preserves and utilizes natural topography and geologic features, scenic vistas, trees and other vegetation, and prevents the disruption of natural drainage patterns.
- A more efficient use of land than is generally achieved through conventional development.

- A development pattern in harmony with land use density, transportation facilities, and community facilities objectives of the Comprehensive Guide Plan.
- Nonresidential developments planned as groups, in park-like surroundings with common ingress points and common parking; with screened loading, storage and parking areas; with buffer areas to adjacent lands which are fully landscaped and with areas set aside for future expansion.[11]

In this example of a series of detailed design criteria, the zoning ordinance specifically relates the qualifications for PUD development with both environmental impacts *and* with mixed use. A problem with identifying specifically how a particular city or county will treat such ordinances may vary. Terms such as *exceptional, innovative,* and *efficient* are not precise although they are widely used in ordinance language. This provides local elected officials and planning departments to apply flexible standards, and variation may be found based on local political mood, the desire (or lack of desire) for new development in a city or town, and previous experience with a particular developer.

Many outcomes are possible, again depending on the local planning department, mood of the citizens concerning new development, and the overall political climate. Because PUD is so often the vehicle for mixed-use projects, and because those projects tend to be large in terms of land use (in comparison to subdivision or single-building construction), the real and perceived impacts can be significant as well. This may include concerns about traffic, crime, availability of jobs or needed changes in the local job market, and the mix of market-rate and affordable housing projects.

CONCLUSION

Anyone who embarks on the process of market analysis—whether studying a proposed mixed use project or some other format—soon discovers that the complexities involved with markets and with other aspects (supply and demand trends, competition, and cost) will be challenging and not subject to specific formulation.

Appraisers can, to a degree, employ recurring processes in valuation of properties. Judgment concerning special situations and individual cases is one aspect of that process, but appraisers are able for the most part to apply well-known methodologies to formulate and document their work. Market analysis and feasibility are not as specific and the processes are not as clear. There are certain tools available, of course, such as the study of penetration and yield on a comparative basis; projections of cash flow for either lenders or investors based on widely understood budgeting techniques and assumptions; and coming to conclusions based on repetitive application of formulas. For example, many of the builders of gated communities in Phoenix, Scottsdale, and Chandler, Arizona, duplicate both style and scope of their projects repetitively. However, markets are not always the same, and even well-understood markets do change over time and as local economic conditions change. At some point in the future, the ability for local municipalities in Arizona to provide medical services, utilities, fire and police protection, and other basic needs will reach a saturation point. This will have an unavoidable effect on supply and demand, competition, and housing prices. The same changes may be expected in other popular areas such as Las Vegas and central Florida.

As the baby boomer generation reaches retirement age, a process that has begun already, massive changes will occur in real estate supply and demand, both in terms of the size and location of properties, and in the pricing of housing. This will further change the trends in commercial and industrial properties, whose markets are invariably factors of residential trends. So historical trends cannot be expected to curve indefinitely in the same manner; as the typical age and income of home buyers changes, due to baby boomer retirement, younger generation home buying patterns, and regional job markets, real estate will have to be studied and adjusted carefully. The United States is moving away from manufacturing at a fast rate and becoming almost exclusively a service economy. For example, in 1885 the United States manufactured nearly one-third of global goods.[12] Today, China has taken over the role of primary world manufacturer, producing 40 percent of laptop computers, 95 percent of shoes, and nearly 100% of denim jeans consumed in the world.

Change is constant, and as economic change occurs globally, real estate prices and markets will change as well. Historical observations of housing and rental trends and related commercial activity are based on well-established trends in the economy. As the economic emphasis shifts away from the United States and toward overseas manufacturing, the type of jobs held by people in the United States will change as well, and accompanying this change may be important shifts geographically. Today's hot region may be cold tomorrow, and vice versa.

This reality is an important indicator to every market analyst: We cannot depend on established demographic or economic trends, because important shifts are occurring. Between now and the year 2030, we should expect to witness many significant changes in global and local economic forces *and* as a result, in how real estate valuation occurs. We can observe the forces at work that directly affect how property values emerge over time, and those same forces of supply and demand will continue to work. However, we may also see that a different set of indicators will come into play. The analyst needs to be prepared to abandon older assumptions that no longer work, and to accept the reality that in our new century, *change* will act as a constant.

Internet Sources for Further Study

Government Statistical Sites

Agriculture Department at http://www.ers.usda.gov/Data/Unemployment; useful employment and median income data by state.

Bureau of Economic Analysis at http://www.bea.doc.gov; part of Department of Commerce, many useful statistical links.

Bureau of Labor Statistics at www.bls.gov; economic and population indicators.

Census Bureau at http://www.census.gov/prod/www/abs/h170sma.html; American housing survey, data for households and housing costs for selected metropolitan areas.

Census Bureau at www.census.gov/popest; population statistics, regional and national.

Census Bureau at http://quickfacts.census.gov; Census data, friendly format, individual state links.

Census Bureau at http://www.census.gov/acsd/www/sub_c.htm; specific statistics and trends in the construction industry.

Census Bureau at http://tiger.census.gov; mapping and cartographic resource, good mapping resources and many free maps.

Economic Development Administration at http://www.eda.gov; part of the Department of Commerce, the EDA works with local agencies to establish economic growth.

Energy Information Administration at http://eiainfo.eia.doe.gov; reports on various energy consumption levels for commercial buildings.

Environmental Protection Agency at http://www.epa.gov; federal regulatory agency supporting environmental professionals and overseeing development and environmental trends.

Fed World at http://www.fedworld.gov; part of U.S. Department of Commerce, useful links to government agency web pages.

Federal Deposit Insurance Corporation at http://www.fdic.gov; real estate, consumer, and lending trends.

Federal Financial Examination Council at www.ffiec.gov; Census tract information and good secondary links.

Federal Housing Administration at http://www.fha-home-loans.com; federal agency providing loans and buy-down arrangements to buyers.

Federal Housing Finance Board at http://www.fhfb.gov; regulatory agency with many useful financing statistical links.

Federal Reserve Financial Services at http://www.frbservices.org; part of the Federal Reserve, online source for information and solutions for financing of real estate projects.

General Services Administration at http://www.pueblo.gsa.gov/cic_text/housing/handbook/handbook.txt; informative online handbook with information about adjustable rate mortgages.

Internal Revenue Service at http://www.irs.gov; source for tax information, forms, publications, and instructions.

Veterans Administration at http://www.va.gov; source for qualified veterans for favorable rates and down payment terms.

World Factbook at http://www.odci.gov/cia/publications/factbook; a CIA site providing a large volume of links by country and by topic.

Nongovernmental Statistical and Industry Resources

American Chamber of Commerce Researchers Association at http://www.accra.org; ACCRA provides economic and policy research in the United States and Canada.

Apartments.com at http://www.apts.com; statistics and trends by state and region on apartment market rates, vacancies, and news.

BRB Publications at http://www.brbpub.com; ties into the Public Record Research System; site includes pay resources and free links.

CACI International at http:/www.caci.com; demographics and real estate economic source.

Claritas.com at http://www.claritas.com; source for demographics, marketing statistics, and other data in a variety of industries.

Demographics USA at http://www.tradedimensions.com; extensive and advanced source for population statistics.

Economy.com at http://www.economy.com; site providing economic information and statistics on a broad range of topics.

Hoovers Online at http://www.hoovers.com/free/; pay site providing members with market analysis and research on a broad range of topics.

Joint Center for Housing Studies at http://www.jchs.harvard.edu; Harvard University-based, provides an annual report on U.S. housing trends, costs, demographics.

National Multi Housing Council at http://www.nmhc.org; good source for news, statistics, legislative trends in residential markets.

NPA Data at http://www.economy.com/default.asp; economic research company for the real estate industry.

Research

Best Places to Live at http://www.bestplaces.net; useful web site providing statistical information on housing costs, crime levels, climate, and other information about cities and towns.

Black's Guide at http://www.blacksguide.com; office and industrial property information, statistics and trends, covering more than 80,000 properties in 19 major metropolitan markets.

Blue Book of Building and Construction at http://www.thebluebook.com; national referral and listing service for the building industry, providing referrals by region and city.

Builder Magazine at http://www.builderonline.com/; online edition providing industry news and referral services.

Chain Store Guide at http://www.csgis.com; information research in the retail and food service industries.

Costar Group at http://www.costar.com; This group offers information services to commercial developers, with a large national and international database including statistics on markets, market values, and tenants.

Housing Zone at http://www.housingzone.com; good source for professionals; news and links to many useful magazines, organizations, and other sites.

LoopNet at http://www.loopnet.com; a service provider in the commercial real estate sector, providing clients with a variety of market and tenant data.

National Real Estate Investor at http://www.nreionline.com; online industry magazine reporting on industry trends.

Real Estate Research Corporation at http://www.rerc.com; source for commercial real estate research, valuation, and consulting.

REIS at http://www.reis.com; research organization providing members extensive industry news, rent, and sales comps by region, valuation of properties, and submarket reports.

Real Estate Research Institute at http://www.reri.org; organization supporting research on real estate investment performance and market fundamentals.

Retail Tenants Directory and Insider at http://www.retailtenants.com; annual publication with detailed information about tenants in retail chains of the United States and Canada.

ShoppingCenters.com at http://www.shoppingcenters.com; publisher of *Directory of Major Malls* and other research materials in the retail industry.

StartRemodeling.com at http://www.startremodeling.com/; referral site by state, news and information as well as handy tips and how to find professionals.

Trade Dimensions at http://www.tradedimensions.com; supplier of guide books, directories, and information products for all sectors of real estate markets.

Magazines and Periodicals

Appraisal Journal at www.appraisalinstitute.org/publications/periodicals.
Builder at www.builderonline.com.
Building Design and Construction at www.bdcmag.com.
Buildings at http://www.buildings.com.
Commercial Investment Real Estate Journal at www.ccim.com/magazine.
Commercial Property News at www.cpnonline.com.
Cooperator at www.cooperator.com.
Economist at www.economist.com.
Engineering News Record at www.enr.com.
Hotel Valuation Journal at www.hotel-online.com/Trends/HVS/Journal.
Housing Market Statistics at www.nahb.org.
International Real Estate Digest at http://www.ired.com.
Journal of Housing Research at www.fanniemaefoundation.org/programs/jhr.shtml.
Journal of Property Management at www.irem.org.
Journal of Real Estate Portfolio Management at www.aresnet.org.
Journal of Real Estate Practice and Education at www.aresnet.org.
Journal of Real Estate Research at www.aresnet.org.
Journal of Shopping Center Research at www.icsc.org/rsrch/research.html.
Journal of the American Planning Association at www.planning.org.
Land Development Today at http://www.landdevelopmenttoday.com.
Metropolis at www.metropolismag.com.
MortgageMag at http://www.mortgagemag.com.
Multi-Housing News at www.multi-housingnews.com.
National Real Estate Investor at www.nreionline.com.
Planning at www.planning.org.
Professional Builder at www.housingzone.com/index.asp.
Real Estate Economics at www.areuea.org.
Shopping Centers Today at www.icsc.org.
Site Selection at www.siteselection.com.

Wharton Real Estate Review at http://realestate.wharton.upenn.edu/review.php.

Low-Income Housing

Association of Bay Area Governments at www.abag.ca.gov; a California regional planning agency involved with housing issues.

City Design Center at www.uic.edu/aa/cdc; provides research and education, based at the University of Illinois at Chicago.

Enterprise Foundation at www.enterprisefoundation.org; advocacy group for low-income and affordable housing.

Family Housing Fund at www.fhfund.org/educational_materials_reports .asp; source for information on affordable housing trends and news.

Habitat for Humanity at www.habitat.org; organization that provides housing with no built-in profit.

Housing and Urban Development at http://www.hud.gov; government site for issues, trends, legislation; and resources for low-income housing.

International Economic Development Council at http://www.iedconline .org; advocacy group supporting legislative development, professional services, and providing publications and certification programs.

Multiple Listing Service at http://www.mls.org; home page for regional real estate listings for member brokerage firms.

National Association of Housing and Redevelopment Officials at http://www.nahro.org; housing and community development advocate for the provision of adequate and affordable housing.

National Fair Housing at http://www.fairhousing.com; online advocate tracking legislation and promoting affordable and low-income housing.

National Housing Institute at http://www.nhi.org; advocacy organization for affordable housing.

National Low Income Housing Coalition at www.nlihc.org; site reports trends on low-income housing, legislation, and local opposition.

Rental Housing OnLine at http://rhol.org/rental/ltlaw.htm#us; landlord/tenant law links; good site for legal questions.

Washington State University at http://niip.wsu.edu; useful Census data for Western states and nationwide.

Professional and Industry Associations

American Bankers Association at http://www.aba.com; industry association and advocacy group for banking institutions, including community, regional, and money center banks and holding companies, savings associations, trust companies and savings banks.

American Builders Network at http://www.americanbuilders.com; useful service matching builders with clients by state.

American Hotel/Motel Association at http://www.ahma.com; national association in the lodging industry, whose members consist primarily of property managers.

American Institute of Architects at http://www.e-architect.com/; trade association for the industry, providing accreditation and ongoing education.

American Land Title Association at http://www.alta.org; national trade association of the abstract and title insurance professionals.

American Planning Association at http://www.planning.org; industry membership group for professional planners.

American Real Estate and Urban Economics Association at http://www.areuea.org; professional site for planners and professionals.

American Real Estate Society at http://www.aresnet.org; association for real estate professionals and educators.

Appraisal Foundation at http://www.appraisalfoundation.org; nonprofit organization that develops standards and qualifications in the industry.

Appraisal Institute at www.appraisalinstitute.org; professional association with 18,000 professional members.

Associated General Contractors of America at http://www.agc.org; trade association and referral service for the building trade.

Association of Construction Inspectors at http://iami.org; the largest professional organization for inspectors and project managers.

Association of Interim Housing Providers at http://test.neton-linc.com/aihp; trade association for organizations that provide temporary housing, including corporate units.

BAI at http://www.bai.org; a professional organization of the financial services industry with emphasis on banking and membership education.

Building Owners and Managers Association at http://www.boma.org; trade organization for commercial owners and managers.

Certified Commercial Investment Member at www.ccim.com; an industry association with 15,000 members.

Commercial Real Estate Exchange at http://www.commrex.com/; association assisting developers in finding commercial mortgages, comparing and evaluating properties, and providing links to other commercial sources.

Community Associations Institute at http://www.caionline.org; resources for homeowner association managers in condominium and cooperative housing.

Contractor.com at http://www.contractors.com/; a referral service by region and contractor specialization.

Corporate Real Estate Network at www.corenetglobal.org; a 7,000-member trade association.

Counselors of Real Estate at http://www.commrex.com; a professional organization that grants the CRE designation to real estate consultants and advisors and enforces professional standards.

Institute of Real Estate Management at http://www.irem.org; members' source for industry research, and education for real estate management professionals.

Institutional Real Estate at http://www.irei.com; free and subscription-based market reports and forecasts for industry professionals.

International Association of Assessing Officers at http://www.iaao.org; professional organization for appraisers and assessors as well as elected officials concerned with property tax policies.

International City/County Management Association at http://www2.icma .org/main/sc.asp?t=0; professional and educational organization for chief appointed managers, administrators, and assistants in cities, towns, and counties.

International Council of Shopping Centers at www.icsc.org; trade association with 39,000 members.

Mortgage Bankers Association of America at http://www.mbaa.org; useful lending trends and economic data.

National Association of Homebuilders at http://www.nahb.org; building industry association with large membership and statistical data base.

National Association of Independent Fee Appraisers at http://www .naifa.com; industry association offering the IFA designation and education courses for members.

National Association of Industrial and Office Properties at http:// www.naiop.org; industry association for commercial and industrial managers and owners.

National Association of Mortgage Bankers at http://www.namb.org; the association of the mortgage banking industry.

National Association of Real Estate Appraisers at http://www.iami .org/narea; industry association serving appraisers, with updates on regulatory trends, publications, and more.

National Association of Real Estate Investment Managers at http://www .nareim.org; trade organization for real estate investment professionals.

National Association of Realtors at www.realtor.org; home page, national realtor membership association, and licensing and standards as well as statistics on property trends.

National Association of Residential Property Managers at http://www.narpm.org; association for property managers and management companies.

National Association of Review Appraisers and Mortgage Underwriters at http://www.iami.org/narea; professional organization for appraisers and loan professionals.

National Council of Real Estate Investment Fiduciaries at http://www.ncreif.org/indices; useful rate and pricing source and statistical summaries.

National Retail Federation at http://www.nrf.com; the world's largest retail trade association, with membership that comprises all retail formats and channels of distribution including department, specialty, discount, catalog, Internet, and independent stores.

Public Housing Authorities Directors Association at http://www.webcom.com/house; membership association providing news, links, and resources.

Real Estate Investment Advisory Council at http://www.reiac.org; association for real estate owners and senior executives of institutions and real estate investment firms.

Retail Leaders Industry Association at http://www.retail-leaders.org; an alliance of retailers and their suppliers, providing legislative tracking, news, and publications within the retail industry.

Society of Industrial and Office Realtors at www.sior.com; a 2,800-member realtor association.

Urban Land Institute at www.uli.org; professional association and publisher with 17,000 members.

Pooled Investments

Axiometrics Inc. at http://www.axiometrics.com; research site specializing in multi-family residential markets for 249 markets, with emphasis on REIT investments.

Dividend Discount Model at http://www.dividenddiscountmodel.com; calculates the discounted cash flow of dividends, useful for comparing current real estate cash flow returns to other investments.

Federal Home Loan Mortgage Corporation at http://www.freddiemac.com; federally chartered agency designed to ensure financing to conventional lenders and to the homer-buying public.

Federal National Mortgage Association at http://www.fanniemae.com/ index.jhtml; information on mortgage pools.

Government National Mortgage Association at http://www.ginniemae.gov; information on mortgage pools.

National Association of Real Estate Investment Trusts at http:// www.nareit.org; industry organization that tracks REIT performance and provides news and information in the REIT industry.

Office of Federal Housing Enterprise Oversight at http://www.ofheo.gov; office within HUD designed to provide oversight for pooled investment programs and to ensure capital structure and other regulatory issues.

Pension Real Estate Association at http://www.prea.org; real estate investment professional organization providing good industry and research links.

REITnetOnline at http://www.reitnet.com; provides research reports, performance models, and industry news and updates in the REIT market.

Growth Management and Legal

Dixieland Law Journal at http://home.hiwaay.net/~becraft/recentcases .htm; informative site for issues such as eminent domain; includes recent court cases.

Findlaw at http://www.findlaw.com; good source for legal information in real estate, court cases and codes, trends, and news.

Georgetown Environmental Law and Policy Institute at http://www.law .georgetown.edu/gelpi/takings/courts; current summary of land use legislation and recent court cases.

Law.com at http://dictionary.law.com; useful online legal dictionary.

National Association of Realtors at http://www.realtor.org/sg3.nsf/pages/ landusezonegrowmgmt?OpenDocument; good listing of state growth management links.

Real-estate-law.freeadvice at http://real-estate-law.freeadvice.com; real estate legal issues, information provided by lawyers; attorney locator, free forms downloads, online query feature.

Snohomish County Camano Association of Realtors at http://www.sccar .com/govern/gmadensity.html; Washington State local realtors' association; good growth management and professional association links.

Other Sites

About page at http://architecture.about.com/cs/buildyourhouse/a/costs
.htm; offers articles as well as a valuable link for estimating costs of
improvements based on square footage.

Academics Education at http://www.selu.edu/Academics/Education/
EDF600/Mod3/; good information about the scientific method.

Bankrate.com at http://www.bankrate.com; source for mortgage referrals
and comparisons.

Bizloan at http://www.bizloan.org; online source for financing; provides
links and referrals.

Century 21 at http://www.century21.com/learn/glossary.aspx; useful real
estate glossary.

Congress for the New Urbanism at http://www.cnu.org; public planning
policy organization founded by architects and involved with trends in
planning, design, and public policy in real estate.

Eastern Connecticut State University at http://koning.ecsu.ctstateu.edu/
Plants_Human/scimeth.html; site with information about the scientific
method.

GlobeSt.com at http://www.globest.com; source for current news and
trends in real estate.

HSH at http://www.hsh.com/calc-amort.html; financial publisher site provides a free mortgage calculator link.

Homeglossary.com at http://www.homeglossary.com; online glossary of
real estate terms.

HomeSearcher.com at http://www.homeresearcher.com; site for people
seeking homes, financing, and comparative pricing information.

Interest.com at http://mortgages.interest.com mortgage calculator, lender
referrals, other links useful to single-family home buyers and investors.

InterestRateCalculators.com at http://www.interestratecalculator.com;
source for a variety of free interest calculators.

Mortgage Guaranty Insurance Corporation at http://www.mgic.com; major provider of private mortgage insurance.

Mortgage-loan-search.com at http://www.mortgage-loan-search.com;
referral service to lenders plus information on comparing mortgage
terms.

MSN house and home at http://houseandhome.msn.com; advice and information on adjustable rate mortgage terms and comparisons.

Owners.com at http://www.owners.com; site matching buyers and sellers,
mortgages and prequalification, and guidelines for buying and selling
property.

Reals.com at http://www.reals.com; a comprehensive directory with links to a wide variety of real estate professionals and information sources.

Rochester University at http://teacher.nsrl.rochester.edu/phy_labs/AppendixE/AppendixE.html; good explanations of how the scientific method works.

State Tax Central at http://www.statetaxcentral.com; useful site providing a range of information for state income tax, available by state.

Yahoo! real estate at http://realestate.yahoo.com/re/homevalues; good site for identifying home values, finding competitive mortgages, and locating other real estate links.

Bibliography

Articles

Belfrage, Eric E. "Business Value Allocation in Lodging Valuation," *The Appraisal Journal*, July 2001.

Bell, Randall. "The Impact of Airport Noise on Residential Real Estate," *The Appraisal Journal*, July 2001.

Berg, Peggy and Mark Skinner. "A New Pricing Index for the Corporate Apartment Industry," *The Real Estate Finance Journal*, Winter 2002.

Brecht, Susan B. "Let the Buyer Beware," *Assisted Living Today*, Winter 1996.

Burrough, D.J. "Golf Deals," *Urban Land*, August 2000.

Caldwell, Douglas A. "Anticipated Value," *The Canadian Appraiser*, Winter 2000.

Canning, George R. "The Contemporary Direct Comparison Approach to Value," *The Canadian Appraiser*, Winter 2000.

Cannon, Michael Y. "Real Estate Market Analysis in the Valuation Process," *Appraisal Institute*, 1993.

_____. "The Role for the Real Estate Appraiser and Assessor in Valuing Real Property for Ad Valorem Assessment Purposes," *The Appraisal Journal*, April 2002.

Cohen, Eric. "Know Your Market Trade Area: The First Steps in a Project Feasibility Study," *Mini-Storage Messenger*, September 1996.

Connery, Thomas W. "FORE! Thought in a Golf Course Market Analysis," *Valuation Insights & Perspectives*, Fourth Quarter 1998.

Craig, C. Samuel et al. "Models of the Retail Location Process: A Review," *Journal of Retailing*, Spring 1984.

Egan, Patrick A. "Mixed Business and Real Estate Components in Hotel Valuation," *The Appraisal Journal*, July 1996.

Epley, Donald R. "Better Real Estate Market Analysis for Metro Areas Through the Use of Unique Sources of Internet Data," *Real Estate Issues*, Summer 2002.

Eppli, Mark J. "Value Allocation in Regional Shopping Centers," *The Appraisal Journal*, April 1998.

_____ and John D. Benjamin. "The Evolution of Shopping Center Research: A Review and Analysis," *Journal of Real Estate Research*, Winter 1994.

Goodman, Jack. "Performance Across Local Apartment Markets," *Real Estate Finance*, Winter 1999.

Hardin, Garrett. "The Tragedy of the Commons," *Science*, 1968.

Hearn, Joy. "How to Analyze Land Values in the Land Market," *The Appraisal Journal*, July 1999.

Jackson, Thomas and Randall Bell. "The Analysis of Environmental Case Studies," *The Appraisal Journal*, January 2002.

Joerger, Albert et al. "Applying Geographic Information Systems," *Cornell Hotel and Restaurant Administration Quarterly*, October 1996.

Jortbert, Richard E. "Retail Market Analysis: An Intermediate Approach to Estimate Demand," *The Appraisal Journal*, October 1996.

Knutson, Daniel. "Feasibility Studies," *Mini-Storage Messenger*, July 2000.

Kummerow, Max. "A Statistical Definition of Value," *The Appraisal Journal*, October 2002.

Lefenfeld, Bob. "Market Analysis Basics, Elements of a Good Study, What to Expect from a Multifamily Market or Feasibility Study," *Multifamily Trends*, Summer 2001.

Lusvard, Wayne. "Valuing Nature Land in Extinct Markets," *The Appraisal Journal*, July 1999.

Madsen, Edgar B. "Timeshare Tax Assessment: Prices Versus Market Value," *The Appraisal Journal*, January 1999.

Martin, Robert S. "Supply and Demand Relationships in Residential Subdivision Analysis," *Appraisal Institute*, 1993.

Miles, Mike et al. "The Graaskamp Legacy," *Real Estate Finance*, Spring 1998.

Morris, Mark L. "Financing Hotel Acquisitions" Issues and Answers About Loan Documents," *The Real Estate Finance Journal*, March 2000.

National Low Income Housing Coalition. "A Second Chance for Victory," *The NIMBY Report*, November 2000, at www.nlihc.org.

_____. "Caught Between a Rock and a Hard Place in Key West," *The NIMBY Report*, August 2003, at www.nlihc.org.

_____. "New Apartments in Columbus, Ohio," *The NIMBY Report*, July 2001, www.nlihc.org.

Nelson, Arthur C. "Reducing Financial Hazard Risk Through Planning Intervention," *Journal of Urban Planning and Development*," March 2000.

Owens, Robert W. "Subdivision Development: Bridging Theory and Practice," *The Appraisal Journal*, July 1998.

Rabianski, Joseph. S. "Retail Area Delineation and Market Analysis for the Appraiser," *Appraisal Institute*, 1993.

_____ "Vacancy in Market Analysis and Valuation," *The Appraisal Journal*, April 2002.

Riggs, Kenneth P. "Property-Level Analysis: The Key to Successful Investing in Today's Changing Landscape," *Real Estate Issues*, Summer 2002.

Rosenberg, Matt. *Zoning—Residential, Commercial, or Industrial?* at http://geography.about.com/library/weekly/aa072801a.htm.

Rushmore, Stephen. "Feasibility Studies: Fact or Fiction?" *Lodging Hospitality*, October 1996.

_____. "Development Cost Can Determine Feasibility," *Hotels*, March 2002.

_____. "Don't Overpay for Hotel Sites," *Hotels*, February 2002.

_____. "Using Hotel Development Cost to Determine Feasibility," *Hotels*, November 1999.

Smith, Charles A. "Using GIS to Improve Estimates of Future Demand," *Journal of Property Management*, July/August 1998.

Staley, Samuel, Ph.D. *Homeowners are Paying Thousands More for Houses Because of Growth Management Acts*," December 18, 2001, *Reason Public Policy Institute*, at www.rppi.org.

Wagner, Richard. "Impact Fees: Truth and Consequences of Bad Policy," John Locke Foundation, at www.johnlocke.org December 10, 2003.

Wilder, Jeff. "Is It Wise to Invest in a Hotel Today?" *Hotel & Motel Management*, November 2001.

Witten, G. Ronald. "Predicting the Multifamily Market," *Multifamily Trends*, Fall 2002.

Viezer, Timothy W. "Simulating and Testing Metropolitan Area/Property Type Returns," *Real Estate Finance*, Winter 2000.

Books

Appraisal Institute. *The Appraisal of Real Estate*. 10th ed. Chicago, IL: Appraisal Institute, 1992.

Armbrust, Betty J. et al. *Practical Real Estate Math*. Cincinnati, OH: South-Western Publishing, 2001.

Barrett, G. Vincent. *How to Conduct and Analyze Real Estate Market and Feasibility Studies*. New York, NY: Van Nostrand Reinhold, 1982.

Benke, William and Joseph M. Fowler. *All About Real Estate Investing*. New York, NY: McGraw-Hill, 2001.

Berges, Steve. *The Complete Guide to Real Estate Finance for Investment Properties*. Hoboken, NJ: John Wiley & Sons, 2004.

Brecht, Susan B. *Analyzing Seniors' Housing Markets*. Washington, DC: Urban Land Institute, 2002.

Carn, Neil and Ronald Racster. *Real Estate Market Analysis*. Cincinnati, OH: South-Western Publishing, 1988.

DeGrove, J. M. *Land Use Plans and Politics*. Chicago, IL: American Planning Association, 1984.

Faber, Marc. *Tomorrow's Gold*. Hong Kong: CLSA Books, 2003.

Fanning, Stephen F. et al. *Market Analysis for Valuation Appraisals*. Chicago, IL: Appraisal Institute, 1995.

Gallinelli, Frank. *What Every Investor Needs to Know About Cash Flow*. New York, NY: McGraw-Hill, 2004.

Garreau, Joel. *Edge City: Life on the New Frontier*. New York, NY: Anchor Publishing, 1992.

Gause, Allen et al. *Office Development Handbook*, 2d ed. Washington, DC: Urban Land Institute, 1998.

McLean, Andrew and Gary W. Eldred, Ph.D. *Investing in Real Estate*. Hoboken, NJ: John Wiley & Sons, 2003.

Peiser, Richard B. and Anne Frej. *Professional Real Estate Development: The ULI Guide to the Business*. Washington, DC: Urban Land Institute, 2003.

Pivar, William A. *Real Estate Investing from A to Z*. New York, NY: McGraw-Hill, 2004.

Rushmore, Stephen. *Hotels and Motels: A Guide to Analysis, Investment Analysis, and Valuation*. Chicago, IL: Appraisal Institute, 1992.

Schmitz, Adrienne et al. *Real Estate Market Analysis*. Washington, DC: Urban Land Institute, 2001.

Thomsett, Michael C. *NIMBYism: Navigating the Politics of Local Opposition*. Arlington, VA: Centerline Media, 2004.

Thrall, Grant Ian. *Business Geography and New Real Estate Market Analysis*. New York, NY: Oxford University Press, 2002.

Urban Land Institute. *Shopping Center Development Handbook*, 2d ed. Washington, DC: Urban Land Institute, 1985.

Willis, Gerri. *The Smart Money Guide to Real Estate Investing*. Hoboken, NJ: John Wiley & Sons, 2003.

Glossary

absorption analysis   a series of tests designed to identify (1) the likely and probable occupancy rate to be expected from a project and (2) the time required before full absorption is likely to be realized.

active participation   a threshold definition used in tax law to define whether or not an individual is allowed to deduct losses in real estate investments; active participation requires a minimal recurring involvement in tenant selection, maintenance of properties, and decisions concerning rent levels and timing of a property purchase or sale.

adjusted gross income (AGI)   an individual's gross income before deducting tax exemptions and itemized or standard deduction.

anticipation   a principle of valuation, stating that market value often is affected by expectations about future events.

appraisal   the process of estimating a property's current value, based on (1) comparison to similar properties and recent sales; (2) income levels for multi-unit investment properties or retail properties; or (3) replacement cost of the property.

asset allocation   the spreading of risk through an expanded form of diversification, in which investment capital is placed in several different markets (such as real estate, stocks, bonds, and the money market) rather than in one market.

availability rate   a comparison between available space and rentable space, usually expressed on a percentage basis of square feet; the purpose is to compare nonrentable areas among projects (utility and common areas, wall space, etc.).

available space   the amount of rentable space on the market, including vacant, occupied, or pending availability in the future.

BANANA   acronym for Build Absolutely Nothing Anywhere, Not Anytime, describing those opposed to *all* types of new development; NIMBYs who want nothing to change in their neighborhoods.

big box   free-standing retail stores, so called due to their cube-shape and name recognition.

business plan   a general description of a document intended to justify a business venture, notably for lenders; plans include narrative descriptions of a proposed course of action; revenue forecasts, cost and

211

expense budgets, and cash flow projections; and biographies of the business owners.

business travelers in the lodging industry, a potential guest whose primary reason for travel is business-related. This group includes the solitary business traveler, corporate small groups, and convention business.

capitalization rate complete meaning of the abbreviated "cap rate," the rate of return used in income properties. It is a comparison between net operating income and sales prices of properties, used by appraisers to estimate value based on similar income property sales in the same area.

capitalization the overall funding of a project; capitalization usually consists of debt (financing provided by lenders) and equity (through capital formation provided by investors). Capitalization may be raised directly between developer and lenders or investors, or indirectly through conduit investment programs, such as real estate investment trusts (REITs).

cash flow projection an estimate of future cash-based revenues and cash payments (including operating expenses, capital expenditures, and debt service); as part of a project's feasibility study, the cash flow projection is intended to demonstrate that cash flow is adequate to ensure that the project will work financially.

CAVE acronym for Citizens Against Virtually Everything, extreme NIMBY interests against any and all forms of new development in a town, city, or county.

CBD The Central Business District of a city, which includes business activity and buildings as well as financial and government areas. This is the center around which all economic activity of the community is organized.

change a principle of valuation, stating that no condition remains the same indefinitely; change is part of the economic cycle.

class A buildings those most attractive to investors, characterized by quality of materials, design, amenities, age, and location; investment-grade; properties commanding the highest rents; prestigious; architecturally exceptional.

class B buildings ones that are older but functional. Rents will tend to be lower and design may be outdated compared with those for class A; characterized by utilitarian space but lacking extra amenities; nonlandmark locations.

class C buildings the oldest inventory, with internal systems, heating and air conditioning, lighting, and amenities that are substandard in comparison to newer construction; basic space offering low rent but typically having had below-average levels of maintenance and inferior internal systems. These buildings are architecturally obsolete.

comparable property   in appraisal, a property that has sold recently, and that is reasonably similar to a subject property, based on condition, lot size, neighborhood, square feet, and other features; used for the purpose of estimating current value.

competition   a principle in valuation, stating that opportunities for profitable investment lead to competition.

competitive analysis   a study of competitive forces for a project, considering the size and location, amenities, and other features of a project; the analysis includes identification of the actual competition and does not assume that *all* properties sharing the same zoning are competitors.

condemnation (or **expropriation**)   the act of changing status of property as part of a government's exercise of eminent domain.

conformity   a principle of valuation, stating that a property is most likely to appreciate in value along with other, similar properties in the same neighborhood.

Consumer Price Index (CPI)   a measurement of inflation published and updated periodically by the Bureau of Labor Statistics (BLS), compiled to report changes in the average prices paid for a basket of consumer goods and services.

contribution   a principle of valuation, stating that improvements add to market value as a factor of current supply and demand, and not necessarily on the basis of actual cost.

convention business   in the lodging industry, customers needing not only rooms, but convenient restaurants, exhibit space and support, and access to shopping and recreational amenities.

corporate contracts   agreements entered between lodging and corporations; these include travel agencies and online travel web sites committing to fill blocks of rooms; airline employees; government and military travelers; and out-of-town employees visiting a home office.

corporate small groups   business travelers who reserve blocks of lodging rooms and interested in business meeting facilities onsite, such as day rooms and small meeting rooms.

cost method   an appraisal method in which current value is based on the current cost that would be required to duplicate the improvements on the same land.

debt coverage ratio   in appraisal of income properties, a calculation of how well operating income is structured to make monthly mortgage payments. To calculate, net operating income is divided by the amount of debt service (principal and interest).

declining balance depreciation   an accelerated method of depreciation in which a greater deduction is allowed in the early years, and less in later years.

depreciation   (1) for tax purposes, a noncash expense real estate investor's claim, based on purchase price of real estate (excluding land). For real estate, depreciation is claimed on the straight-line basis (the same amount claimed each year) over 27.5 years (for residential property) or 39 years (for nonresidential property); (2) for appraisal purposes, a reduction in appraised value based on the age and condition of property.

diminishing returns   a concept in valuing real estate, recognizing that while improvements to property tend to increase market value, investment return will begin to fall when improvements exceed the natural rate of growth in market value.

direct capitalization   in appraisal, the use of gross rent multipliers on similar properties to estimate market value of a subject income property.

diversification   the spreading of risk within a market, by placing investment capital in several different products rather than in a single product.

due diligence   a series of tests and analyses designed to ensure that potential risks, cash shortfalls, and other feasibility-related problems have been anticipated; and also to ensure that likely problems such as project delays, have been studied as part of an overall risk evaluation of a project.

economic demand   a shortage of supply given current economic conditions (compare to **political demand**).

economic life   in appraisal, an estimate of the current condition of property, used to calculate annual depreciation of value due to condition and obsolescence.

economic rent   the rent from income property on the basis of rent per unit, per room, or per square feet (or all three), used in appraisal to compare subject properties to comparable income properties.

effective age   in appraisal, an estimate of the age of a property based not on when improvements were constructed, but on current condition.

effective gross income   total rental income that can be earned, minus the value of rents based on vacancy rates.

eminent domain   a legal power granted to the government and found in the Fifth Amendment. It provides that the government (federal, state or local) has the power to take private property for public use; and that upon exercise of that right, the landowner must be given adequate compensation.

equity REIT a real estate investment trust organized to assume ownership positions in large-scale real estate projects such as shopping centers, office/industrial parks, urban office buildings, and residential subdivisions.

essential public facility under growth management rules, facilities necessary for the public, but not necessarily desirable when placed in certain neighborhoods. This category includes hospitals and convalescent homes, prisons, transportation yards and facilities, airports, landfills, and utility plants. The importance of essential public facilities allows governments to override the property rights of individuals and when necessary, to enact takings in order to free up land for the proposed construction.

exchange traded fund (ETF) a type of mutual fund that trades like stocks on public exchanges. ETFs specialize in specific products or stock types, including real estate. Investors can buy or sell shares with the same liquidity as with stocks.

exclusionary zoning any zoning regulations designed specifically to keep out newcomers and to prevent growth, rather than to serve a legitimate purpose.

expense ratio in appraisal of income properties, a comparison between expenses and income. To calculate, divide operating by effective gross income.

feasibility study an analysis of specific financial expectation involved with a project, based on a study of existing and anticipated demand levels; competition; the cost of construction and financing; time to completion of a project; cash flow and taxes; and risks to investors, lenders, and developer.

free independent travelers (FITs) in the lodging industry, individuals whose needs are very individual and local, including discount and wholesale travelers, members of charter groups, and secondary travelers such as spouses of convention attendees.

fundamental analysis a study of basic financial status and potential for a real estate project; while this concept is usually applied to stock investments, its value is equally important to real estate investors.

gross absorption change in occupied space over time, indicating trends in occupied and vacant space within one market.

gross rent multiplier (GRM) the factor used by appraisers for the income method of valuing properties. Sales prices of comparable properties are divided by gross income (either monthly or annual) to arrive at typical GRM levels; the average or a representative GRM factor is used to estimate the market value of the subject property.

growth management laws   legislation enacted in several states to control land use and development; these laws often expand local zoning and place further restrictions on how and where development will be allowed.

heavy industrial   a specialized subzone of industrial reserved for land uses including toxic material, flammables, or specialized use such as rail car storage, quarries, and other manufacturing uses, and any land use that may pose an environmental or health threat.

highest and best use   a principle in valuation, stating that real estate valuation is maximized when land is utilized in the best possible way.

hybrid REIT   a real estate investment trust containing varying levels of equity, construction, and mortgage features.

improved property   That portion of real estate inventory including the top 25 percent of inventory, normally in ready-to-build condition and with basic services available.

income method   in appraisal, a method for estimating market value of an income property based on its potential to generate income. In most calculations, the sales prices of comparable properties are divided by monthly or annual gross rental income, to arrive at a gross rent multiplier (GRM). The GRM for several comparable properties is used as a basis for identifying market value for the subject property.

increasing returns   a concept in valuing real estate, recognizing that improvements to property may cause growth in market value to an extent, but not without limit.

internal rate of return (IRR)   A calculation of investment return including a calculation of market-rate comparative returns on periodic cash flow; return on capital invested based on the assumption that cash flow may be invested at a current assumed rate of return.

inventory   The available rental space in a specific area, either vacant or occupied, including space of a specific property type (residential, commercial, or industrial) but excluding property occupied by government offices, hospitals, schools, and other essential public facilities; expressed as a number of square feet of space.

larger malls   retail malls sized between 750,000 and two million square feet of retail space and with three or more anchor tenants, each with more than 100,000 square feet of retail space.

leisure travelers   in lodging, guests whose primary purpose for travel is vacation and leisure. Interest is primarily on proximity to travel destinations, comfort, and convenience.

leverage   the use of borrowed funds; investors use leverage by investing a minimal amount and financing the balance. This is common practice in the stock market (via the use of margin accounts) and even more so in real estate. Some investment analysts identify three possible methods to invest: equity (ownership position such as stocks), debt (lending money through notes or bonds), and leverage (using a small amount of money to control a larger investment base).

light industrial   the most common form of industrial zoning sharing similar impact levels with office zoning; light industrial areas often coexist with other land uses in mixed use office/industrial parks.

LIHTC   Low Income Housing Tax Credits, a federal incentive program designed to encourage the development of low-income and affordable housing. Developers are granted tax credits in exchange for constructing below-market rate housing.

limited partnership   a type of investment program in which general partners manage investment properties and limited partners (who purchase equity units in the program) have limited liability but no management control. Losses from limited partnerships are passive losses and cannot be deducted except to the extent that they offset other passive gains.

liquidity   an attribute of investments, useful for comparisons between two dissimilar products. Directly owned real estate is highly illiquid because cash can be removed only through borrowing of equity or sale of the property. In comparison, stocks are highly liquid because they can be bought or sold with minimal cost.

loan-to-value ratio   a ratio reporting the relationship between the current mortgage debt and market value of the property. To calculate, divide the current amount due on mortgage loans, by the current value of the property.

local area   the immediate neighborhood in proximity to a subject property.

local market variables   factors contributing to real estate valuation, which are local in nature and not attributable to any regional or national economic trends.

LULU   acronym for Locally Unwanted Land Use, an alternative descriptor of antigrowth forces commonly called NIMBYs.

market analysis   a study of the market for a project, to include a demand study, analysis of the competition, and other local factors.

market area   the range in which the forces of supply and demand operate; often defined in terms of geographical markets, the true market area may involve a nongeographical base such as a type of traveler in a lodging facility; a family on vacation; or a family moving to find employment.

market or sales comparison   a method of appraising real estate based on market values of similar properties or on recent sales prices.

market share   in analysis of competition, an estimate of the amount of current and future demand that a specific project is likely to absorb.

market study an analysis of level of demand and competition for a proposed project, to include identification of financing methods.

marketability a feature of investments, reflecting the ability to buy or sell. In a soft market, it may be difficult to obtain an asked price for real estate, meaning that marketability is poor. For example, an owner of limited partnership units may be unable to locate a secondary market purchaser, in which case marketability is at zero. Marketability may also refer to obsolescence, or to loss of equity value. A highway store may be obsolete when the highway is rerouted, losing marketability; or a house may lose marketability because the cost required to make repairs exceeds the equity in the property.

marketability analysis a kind of market analysis, in which the market for a specific project is evaluated, which may mean a potential buyer or potential tenants or customers.

mixed use land use involving a coordinated application of two or more different zoning types (residential, commercial, and industrial); one variety mix use includes varying densities of housing.

Modified Accelerated Cost Recovery Systems (MACRS) the current system used for federal income tax calculations of depreciation, which has been in effect since 1986. Under MACRS, real estate depreciation calculations must be straight-line and extend at least 27.5 years (for residential) and longer (for commercial). Recovery periods are strictly defined and annual rates of depreciation are mandated within the MACRS system.

modified adjusted gross income an individual's AGI with adjustments, used to determine the total amount allowed as a loss on real estate investments for federal income tax purposes.

mortgage REIT a real estate investment trust formed specifically to lend money to developers to fund projects.

multi-unit residential a variation of residential zoning with higher density than single-family housing; this includes duplex, triplex, fourplex and apartment projects.

neighborhood-specific shopping centers small-sized malls or expanded strip malls including grocery store anchor tenants, with the entire mall size not exceeding 150,000 square feet.

net absorption changes in occupied space over time (whereas gross absorption includes vacant space, net does not); used to analyze strength of rental demand in the market.

NIMBY acronym for Not In My Back Yard, an individual or citizens' group opposed to development in their neighborhoods.

occupancy rate the historic percentage of occupied units, usually expressed as the dollar amount of rents over maximum potential rates;

used to track and compare demand for rental units within a project and over a period of time, or for a market as a whole.

occupied space all rental space physically occupied by a tenant, excluding all vacant space, even if under lease.

operating expenses the expenses involved in operating real estate investment properties. The most common among these expenses are real estate taxes, insurance, and utilities.

outside CBD/suburban areas removed from the central business district (CBD) and including both suburban and urban-style development (highly concentrated urban clusters).

passive income or loss profit or loss from investments that are subject to tax restrictions. Passive losses may not be deducted except to the extent that they apply against passive gains. The general exception is a provision allowing individual real estate investors to deduct annual losses, subject to both dollar limits and income limits. The restriction in annual losses applies to investors, but not to active real estate professionals.

penetration a formula demonstrating the occupancy rate of a specific site, in comparison to occupancy rates for the entire market. To calculate, the occupancy rate for a subject property is divided by the occupancy rate for the entire market. The result is expressed as a percentage.

planned unit development (PUD) a provision in a zoning ordinance providing developers methods for building mixed-use projects, including exceptions to other zoning laws, in exchange for innovative design, notably allowing higher density or reduced setbacks.

plottage a principle of valuation, stating that land values tend to increase when adjacent lots are combined into single ownership and put to a single zoning or use.

political demand a distortion of economic demand based on local sentiment regarding growth; when local sentiment is opposed to further growth, political demand may be at zero, even when economic demand is strong.

prime industrial building a building defined as belonging in the top 25 percent of local buildings in terms of available inventory.

principles of valuation ten concepts that collectively define real estate valuation; these are progression, regression, conformity, substitution, change, anticipation, contribution, plottage, highest and best use, and competition.

pro forma (Latin for "for the same form") a financial presentation based solely on an educated guess, derived from estimates of future revenue, expenses, profits, and cash flow—an overall financial and cash budget based on underlying assumptions concerning costs, financing, income levels, and time involved to complete a project.

profitability   the difference between a sale price and original purchase, adjusted for interim costs and taxes; the most common method for establishing valuation in real estate.

progression   a principle of valuation, stating that a property's value may increase due to the existence of similar properties in similar locations, containing greater quality.

rate of return   An investment calculation, usually comparing operating income to the purchase price (net operating income is divided by the basis in property).

real estate investment trust (REIT)   a corporation that does not pay federal income taxes directly, but passes tax liabilities through to its shareholders (conduit tax treatment). REITs are classified as equity, mortgage, or hybrid, depending on the position they take in real estate investments. Shares of REITs are traded on public stock exchanges.

real estate market   the combined group of sellers and buyers who exchange property among themselves; further defined by property type and location; income production; and investor, tenant, or customer attributes.

recovery period   the number of years over which specific classes of capital assets can be depreciated.

regional centers   also called *power centers* or *regional malls*, these range between 250,000 and one million square feet of retail space and normally include at least three anchor tenants, typically *big box* stores.

regression   a principle of valuation, stating that a property's value may decrease due to the existence of similar properties in similar locations, containing lower quality.

replacement value   the value required to replace current improvements, based on both the cost of construction *and* duplication of the quality of workmanship (for example, handmade fixtures in older homes).

scientific method   an objective method for evaluating questions of fact, premised on the belief that an original hypothesis may or may not be true; that such a hypothesis may be verified or disproved through a series of tests; and that the outcome of such tests should be conclusive in either direction because of the overall validation of information. The method has four steps: observation, hypothesis, prediction, and experiment.

second home   as defined for tax purposes, a second residence; deductions of mortgage interest and property taxes are deductible by individuals on second homes when they are used as part-year residences.

secondary market   a market for the resale of investments; in the mortgage business, an active secondary market exists to purchase mortgages from lending institutions; package those mortgages into pools; and sell pool shares to investors. Programs performing secondary market services include the Government National Mortgage Association (GNMA) and the Federal National Mortgage Association (FNMA). In some forms of investment, a secondary market may not exist or it may be expensive to complete a transaction.

site evaluation   comparative analysis of a specific site's physical properties such as topography, shape of the land, surrounding uses, proximity to important features; and of the locational features such as off-site visibility and access to transportation routes such as freeway off-ramps or commuter stations.

site specific attributes   the features of a specific site including size, shape, and topography, that affect or contribute to market value.

small-scale mall   a mall with between 100,000 and 300,000 square feet of retail space, sited on 20 to 30 acres with one to two anchors.

solitary business traveler   a business person traveling alone and primarily interested in convenience of a site to transportation and local business districts.

spread   the difference between asked and sale prices in residential real estate; trends in spread are indicative of the overall supply and demand trend.

straight-line depreciation   a method of calculating depreciation in which the same amount is deducted each year until the full value has been deducted.

strip mall   a very small retail shopping area, located on primary roads and consisting of limited retail space and parking; typically, 5 to 10 shops and stores are found in the strip mall.

submarket   geographically distinguished market boundaries identifying a grouping of buildings or land use, which make up a competitive set; located within a larger market with contiguous boundaries, such as an office-zoned downtown area, or an industrial park.

subsidized housing   a program of incentives provided by the government in the form of tax credits and other financial incentives, designed to encourage affordable and low-income housing developments.

substitution   a principle of valuation, stating that a property's greatest potential market value is limited by the market value of other, similar properties.

supply and demand   an economic comparison that affects pricing of all products and commodities; the analysis of supply and demand recognizes that prices rise and fall as a direct result of changes in both supply and demand of a particular product. In real estate, three distinct supply and demand markets coexist: for properties (reflected in prices of real estate); for rentals ("rental demand" is a comparison between the demand among tenants and the supply of rental units); and for financing of real estate purchases and developments.

sweat equity   appreciation in market value derived from the owner's individual efforts, usually relating to improvements and renovations to run-down properties.

takings   limitations on development activity, changes in zoning that prevent an owner from using land as intended or desired, or the requirement by a city or county that in order to gain approval, a developer must pay for additional benefits or donate land.

tax incentives   tax provisions and rules designed to encourage investment in a particular product, such as real estate. Incentives for individuals include allowance for deduction of annual losses on real estate investments that are managed directly.

time on the market   in residential real estate, a test of a market's trend. As the average time on the market between listing and final sale changes, analysts may judge the broader trend in residential supply and demand.

trade area   the area where the entire potential customer base is found, which may extend beyond the primarily geographic market area. The trade area is defined based on a project's attributes; location and drive times; population and competition distances; and demand features.

transition   an observed trend in a neighborhood that will affect valuation; a transition may be either positive or negative, and is an important aspect of judging investment value for a project.

under construction   descriptive of a project whose status specifically resides between the beginning date of actual construction and extending until a certificate of occupancy has been issued.

vacancy rate   the percentage of total potential gross income, representing vacant units. This rate is usually expressed as a percentage of dollar amounts, but may also be reported on the basis of square feet or number of units.

vacant inventory   The currently available rental space, normally expressed in the number of square feet.

weighted average rental rate   A calculation of "average" rental rates that is adjusted to reflect exceptional features, location, or desirability of a specific project.

yield   a specialized calculation in the lodging industry, reflecting a comparative penetration between a subject property and the entire market. To calculate, three steps are required. (1) Multiply a subject property's occupancy rate by the average daily room rate. (2) Multiply the entire market's occupancy rate by the market's average daily room date. (3) Divide the result of (a) by the result of (b) to arrive at yield; it is expressed as a percentage.

zoning ordinance a rule imposing rules and restrictions on how and where development may occur. The broad zoning classifications of land are residential, commercial, and industrial. Zoning originated in New York City in 1916 to prevent industrial land use in Manhattan's office and shopping districts.

Using a GIS Tool in Real Estate Market Analysis

By Steve Benner

This section shows how Geographic Information System (GIS) applications can be used for every type of real estate market analysis. Our goal is to explain what's available today and how you can take advantage of it—to reduce risk and vastly improve the analytical process of defining market and trade areas.

WHAT IS A GIS?

A GIS is computer software that links geographic information (where things are) with descriptive information (what things are). The "where" can be physical, real-world natural or manmade objects such as mountains, rivers, roads, and buildings. They can be legal or administrative constructs such as parcels, rights-of-way, census tracts, taxing districts, neighborhoods, or land use zones. They can also be computer-derived constructs such as flood plains or fire or storm surge zones.

Level of detail is a crucial advantage. In a GIS program, each of the things is stored in a computer in a separate file: one for each type of object. Rivers and roads may be stored as lines, just as you'd see them on a map. But because rivers have different descriptive properties than roads, each would be in its own separate file. Rivers may have information on average depth, flow direction, and channel type stored in the file with each river. Roads would information such as pavement type, speed limit, and number of lanes stored with each road.

Likewise, parcels and land use zones would be stored in separate files with their unique descriptive data on ownership and permitted uses. Census tracts would also be located in a separate file with descriptive information on the population within each track.

In a GIS, these separate files are called "layers" and can be thought of conceptually as separate, transparent maps for each layer that you could lay on top of one another as needed for a particular type of analysis. For example, you might take the land use layer and put the parcel layer on top of it to find out what parcels fall within commercial zones. In a GIS, these layers are stored digitally and can be called up and overlaid with a simple click or two, and displayed on your monitor. These themes can be used to create a stack of information about the same geographic area. Each layer can be turned off and on, based on your specific requirements and desired level of detail. You control the amount of information about an area that you want to see, at any time, on any specific map.

There are added benefits from storing this information in the computer: You can use powerful spatial analysis tools in unique ways. For example, you may call up the roads, rivers, zoning, census, and parcel layers and instruct the GIS to search for all parcels within two miles of a major highway, at least 100 yards from any rivers, zoned commercial, with a population of less than 200 people within a one-mile buffer around the parcel. These valuable features make your job easier than it could ever be doing the same task by hand—not to mention the time involved.

GIS Analysis

GIS systems enable you to employ queries as "cookie cutters," extracting demographic, economic, competitive, and other information from within the bounds of the spatial query.

Consider an example such as a trade area analysis. For many investments, such as retail or apartment housing, the success of an investment will be determined by defining its trade area, the zone containing the majority of its patrons or end-users. There are many ways to create trade areas, including by hand. Static rings are simple rings around an existing or proposed location, often based on simple distance. Often, concentric rings are used at various mile-based levels.

Once rings are established, the "cookie cutter" power of GIS takes over, extracting demographic, segmentation, competitive, economic, and other data from within the rings and presenting it in both tabular report and mapping formats. Rings are very simple and provide a basic starting point for analyzing the area surrounding a proposed investment. More sophisticated analysis methods are also available based on drive times; bounding some percentage of a sites' customers (such as 80%); or areas calculated from various models that take distance, attractiveness, competition, or other factors into account. Of course, hand-drawn trade areas are also possible.

In all cases, the analyst is trying to best define the area from which customers, tenants, labor, or other resources important to the investment will be drawn and assess their availability, purchasing power, and other characteristics. These considerations vary by locality, and their relative weight will vary depending on the type of investment (mall, apartment complex, industrial building, etc.).

ADVANCED SPATIAL ANALYSIS

In addition to trade area analysis and the ability to aggregate data using spatially derived boundaries, there are many more spatial analysis tools available in a business GIS:

- *Thematic mapping*—maps colored by numeric and nonnumeric data to provide a visual tool for discovering spatial patterns such as concentrations of customers. With these, you can simultaneously display maps with charts and use graduated symbols, dot density, and other visualization tools.
- *Complex spatial queries*—such as overlay, buffer, and network traces. For example, you can calculate total spending potential for fast food within a two-minute drive time buffer around a freeway.
- *Customer profiling and prospecting*—enabling you to augment and enhance profiling capabilities by inference based on customer location, such as demographic and lifestyle segmentation.
- *Demand forecasting*—providing various predictive models for sales using geographic relationships such as distance to store, proximity to complementary stores, and other spatial factors.
- *Cannibalization models*—used to assess the revenue impact of opening a new facility close to an existing one.
- *Location-allocation models*—used to evaluate all combinations of possible sites for multiple facilities to meet some defined objective such as to maximize revenue from a fixed number of stores, to minimize the number of facilities to provide some given level of service, or to reduce competition between multiple stores in the network.
- *Competitive analysis*—used to locate and assess the competition.
- *Market penetration/trade area penetration tools*—used to assess market potential and competitive position.
- *Cluster analysis*—advanced tools to evaluate whether the geographic features or attributes in a data set tend to be clustered, dispersed, or random within a region as well as identifying statistically significant outliers and clusters of hot spots and cold spots.
- *Drive time analysis*—used to calculate drive time by traversing a street network attributed with speed limit, turn, and other restrictions as opposed to an "as the crow flies" distance/time calculation.

Many more features enable you to add a sophisticated and highly detailed dimension to your analysis. The tools available from leading GIS vendors rival those of other nonspatial vendors in terms of complexity and robustness. ESRI Inc.'s ArcGIS® Geostatistical Analyst provides tools for advanced data exploration, modeling, and surface generation, and has been used for demand analysis by generating municipal and urban clusters that are similar in regard to investment potential, infrastructure development, and cultural levels derived from 130 socioeconomic variables. In addition, ESRI has partnered with other nonspatial vendors such as SAS to provide access to advanced statistical functions as part of its geoprocessing models. Today, there is no shortage of sophisticated tools for locational analysis.

GEOGRAPHIC DATA

Of course, all of these tools are of little use without some material on which to use them. That material comes in many flavors and has varying quality and price. Our goal here is to introduce the major categories of data that are generally available and used for locational analysis. Each type of investment opportunity will require both common and unique data sets. A retailer will be concerned with spending potential in the particular category. Someone building an airport or landfill will want more environmental data.

The common types of geographic data used in locational analysis include:

Base map data—general-purpose data used mainly as a background reference layer; includes state and county boundaries, major roads, major water features, railroads, and points of interest.

Street data—detailed street network for geocoding (finding locations on the map) and for calculating trade areas based on drive times.

Environmental data—includes natural features such as lakes, rivers, land cover, subsurface, or vegetation, as well as flood plains, fire areas, earthquake zones, and other areas of risk. This is used for risk mitigation, compliance analysis, cost avoidance, and cost estimation.

Boundary data—the most common boundary data are census boundaries (tracts, blocks, and groups, for example) and postal boundaries (zip codes). Demographic and economic data are typically aggregated by these common boundaries.

Demographic data—more than 1,000 demographic variables are available, including estimates and projections. Race, age, income, home ownership, employment, family composition, and a variety of other variables come into play.

Segmentation data—the grouping of individuals into clusters based on common socioeconomic and demographic characteristics and behaviors. These would be used to profile customers, identify new markets, and predict sales of specific goods and services. The data are available for standard census and postal boundaries.

Business data—including analysis of more than 12 million businesses in the United States categorized by industry, sales volume, number of employees, and other attributes.

Consumer expenditure data—detailed information on specific products and services purchased, including total expenditures, average spending per household, Spending Potential Index, and more.

Retail sales potential—market potential indexes for products and services, and leakage/surplus indexes to assess the potential of future sites.

Traffic counts—used for trade analysis, sales forecasting, and modeling.

Satellite and aerial photos—essential for site selection, these provide a bird's-eye view of the area surrounding a proposed investment.

Land use—information on the permitted uses of land such as commercial, residential, or industrial.

Weather—real-time and historic tracking for demand modeling and risk assessment.

Daytime/occupation—the population of workers in an area during the day.

Crime data—used to gauge the quality of a location and to assess risk.

Specialized data—collected for specific industries or purposes including:

> Health care—expenditures by illness or forecasts.
> Shopping centers—gross leasable area, space availability, or planned/proposed centers.
> Construction projects—type of project, value, and owner.
> Restaurant data—type of sales, size, and specific location.
> Industrial facilities—type, product, and size.
> Survey data—consumer expenditure, teen and young adult, or levels of affluence.

Obtaining all the relevant data and loading them into a spatial tool could take a lot of time and cost a good deal of money. Some vendors, such as ESRI, have bundled much of the data with the tools, and also offer data via Internet services on a transaction basis. In any case, be prepared to spend some time identifying, sourcing, and understanding your data. The quality of your analysis directly depends on this.

LOCATION ANALYSIS IN THE MARKET ANALYSIS PROCESS

Geographically speaking, you are going to work with two main questions with respect to location analysis:

1. Where are the locations that satisfy the unique needs of the target market (site selection) as well as other economic, environmental, competitive, political, and site-related constraints?
2. What are the values of those locations?

Both of these questions draw upon the same basic locational techniques. The difference lies in the geographic scale of the analysis. Site selection typically involves a both a macro- and a microanalysis. Valuation is typically focused on a micro scale only.

SITE SELECTION

Site section usually involves two major steps. First, a macro search is done to find candidate areas where there are enough customers who match the target market profile with the required purchasing power, located in an area that also meets the local economic, infrastructure, political, and other factors specific to the success of the investment.

A major mall, used by patrons from adjacent areas as well as by those who come a great distance, is usually sited in relation to major cities and transportation infrastructure. Boutique retail chains require specific demographic and lifestyle segments and may be interested only in areas of high foot traffic in affluent neighborhoods. Convalescent care providers may look for areas with a large population of elderly people in temperate climates. An apartment developer may look for areas of young singles that are close to social or recreational facilities. A county looking to site an airport would look for sites that met all environmental, transportation, airspace, and other restrictions.

GIS systems are ideally suited to facilitate these analyses. Rather than considering a number of potential sites spread across a large geographic area, many can be eliminated through simple spatial analysis. Overlay analysis can identify areas that meet (or violate) criteria based on common location. Drive time analysis can help gauge accessibility. Location-allocation models can help assess cannibalization in a multistore expansion. Thematic mapping can identify areas with the required demographic or economic criteria. Not every GIS tool will be used in all cases. Some will be used heavily, others not at all. The success criteria for the investment will determine the type of tools and analysis used.

Once a potential site or set of sites has been identified, the next step is to conduct a more detailed analysis for each candidate site. Again, the first pass at this should be done with the GIS, only now at a more granular level and with an expanded set of tools better suited to local site evaluation.

For a retail investment, a detailed, block-group demographic analysis should be conducted to better understand the market composition and to validate that it meets the investment criteria for customer profile. Trade area analysis based on rings or drive times should be conducted to validate that demand is adequate.

Housing investments require many of the same concerns that retailers have. Trade area analysis tools work equally as well here on different demographic and socioeconomic variables.

Lodging and tourism investments are analyzed equally well with the basic tools and data of GIS. For example, proximity to local attractions, trends in crime rates, air and ground transportation, conference facilities, and labor availability will impact the feasibility of the proposed investment.

GIS ON-SITE

GIS can help prepare for the on-site visit by identifying competitive locations, points of interest, trade area boundaries, and other features worthy of your direct observation. This can all be taken to the field on a laptop, tablet PC, or handheld device. Once on-site, some information is found to be outdated (a competitor has moved) or missing (a competitor has moved in). Nearby vacant land under development may be observed, the overall condition of the area assessed, site-specific physical details noted, and so on. This all needs to be captured and fed back into the analysis. Taking the GIS into the field not only provides the data and analysis results to the analyst but also provides a means to update the data and create new data. Absent GIS, this data typically ends up in a presentation or a report instead of in the corporate database where it can be used for future analysis.

VALUATION

Geographic location plays a significant role in property valuation. Three common approaches to valuation—*comparable sales method, income approach*, and *cost approach*—all include location as a factor. Additionally, GIS can be effectively used to present findings and conclusions in the final valuation document.

Single-family housing is typically valued based on comparable properties sold in the same general area. Plotting comparables on a map and looking at spatial relationships can often explain differences in price. Location is everything. Unfortunately, residential real estate brokers seldom provide much information on the area surrounding a house other than comparables, what's required by law (flood zones), and some local knowledge based on experience. Buyers must do some research and validation on their own. The good news is that for less than $100 you can go to a web site today and get a very detailed profile of the demographics around a specific location, including trends and projections.

Apartment complex investments must consider many of the same factors as single-family residences as well as longer-term population, socioeconomic, and employment trends. GIS analysis can help understand these trends and remove some of the risk in the investment.

Retail valuation can also be facilitated with GIS analysis. Lessors use GIS to demonstrate to prospective lessees that the area surrounding the site is perfectly suited for their product or service, for example.

GIS output is uniquely suited to communicate the results of a valuation study. The ability to convey a great deal of interrelated data visually communicates more quickly and clearly than thumbing through pages of detailed reports. GIS may be used to:

- Display comparable sales.
- Show neighborhood boundaries.
- Show influencers of value:

  - Flood plains.
  - Contamination sites.
  - Demographics (e.g., areas of growth).
  - Zoning.
  - Traffic counts.
  - Taxing districts.
  - Protection districts.

- Show existing inventories.
- Show adjacent and nearby properties by type or size.

The particular data layers selected will determined by the type of valuation.

SUMMARY

Modern GIS systems provide a wide range of tools, and the data they work on, in packaged applications that do not require advanced training in GIS. A good deal of it is available via the Web to anyone who knows how to use a browser.

Market analysis and valuation in many forms is enriched through GIS, and reports may be presented on a truly detailed level with considerations for *all* of the relevant market, trade area, and supply-and-demand factors that the decision maker requires. It is also quite likely that the investment made in GIS technology will produce greater efficiency and lower research costs, thus providing lower cost in the overall analytical process.

Notes

CHAPTER 1   The Essence of Analysis

1. Appraisal Institute. *The Appraisal of Real Estate*, 10th ed. Chicago, IL: Appraisal Institute, 1992.
2. Schmitz, Adrienne et al. *Real Estate Market Analysis*. Washington, DC: Urban Land Institute, 2001.
3. Owens, Robert W. "Subdivision Development: Bridging Theory and Practice," *The Appraisal Journal*, July 1998.
4. Lefenfeld, Bob. "Market Analysis Basics, Elements of a Good Study, What to Expect from a Multifamily Market or Feasibility Study," *Multifamily Trends*, Summer 2001.
5. Miles, Mike, et al. "The Graaskamp Legacy," *Real Estate Finance*, Spring 1998.
6. Knutson, Daniel. "Feasibility Studies," *Mini-Storage Messenger*, July 2000.
7. Cannon, Michael Y. "Real Estate Market Analysis in the Valuation Process," *Appraisal Institute*, 1993.
8. Rushmore, Stephen. "Feasibility Studies: Fact or Fiction?" *Lodging Hospitality*, October 1996.
9. Schmitz, Adrienne et al. Ibid.
10. Smith, Charles A. "Using GIS to Improve Estimates of Future Demand," *Journal of Property Management*, July/August 1998.
11. http://www.sccar.com/govern/gmadensity.html.
12. Martin, Robert S. "Supply and Demand Relationships in Residential Subdivision Analysis," *Appraisal Institute*, 1993.
13. Martin, Robert S. *ibid*.
14. Brecht, Susan B. "Let the Buyer Beware," *Assisted Living Today*, Winter 1996.
15. Ibid.

CHAPTER 2   Using Analysis Effectively

1. Cannon, Michael Y. "Real Estate Market Analysis in the Valuation Process," *Appraisal Institute*, 1993.

2. Martin, Robert S. "Supply and Demand Relationships in Residential Subdivision Analysis," *Appraisal Institute*, 1993.
3. www.census.gov/popest December, 2004.

CHAPTER 3   Valuation of Real Estate

1. Cannon, Michael Y. "The Role for the Real Estate Appraiser and Assessor in Valuing Real Property for Ad Valorem Assessment Purposes," *The Appraisal Journal*, April 2002.
2. Cannon, Michael Y. "Real Estate Market Analysis in the Valuation Process," *Appraisal Institute*, 1993.
3. IRC Sec. 469(c)(7).
4. Martin, Robert S. "Supply and Demand Relationships in Residential Subdivision Analysis," *Appraisal Institute*, 1993.
5. Canning, George R. "The Contemporary Direct Comparison Approach to Value," *The Canadian Appraiser*, Winter 2000.
6. Matt Rosenberg. *Zoning—Residential, Commercial, or Industrial?* at http://geography.about.com/library/weekly/aa072801a.htm.
7. *Euclid, Ohio v. the Ambler Realty Company* (1926).
8. *Dolan v. City of Tigard, Oregon* (1994) and *Nollan v. California Coastal Commission* (1987).
9. *County of Wayne v. Hathcock* (Michigan case, 2004) and *Bailey v. Myers* (Arizona case, 2003).
10. Staley, Samuel Ph.D. *Homeowners are Paying Thousands More for Houses Because of Growth Management Acts,*" December 18, 2001, *Reason Public Policy Institute,* at www.rppi.org.
11. Statistical industry summaries located at http://www.reitnet.com/reits101/.

CHAPTER 4   Single-Family Home and Condo Analysis

1. Schmitz, Adrienne et al. *Real Estate Market Analysis.* Washington, DC: Urban Land Institute, 2001.
2. Wagner, Richard. "Impact Fees: Truth and Consequences of Bad Policy," John Locke Foundation, at www.johnlocke.org December 10, 2003.
3. Nelson, Arthur C. "Reducing Financial Hazard Risk Through Planning Intervention," *Journal of Urban Planning and Development,*" March 2000.
4. Hardin, Garrett. "The Tragedy of the Commons," *Science* 1968. This is a reference to the conflict between individual motivation and the

common good of society. The metaphor describes a shared plot of grassland. There is adequate land for each of a number of farmers to graze a limited number of livestock. However, individual self-interest leads to every farmer overgrazing, which ultimately depletes the soil and destroys the commons. Consequently, everyone in the village dies. The metaphor is used often to describe motivation in the free market.

5. Garreau, Joel. *Edge City: Life on the New Frontier*. New York, NY: Anchor Publishing, 1992.
6. Dickens, Charles, describing London in 1848 and referenced by author Garreau in his book *Edge City* as "The best one-sentence description of Edge City extant." The full Dickens sentence: "There were a hundred thousand shapes and substances of incompleteness, wildly mingled out of their places, upside down, burrowing in the earth, moldering in the water, and unintelligible as in any dream."
7. http://www.sixflags.com/.
8. http://www.proximityone.com/hpi.htm.
9. Bell, Randall. "The Impact of Airport Noise on Residential Real Estate," *The Appraisal Journal*, July 2001.
10. Ibid.
11. Owens, Robert W. "Subdivision Development: Bridging Theory and Practice," *The Appraisal Journal*, July 1998.
12. The Custer Rezone, 1994–96, Whatcom County, Washington.
13. National Low Income Housing Coalition. "A Second Chance for Victory," *The NIMBY Report*, November 2000, at www.nlihc.org.
14. www.peopleservingpeople.org.
15. National Low Income Housing Coalition. "Caught Between a Rock and a Hard Place in Key West," *The NIMBY Report*, August 2003, at www.nlihc.org.
16. Stein, Debra. "A Strategic Plan To Avoid Nimby Problems," *Affordable Housing Finance Magazine*, September 2002.

CHAPTER 5   Multi-Unit Rental Property Analysis

1. Society of Industrial and Office Realtors, at www.sior.com.
2. U.S. Census Bureau. *Housing and Vacancy Survey* (New York City), 2002.
3. National Low Income Housing Coalition, at http://www.nlihc.org.
4. Witten, G. Ronald. "Predicting the Multifamily Market," *Multifamily Trends*, Fall 2002.
5. Berg, Peggy and Mark Skinner. "A New Pricing Index for the Corporate Apartment Industry," *The Real Estate Finance Journal*, Winter 2002.

6. Lefenfeld, Bob. "Market Analysis Basics, Elements of a Good Study, What to Expect from a Multifamily Market or Feasibility Study," *Multifamily Trends*, Summer 2001.
7. Seldin, Maury and R. Thomas Powers. "Absorption Analysis" (Chapter 9), *Real Estate Market Analysis*, 1988.
8. Hearn, Joy. "How to Analyze Land Values in the Land Market," *The Appraisal Journal*, July 1999.
9. Goodman, Jack. "Performance Across Local Apartment Markets," *Real Estate Finance*, Winter 1999.
10. Liedtke, Michael. "Apartment Rents: LV Rental Costs Up Slightly," January 21, 2003, *Las Vegas Review Journal*, at http://www.reviewjournal.com/lvrj_home/2003/Jan-21-Tue-2003/business/20514487.html.
11. Goodman, Jack, *Op cit.*, indicating that in the period 1988–1997, both Houston and Philadelphia reported the highest vacancy rates among 23 metro areas studied, but both also reported annual rent increases above the average of the same markets.
12. Goodman, Jack, *Op cit.*

CHAPTER 6   Retail Real Estate Analysis

1. Cohen, Eric. "Know Your Market Trade Area: The First Steps in a Project Feasibility Study," *Mini-Storage Messenger*, September 1996.
2. http://www.thenewparentsguide.com/vacations-north-dakota.htm.
3. http://www.hilton.com/en/hi/hotels/index.jhtml?moreDesc=true&cty-hocn=LASLHHH.
4. http://www.oldsacramento.com/home.html.
5. http://www.drinkmorethinkless.com/hrs/dict5.html.
6. http://www.ardenfair.com.
7. Montaño, Ralph. "Florin Mall vacancies are targeted," *Sacramento Bee*, December 16, 2004, at http://www.sacbee.com/content/business/commercial_realestate/story/11772997p-12657733c.html
8. www.claritas.com.
9. Appraisal Institute. *The Appraisal of Real Estate*, 10th ed. Chicago. IL: *Appraisal Institute*, 1992.
10. Used with permission, Stephanie Delaney, Hayward, CA, December 19, 2004, published at http://nooksack.blogs.com/steph/2004/12/the_mall_by_my_.html.
11. Urban Land Institute. *Shopping Center Development Handbook*, 2d ed. Washington, DC: Urban Land Institute, 1985.

12. Rabianski, Joseph S. "Retail Area Delineation and Market Analysis for the Appraiser," *Appraisal Institute*, 1993.
13. Sacramento Economic Development, at http://www.co.sacramento.ca.us/economic/business-incentive-programs/.
14. Eppli, Mark J. "Value Allocation in Regional Shopping Centers," *The Appraisal Journal*, April 1998.
15. Jortbert, Richard E. "Retail Market Analysis: An Intermediate Approach to Estimate Demand," *The Appraisal Journal*, October 1996.

CHAPTER 7   Office and Industrial Real Estate Analysis

1. Muschamp, Herbert, in the *New York Times*, cited at www.wired newyork.com.
2. "Highlighting High Performance," *U.S. Department of Energy, Office of Building Technology*, November 2001.
3. Gause, Allen, et al. *Office Development Handbook*, 2d ed. Washington, DC: Urban Land Institute, 1998.
4. Society of Industrial and Office Realtors, at www.sior.com.

CHAPTER 8   Lodging and Tourism Industry Real Estate

1. Schmitz, Adrienne et al. *Real Estate Market Analysis*. Washington, DC: Urban Land Institute, 2001.
2. Rushmore, Stephen. "Development Cost Can Determine Feasibility," *Hotels*, March 2002.
3. Madsen, Edgar B. "Timeshare Tax Assessment: Prices Versus Market Value," *The Appraisal Journal*, January 1999.
4. Belfrage, Eric E. "Business Value Allocation in Lodging Valuation," *The Appraisal Journal*, July 2001.
5. Joerger, Albert et al. "Applying Geographic Information Systems," *Cornell Hotel and Restaurant Administration Quarterly*, October 1996.
6. http://disneyworld.disney.go.com/wdw.
7. http://www.branson.com.
8. http://www.guinnessworldrecords.com.

CHAPTER 9   Mixed-Use Real Estate Analysis

1. Ross, Lynn. "Growth Management and Affordable Housing," *American Planning Association*, April 25, 2004 at http:/www.planning.org/conferencecoverage/2004/sunday/grwthm.

2. Staley, Samuel Ph.D. Homeowners are Paying Thousands More for Houses Because of Growth Management Acts," December 18, 2001, *Reason Public Policy Institute*, at www.rppi.org.
3. Proust, Marcel. *Remembrance of Things Past*, 1913–1926.
4. Schmitz, Adrienne et al. *Real Estate Market Analysis*. Washington, DC: Urban Land Institute, 2001.
5. www.wirdenewyork.com.
6. http://www.mandarin-oriental.com/.
7. National Low Income Housing Coalition. "New Apartments in Columbus, Ohio," *The NIMBY Report*, July, 2001, National Low Income Housing Coalition, at www.nlihc.org.
8. www.celebrationfl.com.
9. Arvada, Colorado, at Arvada, CO zoning ordinance, at http://www.ci.arvada.co.us/forms/25062sketchplan.pdf.
10. "The Zoning Ordinance," February 2001, Iowa State University extension, at http://www.extension.iastate.edu/Publications/PM1868G.pdf.
11. Marshalltown, Iowa zoning ordinance, Chapter 28 (Planned Unit Development), Section 3 (Application), paragraph 4, at www.ci.marshalltown.ia.us.
12. Faber, Marc. *Tomorrow's Gold*, Hong Kong: CLSA Books, 2003.